Death and Dying
A sociological introduction

GLENNYS HOWARTH

polity

First published in 2007 by Polity Press
Reprinted 2008

Polity Press
65 Bridge Street
Cambridge, CB2 1UR, UK

Polity Press
350 Main Street
Malden, MA 02148, USA

ISBN-13: 978-07456-2533-1

ISBN-13: 978-07456-2534-8 (pb)

A catalogue record for this book is available from the British Library.

Typeset in 11 on 13 pt Bembo
by Carnegie Publishing Ltd
Printed and bound in Great Britain
by MPG Books Ltd, Bodmin, Cornwall

For further information on Polity, visit our website: www.polity.co.uk

Contents

Acknowledgements

I would like to thank Polity Press for commissioning me to write this book and especially Emma Longstaff for her encouragement and patience with the project. I would also like to thank Steven Gallery who, once again, read and commented on a succession of drafts of each chapter. Particular thanks are due to David Field, Jeanne Katz and Allan Kellehear, who gave extremely detailed and helpful comments on an earlier draft of the book.

Glennys Howarth
University of Bath, UK

Introduction

In Western societies we appear to be living in a period where the study of death and the recognition of mortality have gained in popularity. At a public level, the entertainment industry has found new ways of bringing death into our lives without the blood and gore of murder thrillers or war movies. In a more sensitive, and some would say more mundane manner, we are treated to cinema that, in keeping with the narrative of ordinary lives, portrays unexceptional deaths, grief and, increasingly, after-death communication with loved ones. We enjoy star-rated soaps with titles such as *Six Feet Under* that depict the everyday lives of a family of funeral directors in the USA, and *Desperate Housewives*, a drama narrated by a woman who has died by suicide. At a more sober level, the news media is busy with documentaries on dying, funeral rituals, grief, memorialization, euthanasia, cryogenics, global risks and the future of death in a possible world where people live into their second century. Alongside these public manifestations of attention to mortality there are also private considerations. These include concerns about living with dying and grief, about quality of life in dying, and about the fear of death in old age. There are concerns about the need for and availability of professionals to assist with dying and grief, the accessibility of support systems for carers of dying people, issues of spirituality and religious belief, and the nature of self-identity and its construction and reconstruction within an ageing or dying body.

Issues of mortality can take many forms and their shape can be influenced by a range of professional and disciplinary approaches, most commonly medicine, biology, psychology and religion. Whilst no individual discipline or profession can justify a claim to privi-leged knowledge of mortality, each offers insights into the relationship between life and death and thus furthers our under-standing of the two. For example, medicine, pathology and biology can provide information about the nature of the physical body and of the diseases to which it may succumb. Theology and philosophy present us with frameworks for different belief systems, values and mores. Psychology claims expertise in understanding individual responses to mortality, both 'normal' and 'pathological'. Anthro-pology and history can inform us about the way in which societies other than our own construct and make sense of mortality.

What of sociology? What do sociologists contribute to the understanding of mortality? Sociologists perceive mortality as a social issue. Our experiences of dying, death and bereavement are embedded within our social and cultural worlds. Mortality may be a universal feature of human societies, but the form it takes and the ways in which we deal with it is complex and reflects the social and cultural diversity among and within every human society. Death takes a particular shape or form in different societies and this pro-vides individuals within society with an acceptable range of responses to it. Responses that fall outside of those deemed socially appropriate may be characterized as madness, heresy or possibly rebellion. Thus, sociologists attempt to understand and to map out the changing nature of dying, death and loss in society. In so doing they ask a range of questions.

- How do experiences of dying, death and grief differ in different societies? What accounts for these differences? What impact do structural factors such as socio-economic status, ethnicity, sexuality, disability and age have on these experiences?

- How do societies come to terms with, or deal with the fact that their members are mortal? How do individuals make sense of their mortality?

- How is death, in its various dimensions, managed within societies?
- How are changes in ways of dealing with death accounted for in society? Are these related to the prevailing discourses of a particular social or historical era?
- Is there a good death in contemporary Western societies? If so, what form might this take?
- How are the dead remembered and why might they be important to us?
- Is death socially constructed as the end of existence?

This book introduces some of the key substantive and theoretical debates in the sociology of death and dying and provides a framework for responding to many of these questions. Prior to embarking on an exploration of these issues, however, this introduction will familiarize us with some of the key sociological perspectives that can be used to assist our understanding of what we observe in society.

Sociological theorizing

There are now many distinct sociological theories that may help us to understand the nature of death in society and these are explored in detail in chapter 1. Here we briefly examine some of the major theoretical schools of thought that have contributed to our understanding of society.

The most significant theories that have framed our understanding of society have been those linked to the debate around structure and agency. There are three broad schools of thought within this debate, usually referred to as the structure-agency divide. These schools emphasize the significance either of the structure of society or of the individuals within it, or a combination of the two. Some sociologists believe that it is the structures of society that require investigation, whilst others consider that it is the individual who is central to the construction of society. A third perspective argues that to understand social phenomena fully it is necessary to bring structure and agency together without privileging either one.

The structure–agency debate stems from a concern with the way in which society is both produced and maintained. Structure focuses on the social context of action and the objective framework within which society is ordered and individuals constrained. Agency, or action, on the other hand, emphasizes the role of individuals in creating the social world around them. It privileges social interaction and meaning rather than organizations and institutions that form the bedrock of social structures. For the early sociologists of the nineteenth century, such as Comte and Durkheim, under-standing social structure was the purpose of sociology. These founders of the discipline viewed sociology as a science akin to the physical sciences. Just as the physical sciences were able to uncover the laws of nature, so too sociology was perceived as able to reveal 'social facts', and in their understanding of these, to determine social laws, predict and modify human society.

Sociologists such as Emile Durkheim, Talcott Parsons and Karl Marx believed that society existed as a reality 'in itself' and that no matter how individuals perceived or experienced their society, its structure would constrain them to behave in certain ways. For example, Durkheim, in his work on suicide (1951 [1897]), focused on suicide rates in order to understand and explain how society coerced the individual. He came to the conclusion that it was the level of social integration in society that influenced the extent of suicide.

From around the 1950s, the 'Chicago School' of symbolic inter-actionism, drawing from the work of Mead (1934), Cooley (1964 [1902]), and the earlier work of Weber (1968 [1914]) and his quest for *Verstehen* (understanding), began to stress the importance of understanding individual motivation. Sociologists who focused their theorizing on agency (see, for example, Goffman, 1959) believed that individuals are able to act in a meaningful way on the social world. According to these theorists people are not simply the passive receptors of social structures but are active in the social construction of their lifeworlds. Although there are a number of distinct theories that fit into this broad approach, many of the sociologists who take this perspective may be referred to as interactionists – concerned with the way in which 'selves' and social structures are constructed through continuous interaction over time' (Charmaz, 1980: 28). In terms of our understanding of death, this perspective assumes that meanings derive from the individual's own experience.

More recently, there have been social theorists who argue that privileging either structure or agency can only provide us with a partial understanding of social life (Layder, 1994). Accordingly, in order to understand how society is both created and reproduced, it is necessary to bring structure and agency together and to overcome this traditional dualism. Sociologists such as Bourdieu (1977), Giddens (1984) and Habermas (1987), therefore, developed theories that show that structure and agency, objective and subjective aspects of society are inextricably linked.

Bourdieu (1977) attempted to combine structure with agency (objective and subjective) by adopting the concept of 'habitus' to explain human characteristics and mannerisms. Habitus essentially refers to a set of dispositions developed in childhood that predispose individuals to behave in certain ways. These dispositions are based on social structural factors such as socio-economic status, gender and ethnicity. In this way Bourdieu combined structure and agency by demonstrating how structural factors are 'mapped' onto the individual. This, however, is achieved by the exercise of power and not in the constraining fashion suggested by the earlier structuralists. Bourdieu's work is especially useful to understanding the connection between structural factors in society as they impact on life chances and individual experiences.

Giddens (1984) has argued that rather than seeing structure and agency as separate, we should recognize them as inextricably linked. He developed the theory of structuration in which structure is defined as a duality – a combination of structure and agency. For Giddens, structure has only a virtual reality, relying on individual practice to retain its existence. Using this approach, he was able to argue that institutions only exist because of continued practice. For example, the institution of marriage in Western societies continues not because of pre-existing structures and constraints in society, but because individuals perceive marriage as a meaningful institution and therefore continue to subscribe to and perform marriage rituals. This approach is helpful in the context of death, dying and grief because it assists in explaining the institutionaliza-tion of death and the manner in which individuals experience mortality and shape the practices that surround it.

Habermas (1987) has developed a theory that identifies power relations in the separation between structure and agency and has formulated these as 'system' and 'lifeworld'. In modern societies system is the domain of expertise and lifeworld refers to the world of the individual. Habermas argues that a characteristic feature of modern societies is that system and lifeworld become separated. As a consequence of this separation, sub-systems of expertise are created within system. These then move back into the lifeworld and colonize it. An example of this might be the way in which medi-cine as a system of knowledge and expertise has been viewed as disempowering dying and grieving individuals by the employ-ment of dominant professional discourses that are inaccessible to lay people. For Habermas, the creation of new social movements (such as the women's movement or the interest in alternative med-icine) provides the key to removing system from the lifeworld and thus ending its colonization. These latter theoretical approaches that attempt to understand the relationship between structure and agency are helpful to our discussion of how mortality is made sense of within societies. As we journey through the different elements of death, dying and loss, the questions we raise and the way in which we approach the answers to these questions will draw from problems raised in this debate around the significance of structure and agency.

Organization of the book

This book focuses on death in contemporary Western societies and is organized thematically in order that it may be approached either as a whole – starting at the beginning and reading through to the end – or to allow chapters to be read independently with cross ref-erences that point the reader to linked discussions. It is also divided into three sections which, broadly speaking, address the chronology of mortality: the social characteristics and attitudes to death; social structures and individual experiences of dying; and, finally, explorations of post-death rituals of remembrance and survival beliefs.

Part I: Social Characteristics and Attitudes to Death

The first five chapters deal with issues of death and mortality. These chapters are designed to introduce the reader to important elements of death as they relate to the structures and power relations within societies.

Chapter 1 begins by asking how societies make sense of mortality. In so doing, it explores the nature of mortality in a range of societies. It considers theories of the nature of death in pre-modern, modern and postmodern societies and tracks these theoretical positions onto changing concerns within sociology. The concept of death-denial will be examined and critiqued. The chapter concludes with a discussion of the impact on Western societies of social and cultural diversity.

The second chapter in Part I is entitled 'When and How People Die'. In attempting to characterize and chart the development of attitudes to mortality in Western societies, it is important to locate these within their global and historical contexts. The chapter, therefore, presents both statistics and a discussion of patterns of mortality within and across societies. It notes the impact of structural factors on death rates and longevity and observes that as Western mortality rates decline, social rituals pertaining to death and attitudes to dying and loss can be observed to change.

Chapter 3 addresses the question of risk in contemporary societies. It is argued that perceptions of risk to mortality impact on the way in which death is perceived and also the structural and individual frameworks that are adopted for understanding and making meaning. For this reason the discussion utilizes the theoretical perspective of Beck (1992), who argued that we now live in 'risk societies' where threats to life are global in nature – for example, damage to the ecosystem, fallout from nuclear accidents or the threat of terrorism. Beck argued that unlike earlier historical periods, where threat to life fell disproportionately on those with lower socio-economic power, in global risk society these threats are more 'democratic' in that whole populations, irrespective of status or power, face them. This assertion is examined in this chapter by comparing the nature of risk of death in developed and less developed societies. In so doing, the discussion considers death risks in terms of individual health, natural and 'man-made' disasters, and threats of terrorism.

The next two chapters consider different aspects of so-called 'popular culture'. Chapter 4 focuses on religion and spirituality, and chapter 5 on the popular media. Whilst Western societies are viewed as being framed by a dominant discourse of science, there exist other interpretations or ways of viewing the world in which we live. The two most significant are religious or spiritual beliefs and the popular media. Spiritual matters have great relevance for attitudes to dying, death and afterlife beliefs and, as such, impact on social and individual characteristics of mortality. The popular media play a role in informing, reflecting and shaping understandings of mortality and this is achieved through a range of genres that include cinematic representations, television and news media. It has been argued that the media are now replacing the role of religion in shaping our awareness of, and attitudes to, mortality (Walter, 2004). This assertion is explored.

Part II: Social Structures and Individual Experiences of Dying

This section is concerned with the nature and experiences of dying in contemporary Western societies. Chapter 6 examines structural responses to dying. The discussion locates dying within an historical framework that dates back to the nineteenth century wherein certain features of life, such as mental and physical illness and crime, were considered to be social problems that required institutional solutions. The combination of institutionalization and the advance in medical science resulted in the mid-twentieth century in the medicalization of dying. This concept is examined and critiqued through the work of pioneers of change, such as Glaser and Strauss (1965) and Sudnow (1967).

Chapter 7 continues with the theme of dying and explores the notion of the good death. With the demise of medicalized, highly technological forms of hospital dying, the hospice movement emerged in the 1960s. Hospice dying has come to be viewed as the model for the 'good death'. This chapter compares the original hospice philosophy with its current form and asks whether hospice dying can continue to be viewed as the good death. The chapter concludes by looking at other ideas of good death in the form of living wills and euthanasia.

Chapter 8 turns to look at the way in which societies deal with bad death – as distinct from the good death surveyed in the previous chapter. Not all death occurs at the end of a period of dying and sudden, unexpected and/or violent deaths are commonly perceived as bad deaths. This chapter examines the social organization of sudden death, first, from the perspective of professionals such as emergency service workers, the police and the coroner or medical examiner. The focus on professionals allows us to understand the structural elements of the management of sudden death. The role of the coroner or medical examiner is considered in some depth, as it is here that distinctions are made between 'natural' and 'unnatural' death and particular death events distinguished according to a range of categories, such as accidental death, misadventure, suicide, unlawful killing. The experiences of people suddenly bereaved are also discussed in this chapter. This focuses on the way bereaved people may experience the medical and legal structures around sudden death and highlights some of the tensions that exist between the public management and private experience of sudden death.

Chapter 9 is the final chapter in this section and focuses on the dying and on the dead body and its role in the construction and continuation of self-identity. The body is crucial to understanding individual experiences of health, dying and of death. Until relatively recently, sociologists have tended to neglect the significance of the body, relying for their understanding of society on social structures. The creation of a sociology of the body has been important to the recognition of individual agency and no more so than in the sociology of death and dying where the body is central to experiences of illness, dying and loss. The chapter explores the assumption that people construct their self-identity in relation to their bodies and raises questions about the impact of illness and ageing (involving changing body forms) on the construction of self-identity. This chapter also looks at the care of the dead body as it is prepared for the funeral and considers explanations for its treatment. The chapter concludes by addressing the question of the separation between life and death – a continuing theme through-out the book – and the distinction, in relation to agency, that this implies for embodiment and disembodiment.

Part III: Post-Death Rituals of Remembrance and Survival Beliefs

The final section of the book examines post-death beliefs, rituals and practices. It does so in the context of memorialization, disposal rituals and survival beliefs.

Chapter 10 is the first chapter in this section and examines theories of grief. It does so from a chronological perspective, beginning with theories of grief developed by psychiatrists and psychologists. These disciplines were the first in the field, as psychiatrists in particular were called upon to deal with what came to be identified as pathological forms of grieving. During the twentieth century emotions such as grief came to be regarded as the rightful domain of psychology and, for this reason, much of the theorizing in this area was, until the 1990s, undertaken from a mental health perspective. As a consequence, theories of grief (as the emotional response to loss) have largely been framed by models of 'normal' and 'pathological' grieving which assume that a separation between the living and the dead is healthy. After charting some of the earlier models of grief, the chapter moves on to explore the theoretical concept of continuing bonds wherein the living continue their relationships with the dead. This concept has marked a significant change in understanding attitudes to grief and has led to a view among some professionals that new models of grief are now required.

Chapter 11 sets the context for understanding post-death rituals of memorialization. Great diversity is demonstrated in practices of remembrance in both traditional and modern societies. These practices are rooted in belief systems that provide insight into social and individual relationships with death and with the dead. The discussion focuses on three primary elements that assist us to understand the nature of memorial practices: (1) religious perspectives and beliefs about the destiny of the soul and the nature of ancestry; (2) the manner in which the corpse is perceived; and (3) prevailing practices around grief. Each of these is considered in relation to a range of societies. The chapter also includes an examination of Warner's classic study (1965) of the symbolic significance of the cemetery and his conclusions are placed in the context of contemporary Western societies.

Chapter 12 builds on the last chapter to examine mortuary rituals in traditional and modern societies. These rituals reveal a great deal about how societies and individuals make sense of loss and this is reflected in the way in which the corpse is perceived, how it is prepared for the funeral, who is responsible for this preparation and the nature of funeral ceremonies and their social and personal benefit. In exploring these themes, the chapter utilizes theoretical insights from anthropology and history and reminds the reader of the social and cultural diversity of the nature of contemporary Western societies to show that funerals fulfil a variety of social objectives. The history and current role of the funeral director is considered, as this expert often provides the key to understanding contemporary rituals – particularly those concerned with the treatment of the corpse (Howarth, 1996). This is followed by a discussion of the natural death movement and current attempts to undermine the commercialization of mortuary rites.

The final chapter is designed to draw together many of the arguments rehearsed throughout the book and to attempt to provide some answers to the fundamental question raised in this introduction, of how societies make meaning when confronted with mortality. It focuses on contemporary Western societies and argues that although life and death have, within modernity, been constructed as separate, contemporary societies are challenging this way of thinking about mortality. This is demonstrated by the growth in cultural and religious diversity and in the emergence of new or resurgent beliefs and practices around dying, death, grief and remembrance. A central feature of some contemporary approaches is the rejection of the notion of an impenetrable boundary between life and death.

Part I
Social Characteristics and Attitudes to Death

1

Death, Denial and Diversity

Introduction

Death raises the problem of meaning for human beings. Whilst the problem of meaning is one with which theorists from a range of disciplines (from philosophers to psychologists) have struggled, for sociologists the response must be found in a social rather than a personal mechanism. This mechanism or strategy somehow allows individuals within a society to put aside what might appear to be the utter futility of existence, to transcend the temporary nature of social life and retain continuity of purpose. The fundamental question for sociologists then, is, 'How is it possible for societies to continue in the face of mortality?' Sociologists drawing from a range of theoretical perspectives have addressed this question, either directly or indirectly.

Some, like Durkheim (1954 [1915]) would argue that society is greater than the individuals that make up its sum and that structures are developed in the form of rituals to allow for the deaths of individuals to be encompassed within the greater social order. These rituals are often religious rituals that may, for example, frame funeral or grieving behaviours and practices to enable both the immediate family and society at large to mark the loss of one of its members without that loss incurring social disruption.

For Berger (1969), religion is the key to understanding how societies continue in the face of death. Mortality threatens human relationships at an individual level but it also threatens to undermine the basis for order in society. To negotiate the terrors of finitude, human societies construct a 'sacred cosmos', a place beyond mundane life and death existence. 'The sacred cosmos, which transcends and includes man [*sic*] in its ordering of reality, thus provides man's ultimate shield against the terror of anomie' (Berger, 1969: 26). Religion, or the sacred, is depicted as a 'sacred canopy' under which members of society shelter against the terrors of mortality. Other sociologists, such as Gorer (1955; 1965), have argued that rather than confronting the 'facts' of mortality, modern societies have chosen to avoid facing death and instead have produced 'death-denying' societies, where death is confined to medical or scientific discourses; anything outside of that is taboo or viewed as 'pornographic'.

More recent analyses have suggested that death in modern societies has been 'sequestered'. This means that it has been removed from the public realm and placed firmly within the private sphere of the family and individual – thus removing the problem of mortality from an overtly public or social context (Giddens, 1991; Mellor, 1993; Mellor and Shilling, 1993; Shilling, 1993). From a further perspective, Bauman (1992) has argued that, whilst we may not acknowledge it, it is the very fact of our mortality that produces the cultures in which we live. Without death, there would be no culture.

This chapter will examine this question of how societies make sense of mortality. In so doing, it explores the nature of mortality in a range of societies and from a number of theoretical perspectives within sociology. In order to examine more closely such varied theories, it is helpful to place them in the context of different and changing societies, as few, if any, of these theories claim application across all societies. For this reason, we will use and critique Walter's (1996a) typology of death in traditional or pre-modern, modern and postmodern societies (see table 1.1). Theories that suggest that contemporary Western societies are death-denying are examined

Table 1.1 The changing nature of death in traditional, modern and postmodern societies

	Traditional death	Modern death	Postmodern death
Authority	Tradition	Professional expertise	Personal choice
Authority figure	Priest	Doctor	The self
Dominant discourse	Theology	Medicine	Psychology
Coping through	Prayer	Silence	Expressing feelings
The traveller	Soul	Body	Personality
Bodily context	Living with death	Death controlled	Living with dying
Social context	Community	Hospital	Family

Source: Walter, 1996a: 195; reproduced with permission of Palgrave Macmillan

and critiqued, as this assertion has become a dominant theme in discussions of mortality where it is commonly asserted that we live in societies where death is either taboo or denied. A major problem with this approach derives from the assumption that Western societies are socially and culturally homogenous and that whole societies can be identified as sharing one cultural approach. The chapter concludes by addressing this problem and pointing to the impact on attitudes to mortality of increased social and cultural diversity.

Before we continue any further, it is important to briefly define Walter's use of these societal types. *Traditional* societies tend to be defined as societies distinct from those that have undergone a period of industrialization. Included under this type are societies as distinct as hunter-gatherer societies, nomadic societies, agrarian societies and those of antiquity and ancient history.

Modern societies, in social science terms, refer to societies that have undergone industrialization and subscribe to notions of progress in human activities related to politics, economics, communication systems, science and technology. In Europe, the historical period of modernity may be dated from the mid-sixteenth century.

Postmodern societies are usually dated as occurring during the twentieth century in the Western world and as particularly prevalent in the latter part of that century. These are depicted as societies in which the values associated with modernity have become fragmented and there has been a significant rise in the importance of the mass media, communication systems and popular culture. The globalization of systems of production and economic arrangements has resulted in challenges to social norms and values. This has led to a proliferation and fragmentation of values, for example, critiques of science and progress.

Prior to discussing Walter's framework, it is important to note that his typology utilizes broad categories that are useful for conceptualizing dominant approaches to death in each society but are unable to truly reflect complexity within societies. Societies cannot easily be typified according to a linear historical or anthropological period; beliefs and practices do not fall neatly or solely into one or other of these categories. For example, the concept of the traditional (or pre-modern) society might be expected to encompass all societies that pre-date Western Enlightenment thinking and those contemporary societies that have not industrialized. This effectively groups together communities as distinct as those of medieval Europe, prehistoric hunter-gatherer tribes and those of the Egyptian Pharaohs. There is little archaeological evidence to suggest that prehistoric societies understood death through the lens of religion. Equally, in archaeological terms, at the time of the Pharaohs, Egyptian people were, in essence, modern people. Similarly, in modern societies there may be found strong traces of beliefs, such as folk beliefs and superstitions that might, according to Walter's schema, be more appropriately associated with traditional societies. Furthermore, although medicine may provide a means of understanding the causes of illness and death and be at the forefront of the struggle for health and longevity, religious practice continues to be fundamental to many people's understanding of mortality. Furthermore, there is much cultural diversity within societies, particularly contemporary Western societies, and although it is expedient to consider each system separately – traditional, modern and postmodern – in reality it is only possible to speak of dominant beliefs, values and practices that marginalize (but do not necessarily eradicate) other approaches. For this reason, Walter's categorization of the nature of death in each type of society should be used as a tool for identifying dominant approaches surrounding death rather than as a portrait of attitudes within any one society.

Having noted the complexity and diversity of the location of mortality within societies, let us begin this exploration of the changing nature of death in Western societies with a brief (and commonly held) portrayal of the character of mortality in each of Walter's types of society.

Walter's typology provides a broad framework for understanding different social approaches to death in each of the three categories he outlines. In short, he argues that religion forms the basis of meaning in traditional societies but that in modern societies this is undermined and usurped by medical science. In postmodern societies, the dominance of either religion or medicine has given way to a greater emphasis on the individual and, in so doing, has privileged psychology and the authority figure of 'the self'. Let us now examine the veracity of this account.

Death in traditional or pre-modern societies

Walter (1996a) argues that in traditional societies religion forms the basis for understanding death. The authority figure is the priest and the dominant discourse (language for understanding) is that of organized religion. People believe in an afterlife that may involve a weighing of life deeds and a subsequent return to mortal existence to gain greater spiritual experience; for others it may be expected to be much longer (possibly eternal) and more pleasant than the one they experience in the mortal world. Whatever the nature of life after death, the social context for meaning-making is the community, and death (like life) is primarily played out in the public sphere.

According to Ariès (1974, 1981, 1985), a social historian and prolific writer on the nature of attitudes to death, pre-modern Western societies perceived of death as an inevitable fact of life. Christianity was the dominant religion in Europe during the Middle Ages and the Church held authority in matters of life and death. Life, particularly for the poor masses, was made sense of in the context of death: poverty, misery and injustice were compensated by rewards in heaven and the promise of eternal joy. The 'good death' was defined as one where people were aware that death was immanent and they therefore had the opportunity to prepare themselves for it, both spiritually and in terms of their earthly business. Unless death came suddenly, awareness of its proximity meant that people were able to receive visits from friends and relatives who would gather to make their farewells and listen to instructions about the disposal of any belongings. Furthermore, a priest would be summoned to preside over the individual's spiritual needs and to administer extreme unction when the time came. A written or verbal testament would be produced and any necessary apologies and confessions made to absolve personal conscience and prepare for a smooth journey into the afterlife. After death the body would be disposed of by burial in consecrated ground. People with wealth and influence could be buried within the church, usually under the floor of the building. The closer to the altar the body was buried, the closer they were believed to be to their resurrection. During this time there was a widespread belief in purgatory. This was a popular conviction in Europe from the fifth century until the Reformation. It was assumed that the souls of the dead had to pass through a place of spiritual cleansing. The prayers of the living could assist the dead on this journey.

Transition to modern deathways in Europe

In Europe during the sixteenth and seventeenth centuries, as intellectuals struggled to critically examine their culture and environment, the seeds of secularization were sown. The physical world was afforded a new significance and, although nature continued to be regarded as glorifying God, the interest in worldly phenomena laid the foundations for scientific understanding. The 'tame death' that Ariès (1981) identified as belonging to the Middle Ages – that is, death that was expected, visible and public – slowly began to give way to a death that was no longer accepted as inevitable and influenced only by petitions to God. It was the perception of death as a social problem – a stance increasingly adopted during the late seventeenth and early eighteenth centuries – that provides clues to changing attitudes to mortality in the early modern period in Europe.

The rise of Protestantism and, in the sixteenth century, its rejection of the doctrine of purgatory, meant that life deeds took on greater importance for the salvation of the deceased as the payment of doles[1] and the efficacy of chantries[2] came to be viewed with disapproval and scepticism (LeGoff, 1984). Gittings (1984) contends that during this period of early modernity there was an increasing awareness of individualism and the notion of the self, and a heightened distinction between life and death. As the eighteenth century unfolded, industrialization led to the rapid growth of towns and urban populations. With the decline in small scale, close-knit *Gemeinschaft* communities, death increasingly came to be perceived as a personal, individual loss and located within the private domain (McManners, 1981).

Large-scale migration from rural areas and the consequent rapid growth of urban populations resulted in the disintegration of previously held values and mores surrounding communities, families, religion and associated hierarchies. This promoted an awareness of the need for stability and social order. Institutions were established, dedicated to solving the problems of social order, and here we locate the forerunners of the modern prison and hospitals for the physically and mentally ill. The dawning appreciation of the greater importance of the individual over the community added death, or rather the social disorder that death threatened, to the list of social problems demanding attention.

Modernity

Ariès (1981) argued of Western European societies that during the twentieth century the burden on religion to provide 'insurance' against mortality declined and attention turned instead to the quality and quantity of life in this world rather than eternal happiness in the next. The role of the clergy dwindled as will-making and deathbed care came to be adopted as roles for the legal and medical professions. Unlike pre-modern Europe, when the will might have been verbal and issued at the deathbed in front of witnesses, the writing of wills began to occur before dying, with the help of lawyers. During the same period, the doctor began to replace the priest at the bedside, taking responsibility for prolonging life and, with the help of narcotics (Porter, 1989), assisting to make death as painless as possible.

During the twentieth century dying was no longer the preserve of the Church, but primarily the concern of medical science. Medical science aims to expand the frontiers of physical existence and to limit death, at least in Western societies, to the realms of accident and extreme old age. Medical knowledge has now firmly located the causes of death within the body rather than by appeal to the supernatural or the will of God. According to Riley (1989), this process, begun in the nineteenth century, has gradually altered the discourse on death to one of sickness, with a related popular mythology trusting that all illnesses can (or eventually will) be cured. The notion of 'saving life' erroneously takes on an air of permanence. Broadly speaking, the 'good death' in the modern Western world has become the death in old age.

In contrast to good death, a 'bad death', is an 'untimely' or premature end. To die in youth brings emotional devastation to the bereaved. Discussion of such tragedies dwells on the 'waste of human life' and, often, the belief that someone must be to blame: with greater care or more sophisticated technology the catastrophe could have been avoided. Under the auspices of saving life and reducing suffering, medical science has developed techniques and remedies to drastically reduce both the incidence of mortality and much of the accompanying physical and emotional pain. Consequently, advanced industrial nations are freed from all manner of terminal diseases such as tuberculosis, cholera and smallpox, and wait patiently on the assumption that sooner or later cures will be found for those that remain to plague us. As Simpson asserts:

> The significance of death has changed in our society. Institutionalised medicine has become so adept at attracting funds and at impressing us with its marvellous achievements that we have almost come to assume that death is somehow avoidable – if you pay enough money and if the medical team works hard enough. Many people behave as if death is, accordingly, always someone's fault, always due to someone's act of omission or commission. (1972: 2)

Unlike religious systems that perceive of death as an integral feature of life, these scientific-rational approaches cast death as the enemy. As such, it is the role of the medical doctor to engage in battle on behalf of the patients.

Postmodern deathways

A number of sociologists have argued that in contemporary Western societies – broadly depicted as 'postmodern' or 'high modern' – death has been *sequestered*. By this they mean that death has been removed from the public sphere and located instead in the private world of the individual. This sequestration of death to which Giddens (1991) and Mellor and Shilling (1993) refer explains the contradiction between the apparent absence of death in the public realm and the presence of death in the private lives of individuals. Death, Mellor (1993) contends, in keeping with the project of modernity, has been removed from public space and relocated as a personal issue.

> [T]his sequestration is manifest as the privatisation and subjectivisation of the experience of death, which in turn results in the increased presence of considerations of death *for individuals*. . . . In high modernity, individuals must create their own identities, drawing upon the reflexive mechanisms and socio-cultural resources available to them, but ultimately having to take individual responsibility for the construction of meanings as well as the construction of identity. In this context, death is particularly disturbing because it signals a threatened 'irreality' of the self-projects which modernity encourages individuals to embark upon, an ultimate *absence* of meaning, the *presence* of death bringing home to them existential isolation of the individual in high modernity. (Mellor, 1993: 12, 19–20)

Sequestration is illustrated in that the majority of people now die in institutions, away from the public gaze. Social strategies that assimilate the knowledge of mortality are fragmented because it is individuals who must create their own sense of meaning in the face of death. For example, in the latter half of the twentieth century, Western societies witnessed the emergence of a variety of approaches for coping with death, such as the blossoming of the hospice movement and an upsurge in new religious movements – arguably as a reaction to secularization and the associated individual search for meaning. This period was one in which there were attempts to construct more personalized death rituals. One feature of this was the creation of the Natural Death Movement (Alberry et al., 1993) that criticizes medical science and the funeral professions for removing control of dying and death from the individual. There has also been a growing movement appealing for the legalisation of euthanasia, in part as a response to the power of medical science to extend life. The grand illusion that science can control mortality has thus been subjected to growing scrutiny.

Having set out the parameters of social understandings of mortality from pre- to postmodernity, we will now critically examine the way in which sociologists have interpreted the place of death in modern and contemporary societies.

From measurement to meaning

Death in nineteenth-century Western industrial societies could be equated with uncertainty, and uncertainty with disorder. In keeping with the scientific ethic of the day, the solution to disorder was perceived as classification. The nineteenth century had witnessed a revolution in the discourse of mortality. Sympathetic with the increasing desire to control or predict social phenomena and to restore patterns of social order lost in the move from rural to urban societies, came a preoccupation with taxonomy: with ordering, counting and measuring aspects of society, including death. Furthermore, the two – classification and control – were viewed as being linked; the former regarded as the means by which the latter could be achieved. Prior (1989) contends that these aims were crucial to the development of the disciplines of demography and pathology. According to Diamond and McDonald (1994), the discipline of demography began with the study of mortality. Its purpose was to identify trends in the causes of death across different populations and, in so doing, to point to social, economic, behavioural and environmental factors that result from these patterns. The discipline of pathology was established in the nineteenth century at a time of increasing concern with the scientific study of disease. Constructing a scientific connection between the causes of death and the human body, it located disease as existing within the body. Sociology was also a new discipline at this time, which, as Prior argues, 'had discovered in death something which both reinforced and reflected the nature of the social' (1989: 7). The accent in all three disciplines was on investigation, explanation, classification and, thereby ultimately, control of the human condition.

Like the disciplines of demography and pathology, sociology perceived of death as a measurable phenomenon and Emile Durkheim was one of the first sociologists to attempt to do just that. Believing sociology to be the scientific study of society, Durkheim's work focused on the distinction between traditional and modern societies. His study of suicide is particularly apposite here and his appraisal of the distinction between traditional and modern societies is significant to an understanding of his approach to mortality. For Durkheim (1954 [1915]), death had a greater significance in societies he described as 'simple', where what he termed 'mechanical solidarity' prevailed. These traditional or 'primitive' societies, he argued, were based on similarity: small, simple, homogenous societies where beliefs, values, meanings and experiences were similar. They were characterized by a strong, coercive collective consciousness (external normative order) that ensured the moral integration of individuals into society. In these simple societies, as anthropologists continue to argue, death had a profoundly disruptive effect on everyday life and was therefore accorded prominence in cultural behaviour. As societies became more highly structured with an increased division of labour, they also became more complex. Durkheim defined these latter societies as containing people with different values, beliefs and attitudes. Drawing on a biological analogy, he identified them as having 'organic solidarity'. This means that although parts of society are dissimilar, like the organs of the body they rely on each other for successful functioning. In these modern, organic societies, Durkheim claimed, there is less awareness of death, fewer public rituals and more privatized forms for acknowledging and grieving loss.

Robert Blauner's (1966) classic analysis of the place of death in traditional and modern societies drew similar conclusions to Durkheim, asserting that death was less significant in complex societies. In concluding that modern societies are more able to control death he reached for quantifiable data as a means of comparing the two types of societies:

Let us take, for instance, one of the average Australian tribes (usually numbering 300–600 members.) The simultaneous loss of 10 persons is therefore an event which quantitatively considered, would have the same significance as the simultaneous death of 630,000 to 850,000 inhabitants in the present Polish state. (1966: 175)

Blauner appeared to be of the opinion that modern societies can control death. The way in which they achieve this has the consequence of reducing the status and power of death:

> But the weakening of religious imagery is not the sole cause; there is again a functional sociological basis. When those who die are not important to the life of society, the dead as a collective category will not be of major significance in the concerns of the living. (1966: 191)

In terms of methodology, Durkheim believed that society generated its own social reality. This social reality was observable in 'social facts' – aspects of the social world that stood alone regardless of the subjective views of individuals – which had similar status to the facts of the natural world and could be discovered using similar scientific methods. This approach to understanding society is referred to as 'positivism' and it assumes that the social world can be observed and knowledge generated in much the same way as in the natural world. According to this perspective, the role of the sociologist is to reveal and explain the social facts on which society is built:

> No recourse to subjective meaning is necessary or desirable. Thus, such an apparently 'subjective' datum as a suicide can be objectified in terms of the rates of suicide, but these can be explained by the conditions of social solidarity or its absence (anomie) ... for Durkheim it is an objective structural fact, measurable in totally objective terms. (Berger and Luckman, 1967: 14)

We will return to Durkheim's study of suicide in chapter 2; suffice it here to acknowledge that he was one of the first sociologists specifically to be concerned with death as a 'social problem'. In terms of social understandings of death, Durkheim set a precedent that was to shape sociological approaches to death for half a century at least. Accordingly, death was viewed as a measurable entity, a social fact that could be correlated with other social facts – for example, by studying mortality rates according to occupation, socio-economic position, wealth, or housing status. This positivist strategy of identifying, categorizing and measuring the causes and impact of death led to a sociological fixation for studying mortality solely through the lens of quantifiable data according to age, birth cohort, gender, economic status, and so on. Death, the great and universal uncertainty, was ordered by sociologists and employed as a social fact of society to clarify other social facts, such as life chances and the impact of poverty.

To some extent this approach to mortality, which views death as controllable by identifying and measuring its causes and impact, continues to shape modern Western understandings of death. This can be seen in contemporary societies where there is an emphasis on delineating causes of death and producing 'league tables' of the 'biggest killers' in the modern world – in Western societies these are identified as circulatory and respiratory diseases and cancer. Armed with this knowledge and the doctrine of new public health (which enshrines personal responsibility for well-being – see chapter 3), it is deemed possible to reduce the number of people dying from each cause and so to improve the health of nations. As Prior (1989) remarks, in modernity death is reduced to a typology of causes, all of which can, in theory at least, be cured or avoided.

We have already noted the nineteenth-century emphasis on institutional solutions to social problems. In part a consequence of institutionalization, was the move to professionalize skills and to create organizations of expertise. These connected processes of institutionalization and professionalization became more developed during the twentieth century. In the field of medicine this led to a reliance on medical science to assist with the battle between life and death. From the mid-century onward, this resulted in the creation of a new way of dying, described in the critical literature as 'medicalized' dying. Medicalization, as we shall see in chapter 6, is a concept used by sociologists to refer to the process by which social life comes to be seen through the lens of medicine – see, for example, Zola (1972) and Illich (1976). According to the medicalization thesis, the emphasis within medical science on the biomedical model has become a dominant discourse in our understanding of social life. Modern medicine is now able to define health and illness and, Zola (1972) argues, has effectively become a mechanism for social control by determining what is 'healthy' and what is 'normal' in society. Furthermore, Illich (1976) claims that medicalization has dehumanized dying by viewing death as a failure of medicine and thus subjecting dying people to a range of technological indignities in attempts to keep them alive.

According to this thesis, medicalization has disempowered dying people. Medical science's commitment to longevity can have a distressing effect on dying people and their relatives. Maintaining the illusion of hope for a last-minute reprieve and, arguably, failing to allow the dying to make adequate preparation, can lead to awkward and embarrassing interaction between patient, staff and relatives (Glaser and Strauss, 1965; Sudnow, 1967). Dying people are discouraged from becoming 'morbidly preoccupied' with death, and their relatives and friends often feel it necessary to collude in the conspiracy to convince the patient that it is simply a matter of time before they will be 'up and around again'. Rather than dying peacefully amongst family, terminally ill people may be moved from home to hospital in the expectation that medical technology may save them. In their criticism of the treatment of dying, sociologists have characterized modern death and dying as occurring within a resounding conspiracy of silence where neither the professionals nor dying people and their families were able to speak of death.

From the 1960s, however, sociologists began to challenge this silence and to concern themselves with the nature of dying in societies characterized as medicalized. This generated a new discourse on dying which spoke of the need to liberate dying people from the prison of silence to which they had been confined. This challenge was initially pursued most fervently in the United States, producing important studies such as Sudnow's (1967) ethnography of the social organization of death in hospital settings and Glaser and Strauss's (1965 and 1967) work on the awareness and timing of dying. One consequence of these new studies was that the preoccupation with measuring mortality rates and the relation to social structures dwindled, and concern focused instead on individual agency and the meaning and experiences of dying and death. Death was no longer construed merely as a statistic but was an individual dying in a hospital setting, surrounded by professionals and family.

These new approaches, which characterized much of the sociological research in this area from the 1960s onwards, essentially explored the way in which people constructed the world around them; thus marking a turn from structural approaches to the study of individual agency and meaning. Critics of the modern, medicalized forms of dying came from a range of perspectives. Some, like Glaser and Strauss (1965), Illich (1976), Sudnow (1967) and Elias (1985) believed that the problems of dying in modern societies lay with the organization of institutions and the emphasis on high-tech, medical solutions which focused on cure rather than palliation. Others, such as Gorer (1955) and Ariès (1981), believed that the problems of mortality in modern societies stemmed from a loss of traditions. Closely associated with this latter view were those who argued that modern, Western societies had become 'death-denying' and were characterized by attempts to avoid the reality of mortality (Becker, 1973).

Loss of tradition and the denial of death

As we have seen, it was not until after the Second World War that sociologists began to question the structural, quantitative analysis of death in modern Western societies. Gorer (1955), subscribing to the view that 'natural' death was hidden, rued the passing of Victorian mourning customs and criticized modern Western societies for a failure to acknowledge and confront the realities of death. This perspective suggests that Gorer was either ignorant of the wealth of data generated by the positivists, or, alternatively, that he did not recognize it as a discourse on mortality. Comparing contemporary attitudes to mortality with the Victorian reaction to sex, he concluded that death had replaced sex as the unmentionable subject. 'Natural' death and the corruption and decay of the body, he believed, had become disgusting where once they formed an ever-present feature of life. In the nineteenth century, sex was disguised and cloaked in euphemism, for example, babies were not born but 'found under gooseberry bushes'. In the modern world, Gorer insisted, death had not simply become a substitute for sex but, rather, violent death had come to reside alongside sex as a legitimate theme for entertainment. 'While natural death has become more and more smothered in prudery, violent death has played an ever-growing part in the fantasies offered to mass audiences' (1955: 173). For Gorer, death had become pornographic. Ariès (1981) held similar views to Gorer and, as noted earlier in this chapter, criticized modern societies for having the most unhealthy approach to mortality of all time. For Ariès and Gorer, death had fallen within the domain of the medical profession and this had resulted in death being hidden, locked away within a hospital setting and mourning privatized and confined to the immediate family.

It was during the 1950s and '60s that the 'denial of death' thesis emerged. This thesis, promulgated primarily by psychologists but supported by sociologists such as Gorer who argued that death had become the 'final taboo', suggested that modern Western societies are 'death-denying'. The protagonists asserted that fear of death is universal and therefore societies have to find ways of dealing with this fear in order for them to continue in an orderly fashion. Where traditional societies may have relied on religion to provide a shelter against death (Berger, 1969), modern societies were constructed around death-avoidance. The medicalization of dying was given as a prime example of this trend where, it was argued, sickness had replaced death, with dying predominantly occurring in institutions, largely hidden from the public gaze, and with patients and professionals generally denying its imminence.

The concept of death-denial derives from the work of Freud (1940) and is based on the idea that individuals use denial as a defence against potentially traumatizing experiences. As the exclusion of awareness of loss or potential loss, denial may be employed to explain behaviour that refuses to acknowledge, '(1) the fact or reality of death, (2) the meaning of a death, or (3) a particular affective or cognitive aspect of grief' (Kauffman, 2001: 151). The notion that societies may be death-denying was developed by Becker

(1973) in his book, *The Denial of Death*. He asserted that whole societies may adopt this maladaptive psychological response to awareness of mortality. Evidence of denial was sought and 'attributed to social institutions such as medical education, burial customs, the nature of modern work, traditional religion or even medical research efforts' (Kellehear, 2001: 152).

There have been a number of sociological critiques of this essentially psychological theory of the place of death in modern societies. The first of these was expounded by American sociologists Talcott Parsons and Victor Lidz (1967). They preferred the concept of 'instrumental activism' to describe the modern approach to mortality and stressed the point that a radical change in death rituals need not represent a denial of death. People in Western society cannot be seeking to avoid death, they argued, when the orientation of science is to control mortality – or at least, its more 'adventitious' aspects. Science, they contended, can hardly be 'grounded primarily in fantasies that deny basic realities of the empirical world'. Death is not denied; rather, it is accepted but in a manner apposite to 'our primary cultural patterns of activism' (Parsons and Lidz, 1967: 32). More recent sociological criticism of the death-denial thesis has centred on the indiscriminate manner in which the theory is applied (Kellehear, 1984) and its inadequacy as a descriptor of responses to death in modern, Western societies (Walter, 1991). Given the popular prevalence of the thesis and its consequent significance for understandings of death in the modern world, we will consider each of these criticisms in some depth.

Kellehear takes issue with the idea that modern societies are necessarily 'death-denying'. He argues that in contemporary Western societies the denial thesis, 'is used indiscriminately to refer to any avoidance of reality – particularly the reality of the labelling observer' (1984: 713). In the context of death, individual behaviour can easily be identified as death-denying without the identifier being required to provide an explanation. As Kellehear suggests:

> As a theoretical construct it has the best of both worlds – valid with and even more valid without – any evidence. As Taylor [1979] has pointed out of attitude research in the area of death, three propositions are widely held: (a) death creates fear; (b)

respondents often profess little fear and therefore, (c) are denying their fear of death. (1984: 713)

Based on an analysis of the individual psyche, the concept of 'denial' is primarily psychiatric and Kellehear objects to its wholesale adoption by sociologists as a descriptor of society. The problem hinges on the confusion this creates between personal and social systems. For example, the thesis suggests that there is a universal fear of death. The question must be asked as to whether this is a personal, individual fear (with all that implies) or a social fear that can then be identified organizationally in society. It is this fundamental confusion that forms the basis of Kellehear's critique. He argues against the widespread use of death–denial on four grounds: fear of death, medicalization, crisis of individualism, examples of social practice.

The fear of death argument

Psychologists have argued that fear of death is a universal phenomenon. If this is so and every individual in every society shares this fear, then it must be a social rather than simply an individual feature. Kellehear rejects this conclusion. First, he points out that many studies have shown that fear of death is not universal. Second, that where individuals do report fear, the nature of it varies. Third, the category of fear is so inclusive that it may well be regarded as a fear of life itself. Fourth, a description of individual fear does not tell us anything about the organizational dynamics that might result.

The medicalization of death argument

The denial thesis relies heavily on the idea that sickness has replaced death in modern societies. The argument suggests that as dying now increasingly occurs in medical institutions, such as the hospital, patients and professionals will deny the imminence of death and focus instead on sickness and healing. In response to this, Kellehear points out that individual beliefs and institutional procedures cannot be equated. A dying person may follow the 'rules' of the hospital by not talking about death (as may a member of staff). This behaviour, however, tells us nothing about their personal beliefs or their interactions with others. There is no reason, he contends, to assume that these are characterized by denial.

The twentieth-century crisis of individualism argument

Ariès (1981) and others have asserted that a further consequence of medicalization has been the loss of the 'good' or 'natural' death. According to this thesis, the individual can no longer preside over his/her own death, as the medical profession has divested them of control. Again, Kellehear takes issue with this analysis. Amongst other criticisms, he points out that in any society the characterization and features of dying will depend on the nature of the prevailing authority. So, for example, in pre-modern societies religion may hold authority over death and this is reflected in the way in which people die. In modern Western societies it is medicine that holds sway over the social organization of death.

Examples of death-denying social practices

The final area that Kellehear critiques is the propensity of death-denial theorists to search for confirming examples rather than examining practice and thus potentially highlighting features that undermine the theory. These confirming instances tend to be taken from observations of the funeral industry, religion and the social expression of grief.

Walter (1991) proposes a further critique of the concept of death-denial in his article entitled, 'Modern death: taboo or not taboo?' Walter focuses on Gorer's (1955) assertion that death is the taboo of modern society, having replaced sex as a source of pornographic entertainment. He takes issue with this by pointing out that death and news of death are everywhere in modern societies. For example, it is almost impossible to read a newspaper or to turn on the television without being confronted with death. Although some of this takes the form of violent entertainment, much of it is the everyday treatment of mortality. Through the media we are presented daily with news of tragic death at home and abroad; with the death of children and adults from cancer, industrial negligence, murder, war, famine, natural disasters and so-called acts of terrorism. The death of celebrities is regularly reported, whether a consequence of illness, accident, violence or old age.

This public presence of death challenges the death-denial thesis. It also raises questions for those who argue that death in modern societies has been sequestered or removed from the public realm (Giddens, 1991; Mellor, 1993; Mellor and Shilling, 1993). Sequestration is said to occur because death poses problems of meaning for the lives of individuals in complex, postmodern societies. Thus death is argued to be publicly absent but privately present. Whilst there is no doubting the privatization of many aspects of dying and grief, it may be that in their quest to uncover hidden death, social theorists have neglected to acknowledge the more public face of death. Moreover, in analysing the nature of death, and evaluating the denial of death thesis, sociologists have tended to adopt a psychological mechanism that was not designed to analyse society. This psychological model focuses on the individual pathology of denial or disavowal and this, in turn, leads to an emphasis on individual or private systems. Centring analysis on these individual aspects of mortality inevitably ignores other areas of public social experience where death is present. Employing the public/private dichotomy, simply serves to obscure rather than illuminate our understanding of death in contemporary Western societies. Death is complex and multifaceted and cannot be moulded to fit into a simplistic public/private dichotomy. It appears in both spheres, in expected and unexpected forms, natural and unnatural, to the willing and the reluctant. It occurs in complex and simple ways and as such challenges attempts to reduce it to a single, simple discourse. A further critique that may be made of the argument that death has been sequestered, is that it fails to take account of social and cultural diversity.

Social and cultural diversity

Modern Western societies are increasingly culturally heterogeneous, yet many accounts of death-denial and the so-called loss of tradition fail to acknowledge this. For example, Ariès presents a rather romantic version of death in traditional societies. According to his account there is little or no cultural diversity in these societies and so dying takes place in the community and conforms to a process overseen by the Church. This explanation places emphasis on the significance of social structures and, as Durkheim (1954 [1915]) would have argued, on the strength of the collective conscience, or moral order in society.

However, as Kellehear (1984) comments, in identifying modern societies as typically death-denying, supporters of this thesis have been searching for confirming instances. These are easily found in the funeral industry, in hospitals, schools, and so on. Thus, what they observe matches their expectations and reinforces the death-denying paradigm. What is hidden or lost in this research is not death but anything that does not fit with the dominant discourse of death in modernity. If, by contrast, the emphasis on research into social attitudes and rituals surrounding death focused on diversity the model would begin to collapse. Unlike the model of traditional societies that is based on similarity (and is itself debateable), in modern societies death, dying and grief comes in many shapes and forms. Unfortunately, most commentators on contemporary death mores have ignored the richness and complexity and looked only for similarities.

In his typology of the changing nature of death (see table 1.1) Walter views death in modern societies as dominated and controlled by the medical profession. In contrast, postmodern death is described as a matter of personal choice and a refusal to accept the authority of either religion or medicine. The dominant discourse is that of psychology and the social context, the family. It may be, however, that neither modern nor postmodern death can be so clearly defined. Alternative discourses exist alongside dominant ones – the former are merely less visible. It might thus be argued that it is not postmodern fragmentation that is being identified but social and cultural diversity. Such diversity has always existed, but has been pushed to the margins by dominant discourses that reflect the power of different social groups, for example, of those seeking only religious or medical understandings. More recently sociologists of death have begun to hear the marginal voices of women, working-class people and ethnic and religious minorities in their scrutiny of death in contemporary Western societies.

Field et al. (1997) have examined a variety of theoretical approaches to understanding social and cultural diversity in relation to mortality. These include functionalist approaches that focus on patterns of behaviour in minority ethnic groups that are perceived as key to understanding social factors or structures that shape experiences. As Field at al. argue, however, this approach results in placing too much emphasis on consensus or shared values systems that are assumed to be normal within such groups. A further approach is the Marxist political economy view that emphasizes distinct power relations in society and focuses on inequalities in material conditions such as income, housing and employment. These assume that differences in health and illness, and thus experiences associated with dying and death, are a consequence of economic position and that minority ethnic groups and women will fare less well 'than more advantaged males and the dominant ethnic group' (1997: 22). Structuralist and post-structuralist approaches tend to draw from anthropological work and take greater account of the symbolic meanings associated with social systems. In the context of death and dying, they suggest the importance of understanding belief systems within the wider social context and the need to interrogate the deeper social meanings of images and what they signify. Linked to this is the approach of the interactionists who focus primarily on the way in which individuals make sense of their illness, dying and death. Unlike the other approaches, however, this emphasizes the agency of the individual in shaping and defining behaviour. Studies using this framework (Roth and Conrad, 1987; Strauss, 1994) have adopted the concept of the 'illness career', examining the manner in which people come to understand their illness and the crises and 'critical turning points' they face in managing illness and incorporating 'altered identities and self-conceptions into new patterns of social life' (Field et al. 1997: 23).

Whilst there are yet other approaches to understanding social and cultural diversity, what is important here is that it is a combination of structural and individual factors that impacts on experiences of death and, furthermore, that these factors are dynamic. It cannot be assumed that members of a particular ethnic group will necessarily share values and belief systems. It is also important to remember that social status, economic position, and a range of other factors such as gender, ethnicity, sexuality, age and disability, will also impact on experiences and beliefs and that these cross-cut each other in their influence.

Although contemporary Western societies may be fundamentally structured by modernity, there is great social and cultural diversity both among and within societies. The concept of social diversity is broad-ranging and not solely confined to ethnic differences. All social distinctions, such as social class, ethnicity, gender, age, sexuality and disability, help to give shape and meaning to experiences of dying, death and grief. Indeed, the recognition of difference should be central to any theoretical understanding of the nature of death in society. Furthermore, as Campbell et al. (2000) illustrate, recognizing diversity is essential in establishing policies on good practice for those who work with dying and bereaved people.

Summary

This chapter has examined some of the major theoretical approaches to the social understanding of mortality. It began by considering Walter's (1996a) model of death in pre-modern, modern and postmodern Western societies. The way in which sociologists have interpreted death was then discussed. The structural accounts of Durkheim were considered, as was the impact that such positivist approaches had on the sociological study of death in the late nineteenth and early twentieth centuries. The development of interactionist sociology in post-Second World War Western societies marked a turning point in the study of mortality, with more emphasis placed on individual meaning rather than the earlier focus on the measurement of causes and impacts of social structures. From the 1950s and 1960s, medical sociologists, such as Glaser and Strauss (1965) and Sudnow (1967), studied the experiences of hospital dying and added their voices to those who criticized the medicalization and institutionalizaton of dying and death. The discussion then examined the denial of death thesis that asserts that in modern societies death is hidden, taboo and denied. This thesis derives from a psychological model that has been adapted to account for what has been perceived as a principle theme in modern, Western societies – that they are death-denying. The work of Kellehear (1984) and Walter (1991) was used to evaluate the validity of this thesis for contemporary societies. The chapter concluded by highlighting the significant of understanding social and cultural diversity in Western societies and by suggesting that what has been viewed as denial of death might more properly be identified as a neglect of marginal experiences and practices surrounding death and dying.

In the next chapter we will demographically explore some of this diversity in a global context.

2

When and How People Die

Introduction

Prior to exploring death, dying and loss in detail, it is appropriate to examine patterns of mortality both within and across societies. Death is one of the few certainties in life. As a biological event it will come to us all, and in virtue of this it has often been regarded as the 'great leveller'. In the eyes of death we are all attractive: rich and poor, black and white, male and female, young and old. Whilst this is true, however, it is only part of the story, for death is also a social event and how we understand and experience it depends on the social environment in which we live. Death may come to us all, but the form or character it takes and the way in which we deal with it will vary according to a very wide range of social and cultural factors.

At a structural level, the nature of mortality will be influenced by political, economic and military stability, by the extent of technological or industrial development, and by government policies on issues such as public health, environmental pollution, workplace health and safety. At an individual level, encounters with death, dying and grief will depend on a person's cultural and religious identification, social and economic status, and on the impact of social attitudes to gender, ethnicity, age, sexuality, disability. In other words, experiences of mortality are complex, as death has a diverse character that reflects the social and cultural diversity among and within every human society. Furthermore, as societies change, so do the social characteristics of mortality and, with that, individual experiences of death, dying and loss. In later chapters we will consider some of the issues associated with the way in which individuals negotiate their lives in terms of their experiences of dying, grief and memorialization.

The discussion in this chapter will focus on the demographics of mortality in different societies. In this way, it will recognize the importance of time, place and disease (Najman, 2000). To highlight the significance of social structural factors, the chapter will begin by noting the prevalence and importance of socio-economic status within societies. Following an explanation of the nature and purposes of the demographic study of mortality, we will then concentrate on the demographics of life expectancy, infant mortality, maternal mortality and old age. As the chapter progresses, the social meanings of death and dying will also be considered through examinations of AIDS and suicide. The thread that runs through much of the discussion of patterns of disadvantage, and which is central to the understanding of mortality globally, is socio-economic status or poverty.

Socio-economic status

Almost all societies have some way of distinguishing socio-economic status or social stratification (for example, the caste system in India). In modern Western societies distinctions of social class tend to exist alongside a commitment to equality before the law and the rights of individuals to move from one socio-economic position to another (Howarth, 2001: 418). Social class affects life experience of housing, areas of dwelling, geographical and social mobility, school attended (private/public, well resourced/poorly resourced), educational qualifications, and occupation and peer

Table 2.1 Life expectancy by social class (ONS longitudinal study) for men and women, England and Wales (1992–1996), by age

Social class	Men	Women
I	77.7	83.4
II	75.8	81.1
IIIN	75.0	80.4
IIIM	73.5	78.8
IV	72.6	77.7
V	68.2	77.0
Difference I –V	9.5	6.4
All	73.9	79.2

Source: Hattersley, 1999; Office of National Statistics. Crown copyright is reproduced with the permission of the Controller of HMSO

group. It impacts on health and access to medicine and care (for example, public/private provision). It is also significant in guiding behaviour, with individuals from lower socio-economic groups thought to be more likely to smoke and to be involved in high-risk behaviour. In contemporary Western societies a person's social class status will affect the nature and timing of death. As can be seen from table 2.1 life expectancy varies according to social class position. In England and Wales, men in Social Class I (the highest socio-economic class) can expect to live, on average, nine and a half years longer than those in Class V, the lowest socio-economic class. Explanations for this are to be found in the greater life chances and better quality of life for people in higher socio-economic groups. Members of lower classes are more at risk of workplace accidents and related diseases such as asbestosis. A lower life expectancy rate for this group is also associated with poor living conditions, environmental hazards and the greater likelihood of dying in sudden or violent circumstances. The impact of social class on mortality rates has been a focus for the sociological study of health and social inequality (Townsend and Davidson, 1982). The outcome of these studies has usually been confirmation that economic factors are centrally implicated as causal indicators of differential mortality rates (Wilkinson, 1996).

In singling out the significance of social class for mortality it is important to recognise that the effects of social class and those that stem from experiences of ethnicity are sometimes difficult to distinguish. Both are frequently implicated in low socio-economic status and may be associated with stereotypically culturally ascribed behaviour. For minority ethnic groups in modern Western societies, socio-economic conditions may be even more damaging to health than those experienced solely as a consequence of social class position. For example, in an analysis of World Health Organization (WHO) statistics on life expectancy and health, Murray (2000) remarks that in the United States, some ethnic groups, such as Native Americans, rural African Americans and the inner city poor, have levels of health more usually characteristic of a poor developing country. In Australia, a country with a crude death rate (deaths per 1000 of the population) for non-Aboriginal people of 6.5 in 1993, the rate for Aboriginal people and Torres Strait Islanders was 13.3 in the same period (Hossain, 2001). Moreover, the experience of dying and death for Aboriginal people is distinct from that of other citizens. As Kellehear and Anderson passionately describe it,

> For Aboriginal Australians, death is more often public, as in custody; or exterior, as from poor environmental conditions. The experience of death is not dominated by medical labels but social ones – violence, poverty, isolation, social and political neglect. For Aboriginal peoples, death is a mark of disadvantage – the very antithesis of urban comfort and life-style. (1997: 12)

It is important to be aware of the consequences of socio-economic and ethnic status, as both impact on an individual's access to power and resources and, therefore, life and death experiences. These elements will be addressed throughout this chapter.

First, however, it is necessary to examine briefly the purpose and mechanisms for studying the demography of mortality and then to make some general observations on changing patterns of mortality across the globe.

The demographic study of mortality and global patterns

According to Essex-Cater (1967) the demographic study of mortality began in Europe in the sixteenth century with the publication of the Bills of Mortality. These were the first attempts to register deaths and record differences in life expectancy between social groups. Susser argues that these Bills were utilized as a method of monitoring plague and effectively warned 'the wealthier classes of the population in time for them to leave the city early in an outbreak' (1973: 17). As these monitoring systems developed and spawned the scientific study of demography, they became more sophisticated and embraced four major purposes (Diamond and McDonald, 1994):

- to identify levels and trends of mortality;
- to compare mortality between populations;
- to identify patterns and trends in the causes of death; and
- to identify social, economic, behavioural and environmental factors that influence these levels and trends.

Mortality rates do not remain constant throughout the life course. For example, the risk of death is higher in infanthood and in old age than it is during adulthood (although it is important to note that the definition of old age will vary according to the social environment and geographical location in which people live). There is a range of indicators of mortality that shed light on the health of populations, as there are a number of methods for measuring the same. Mortality may be indicated via age at death, infant mortality or maternal mortality. Measures used include 'crude death rate' (the annual number of deaths per 1,000 of the population) and, a more precise measure, 'age-specific death rate' (the number of deaths per 1,000 of the population according to specified age groups). In gathering accurate mortality data, most registration systems collect information on cause of death by age and sex (Hossain et al. 1996).

According to Hossain, one of the most striking demographic

features of the last four hundred years has been the 'unprecedented increase in population' (2001: 306). This has largely been attributed to a dramatic decline in mortality. Yet the rate and impact of this decline has been experienced differentially across the globe. Rates in developed countries, such as those of Western Europe and North America, have been reduced slowly and steadily, particularly throughout the twentieth century. In contrast, countries that have developed rapidly have witnessed an accompanying sharp decline in mortality. In Japan, for example (see table 2.2) mortality rates have plummeted since the 1940s to the current situation where life expectancy is now greater in that country than many countries in Europe. In less developed countries (see table 2.3) the rate of mortality has declined less dramatically and there are stark differences between life expectancy in countries in Africa and some parts of Asia, for example, when compared with those enjoyed in Western developed societies. In some African countries mortality rates are actually increasing, and this is largely a consequence of the AIDS epidemic.

We will now explore in more detail the nature of death rates and consider some of the socio-cultural explanations for these differing patterns of mortality.

Socio-cultural status

Life expectancy

A dramatic decline in infant mortality and increased longevity is a hallmark of modernization. In countries such as Australia, England and the USA, life expectancy at birth increased from around 55 years in the first decade of the twentieth century to the mid- to late 70s by the end of the century (OECD, 2001). Table 2.2 shows trends in life expectancy in several OECD countries, with Japan enjoying the greatest expectation of longevity for men in 1998 (77.2 years); Hungary, Turkey and Korea had the lowest (66.1, 66.4 and 70.6 respectively); and the remainder clustered around the mid-70s. There are, as can be seen from table 2.2, differences in the life

Table 2.2 Trends in life expectancy at birth and at age 65 for selected OECD countries (1960–1998)

Country	Men at birth			Women at birth			Men at 65			Women at 65		
	1960	1980	1998	1960	1980	1998	1960	1980	1998	1960	1980	1998
Australia	67.9	71	75.9	73.9	78.1	81.5	12.5	13.7	16.3	15.6	17.9	20
Belgium	67.7	70	74.8	73.5	76.8	81.1	12.4	13	15.6	14.8	16.9	19.8
Canada	68.4	71.9	75.8	74.3	79.1	81.4	13.6	14.6	16.3	16.1	18.9	20.1
Germany	67.6	69.9	74.5	72.4	76.6	80.5	12.4	13	15.3	14.6	16.7	19
Hungary	66.7	65.5	66.1	70.1	72.7	75.2	12.3	11.6	N/A	13.8	14.6	N/A
Japan	65.3	73.4	77.2	70.2	78.8	84	11.6	14.6	17.1	14.1	17.7	22
Korea	N/A	62.3	70.6	N/A	70.5	78.1	N/A	11.2	13.6	N/A	15.1	17.3
Mexico	56.2	64	72.4	59.5	70	77	13.8	15.3	17.6	14.4	16.5	18.7
New Zealand	68.7	70	75.2	73.9	76.3	80.4	13	13.2	16.1	15.6	17	19.5
Poland	64.9	66	68.9	70.6	74.4	77.3	12.7	12	13.4	14.9	15.5	17
Spain	67.4	72.5	74.8	72.2	78.6	82.2	13.1	14.8	16.3	15.3	17.9	20.3
Switzerland	68.7	72.3	76.5	74.1	78.8	82.5	N/A	N/A	16.7	N/A	N/A	20.6
Turkey	46.3	55.8	66.4	50.3	60.3	71	11.2	11.7	12.7	12.1	12.8	14.3
United Kingdom	68.3	71	74.6	74.2	77	79.7	11.9	12.9	15	15	16.9	18.5
United States	66.6	70	73.9	73.1	77.4	79.4	12.8	14.1	16	15.8	18.3	19.1

Source: OECD Health Data, 2000

Table 2.3   Life expectancy at birth in selected less developed countries (2002)

	Men	*Women*
Afghanistan	41.9	43.4
Albania	67.3	74.1
Bangladesh	62.6	62.6
Botswana	40.2	40.6
Cambodia	51.9	57.1
Chad	46.1	49.3
Ethiopia	46.8	49.4
India	60.1	62.0
Kenya	49.8	51.9
Sierra Leone	32.4	35.7
South Africa	48.8	52.6
Swaziland	36.9	40.4
Viet Nam	67.1	72.2
Zimbabwe	37.7	38.0

Source: Adapted from World Health Organization online statistics, 2002

expectancy of men and women, and these will be discussed shortly. Explanations for this radical shift have emphasized improvements in living standards (for example, diet and housing), public health, medical technology and the decline in infectious diseases such as tuberculosis, diphtheria and gastroenteritis (McKeown, 1975; McKinlay and McKinlay, 1977; Powles, 1973). However, there remain significant differences in life expectancy between ethnic groups in Western societies. For example, in the USA white women, on average, live five years longer than black women (US Department of Health and Human Services, 2002). This trend of lower life expectancy for black and ethnic minority groups is true for most Western countries. As noted earlier, Aboriginal Australians have higher mortality rates than the non-Aboriginal population.

Similar average advances in health have not been in evidence in non-industrialized countries and this has resulted in continuing disparity between life expectancy in developed and less developed societies. Table 2.3 presents statistics on life expectancy in some less developed countries. These figures reveal the shocking inequalities in health between developed and less developed countries. At birth, a female child in Japan might expect to live to the age of 84, whereas a girl born in Sierra Leone would, in 2002, have a life expectancy of only 35.7 years. Life expectancy globally has increased by almost twenty years in the last half century, from 46.5 in 1950–5 to 65.2 in 2002 (Mason, 2004). What this statistic disguises, however, is the fact that in some poorer countries life expectancy is actually declining. In Botswana and Lesotho, for instance, the life expectancy rate had reduced by twenty years. In Zimbabwe a girl might expect to live to the age of 38. One of the major factors in this decline in life expectancy is the Acquired Immune Deficiency (AIDS) epidemic. We will return to this later in the chapter.

Infant mortality

The expectation in developed nations that death will occur in old age is a relatively recent phenomenon. In previous centuries in Europe, and until the early decades of the twentieth century, people frequently witnessed death in infancy, youth and middle age (Ariès, 1981; Howarth, 1998). Due to a high infant mortality rate, children were encouraged to contemplate their own, routinely premature death (Walvin, 1982). Measured as the number of deaths of infants younger than the age of 1 per 1,000 live births, the infant mortality rate (IMR) in England and Wales in 1909 was 120. Advances in medical science, better sanitation and a greater understanding of public health, meant that mortality rates began to improve and health and longevity increased. In particular, the infant mortality rate declined to the point where in 1896, for the first time in British history, upper- and middle-class parents could reasonably expect that their children would outlive them (Mitchison 1977). It was not until the 1920s and 1930s that working-class parents could enjoy this privilege.

In Western developed societies in 1999 the IMR rate in the UK was 5.78, in the USA 6.33, with the lowest rate registered as 3.80 in Finland (see table 2.4). Thus, in parallel with the increase in life

Table 2.4 World infant mortality rates[a] (1999)

Lowest		*Highest*	
Finland	3.80	Pakistan	91.00
Sweden	3.91	Bangladesh	69.68
Japan	4.07	India	60.81
Switzerland	4.87	Kenya	59.07
Norway	4.96	South Africa	51.99
Austria	5.10		
Australia	5.11		
Denmark	5.11		
Germany	5.14		
Canada	5.47		
United Kingdom	5.78		
United States	6.33		

Source: Hossain, 2001: 308; reproduced with permission from Thompson Publishing Services, on behalf of Taylor & Francis Books (UK)

[a] IMR defined as the number of infant deaths under the age of 1 in a particular year per 1,000 live births registered in the same year.

expectancy there has been an equally dramatic decline in infant mortality rates and these are understood as good indicators of the overall well-being of a population, with high IMR equated with a high birth rate and elevated levels of poverty (Hossain, 2001). However, this focus on the overall decline in infant mortality disguises substantial differences among distinct socio–economic and ethnic groups within societies. Distinctions in IMR exist that are related to mother's educational and nutritional status, socio-economic status and ethnic identity. Haynatzka et al. (2002) argued for the need to address high infant mortality rates among black people living in cities in the USA. They noted that although the IMR nationally had declined by 90 per cent during the twentieth century, the rates for black people were disproportionately high – a median black IMR of 13.9 per 1,000 live births compared to white IMRs of 6.4. They were able to identify a number of factors that contributed to this position: 'very low- and moderately low-birth-weight infants, more births to teenage mothers, more late or absent prenatal care, and more racial segregation' (2002: 330).

With regard to non-Western countries, as illustrated in table 2.4, infant mortality continues to claim a great number of lives in less developed societies. In stark contrast with the low rates in Western developed countries, the rate in Kenya is 59.07 per 1,000 live births, in Bangladesh 69.68 and in Pakistan an especially alarmingly high rate of 91.0. Whilst IMRs in developed countries are usually explained in terms of congenital disorders, low birth weight and 'sudden infant death syndrome' (Hossain, 2001), they have also been shown to be related to social factors such as teenage motherhood, mothers over the age of 40, those relatively uneducated and mothers who smoke (NCHS, 2000). In less developed countries these high rates are usually attributed to poor health and sanitation, malnutrition and poverty (Sen and Bonita, 2000). In sub-Saharan Africa the causes of infant mortality are predominantly malnutrition, diarrhoea, malaria and infections of the lower respiratory tract. Many of these deaths could be prevented by the provision of clean water supplies, adequate diet and basic measures such as anti-malarial drugs and insecticide-treated nets (Mason, 2004).

The wealth of a country will determine the resources available for health measures such as immunization programmes, and social services, such as those associated with welfare and education provision. Indeed, infant mortality rates have been correlated with maternal literacy, the suggestion being that with greater resources devoted to the education of women in society, life chances improve and mothers have better access to information about health and the care of children.

Maternal mortality

In turning now to examine gender differences at death in younger age groups, the incidence of maternal mortality is clearly significant and again provides insights into differences in life expectancy rates between wealthy and poorer societies.

Table 2.5 provides maternal mortality rates (MMR) in selected World Health Organization member states. MMR is defined as the

Table 2.5 Maternal mortality rates (estimates for UN regions, 1995)

	Maternal mortality ratio (maternal deaths per 100,000 live births)	Maternal deaths (thousands)	Lifetime risk of maternal death, 1 in:
World total	400	515,000	75
More developed countries	21	2,800	2,500
Less developed countries	440	512,000	60
Least developed countries	1,000	230,000	16
Africa	1,000	273,000	16
Asia[a]	280	217,000	110
Europe	28	2,200	2,000
Latin America & the Caribbean	190	22,000	160
Oceania[b]	260	560	260

Source: Adapted from World Health Organization, 1995 (<http://www3.who.int/whosis/mm/mm_region_1995.cfm>). Reproduced with kind permission of WHO

[a] Japan has been excluded from the regional averages as it is considered to be a more developed country than others in the region. It is included in the average and total for more developed countries.

[b] Australia and New Zealand have been excluded from the regional averages as they are considered to be more developed countries than others in the region. They have been included in the average and total for more developed countries.

number of deaths of women due to childbirth and complications of pregnancy for every 100,000 births (Pollard et al., 1990: 82). Hossain et al. (1996) observe that the highest MMR is found in countries in Africa where an average of one in seven women die from pregnancy-related causes. In sub-Saharan Africa the rate is 100 times that of Europe. Asia, with 61 per cent of the world's births, accounts for 55 per cent of all maternal deaths. Explanations for the high mortality rate of women in childbirth can be traced to lack of access to medical technology, ignorance of sanitation and nutritional requirements, and the vagaries of traditional labour and birthing practices, all of which in the contemporary world can be directly connected with poverty.

These rates differ greatly from those found in Western developed countries, which now account for 11 per cent of all births and have a 1 per cent maternal mortality rate (Vogeler, 1996). In previous centuries in Western societies, MMR were similar to those in less developed societies today. For Western women the major risk of death as a consequence of pregnancy and childbirth is related to age. Women over the age of 35 have a higher MMR than younger women. However, once again, the risk is increased for black and ethnic minority women. In 1999 in the USA, the MMR rate for black women (23.3) was more than four times that for white women (5.5); black women aged 35 years and older had the highest rate of maternal mortality of nearly 70 deaths per 100,000 live births (US Department of Health and Human Services, 2002: 58).

Let us turn now to consider death in old age.

Old age

Every society has beliefs about what is the 'right' time to die, and in contemporary Western societies this is usually deemed to occur in old age. It is assumed that elderly people accept death as an inevitable and natural event in old age – an event that loses its frightening character as the individual becomes older. According to Stedeford, an elderly person sees death, 'as a natural event, to mark the completion of his [sic] life... For such a person, death may come easily, as it should. Mortality is less alien for him, for he has had plenty of time and opportunity to accept its gradual approach as his life has progressed' (1984: 76). In this depiction, the 'good death' (which is equated with 'natural' death) is one which characteristically occurs in old age with life projects complete. In this representation, death adopts a rather benign persona, visiting only those who, aged and frail, welcome its approach as a merciful release from the trials of life.

The accuracy of this description is debatable and the notion of old age as the 'right time to die' may not be as straightforward as is generally assumed. Modern society has witnessed increased longevity and this has raised expectations that the life span will continue to be stretched. As people age they may no longer think of death as appropriate at 65, 75 or even 85 years. The contemplation of death is discouraged throughout life and, therefore, in later life, elderly people are likely to be left to deal with their fears and anxieties in private. Characterizing death in old age as easy and natural implies acceptance or resignation on the part of elderly people. Yet, my own study of attitudes to death and dying among people over the age of 75 years (Howarth, 1998) revealed that death in old age is not always the easy and welcome experience that many in the younger generations would like to believe.

Moreover, Hockey and James argue that in Western countries mainstream adult society is unable to contemplate old age and the inevitable decline into death. For this reason, death is masked by the infantalization of elderly people and a cultural emphasis on life as a cycle of death and rebirth: 'The young are green striplings, who are burgeoning, blossoming forth in the springtime of their youth... By contrast, the old are shrivelled sticks, who overripen to face the autumn of their days' (1993: 27). To counter this negative representation of old age, elderly people are constructed as metaphorical children and are thus able to share in the promise of the child's upward growth. In utilizing this 'metaphorical restructuring of time, the wheel turns and death is seemingly subverted' (1993: 28).

Although increased longevity in societies is broadly heralded as a positive phenomenon, this is balanced by the image of old age as a period associated with poverty, loss of control, failing health, disability and stigmatization. This culturally constructed link between old age and deterioration has, as a consequence, stimulated stereotypical representations of later life that have induced fear and distancing of elderly people by younger generations (Bytheway, 1995; Hazan, 1980; Jefferys and Thane, 1989). This in itself has led to stigmatization and ageism whereby elderly people are represented in a negative fashion and discriminated against due to their age. Markides and Miranda (1997: 11) comment that this is particularly distressing for older people from minority ethnic communities as they face the triple burden of being old, poor and of minority status.

In societies that focus resources and power on those with economic value, elderly people are frequently marginalized and, as old age progresses and personal funds run low, they may find themselves slipping into poverty. This is particular true for women who may have spent substantial periods of their adult lives devoted to the care of children. Since women tend to outlive men (see the discussion below) this has resulted in the feminization of poverty in later life (Garner and Mercer, 1989). As Arber and Ginn argue, '[f]or elderly women (in Britain at least), personal poverty is the price of fertility, and their relative poverty is likely to increase as occupational and private pensions become more widespread' (1991: 100). Reliance on state support for pensions and welfare payments requires relinquishing primary control over financial decision–making.

The experience of old age for many people is also one of failing health or chronic disability. Whilst there has been a decrease in mortality due to a reduction in cardiovascular diseases and acciden-tal deaths, there has also been an increase in degenerative conditions, such as arthritis, experienced in later life. These illnesses may not be the primary cause of death but they do have major impact on quality of life. As McCallum suggests, '[q]uality of health in old age has become an even more important issue for older peo-ple than quantity of life' (1997: 58). The effects of loss of economic status and poor health might result in individuals entering or being placed in care homes and this, too, will result in further loss of con-trol over the quality of their life (Nettleton, 2006). Moreover, in the context of a discussion of death and dying, it will have important consequences for the experience of dying (Hockey, 1990).

Having addressed the notion of old age as the 'right time to die' in modern Western societies, let us now consider gender differences in ageing. As table 2.2 shows, the life expectancy of men and women differs. Although the gap is gradually shrinking, in OECD countries women typically live longer than men by roughly five years. Whilst the reasons for this discrepancy are unclear, the fact that life expectancy for women in poorer countries may be equated with that of men suggests that the explanation is not wholly bio-logical. Male mortality in adulthood and in 'early old age' in Western societies tends to be ascribed to a greater incidence of heart disease than that found in women, and to be related to events that typically occur in the public domain (such as road fatalities and violence, often perpetrated by a stranger). Women, on the other hand, are more susceptible to cancer, especially breast cancer, and if death is caused by violence this is more likely to occur in the home (Ardener, 1993).

The implication of this difference in life expectancy in Western societies is that old age is a largely gendered experience (Arber and Ginn, 1991; 1995; Estes et al., 1984). Widowhood, too, is more a female experience that a male one. There are more widows than widowers and the numerical gap between the two widens with age. Men are more likely to continue to be in marriages to the end of their lives and this in turn means that there is a greater likelihood that women, rather than men, will carry any burden of care for a spouse. When these women themselves become frail, they are less likely than men to have a resident carer and may be more reliant on formal systems of support, informal care provided by children, or sometimes by neighbours, or residential care. In a discussion of gender differences in caring in the USA, Montgomery and McGlinn Datwyler note that, in chronic illness towards the end of life, '[s]pouse caregivers make up the greatest number of sole caregivers – husbands and wives who are providing care to their spouses without the help of others.' These carers, they observe, 'are often viewed as the most vulnerable of caregivers: Typically, they are older, in poorer health, with lower incomes, and have been providing more intensive care for longer periods of time' (1992: 62). When a partner becomes sick, the first port of call for care is usually the spouse. This is an ongoing relationship of reliance in ill-health and, as Rose and Bruce (1995) point out, throughout the life course, there is a continuum of care and a shifting balance between partners. Longevity, however, plays a role in disturbing any equilibrium that exists among elderly spouses as differences in morbidity and mortality rates between women and men affect the potential for giving and receiving care. 'Older women therefore suffer serious structural disadvantages, meaning that they tend to approach their deaths feeling a greater sense of being alone and powerless in the world' (Seale, 1998: 46).

Having considered some of the demographic characteristics of mortality across the globe we will examine some of the social meanings of death and dying. This will be framed within discussions of Acquired Immune Deficiency Syndrome (AIDS) and suicide.

Social meanings of dying and death

Acquired Immune Deficiency Syndrome (AIDS)

In sub-Saharan Africa, where the life expectancy rate has dropped dramatically over the last ten years, AIDS is the leading cause of death (see table 2.6). It exceeds that caused by malaria, tuberculosis, pneumonia and diarrhoea. AIDS accounted for the deaths of 2.2 million Africans in 1999, in contrast with 300,000 ten years previously (Murray, 2000). It has been estimated that half of all 15-year-olds in Botswana, South Africa and Zimbabwe can expect to die of AIDS. In Swaziland, a country in the north-east corner of Southern Africa with a population of one million, it is estimated that two in every five adults is infected with the HIV virus – the virus that causes AIDS; 38.6 per cent of the population have HIV/AIDS (USAID, 2005). The majority of deaths from AIDS occur in the 15–49 year age group.

These infection and death rates have a resounding significance not only for individual health and well-being but also for the economic and social fabric of these African societies (Small, 2001a: 6). Epidemics throughout history have tended to target the weak and vulnerable, typically the very young and the older sectors of the population. In contrast, the highest rate of death from AIDS falls upon the economically active members of society. This has a devastating effect on the economy and plunges many families into poverty as grandparents and teenagers take responsibility for caring for the orphaned children of AIDS victims. It is estimated that 12.3 million children have been orphaned by AIDS (<wvi.org/wvi/aids/africa_aids.htm>); 50,000 children in Swaziland have lost parents (UNAID, 2005), and in the majority of cases this results in a loss of future for this generation of children. An article in the *New York Times* presented a number of accounts of the impact of AIDS on families in Swaziland. Here is reproduced one typical example from that report. This is the story of Nomfundo, a 15-year-old girl, and her 10-year-old brother, Ndabendele.

Table 2.6 Regional HIV/AIDS statistics at the end of 2003

	Adults and children living with HIV/AIDS	Adult prevalence rate (%)	Adult and child deaths due to AIDS
Sub-Saharan Africa	25.0–28.2 million	7.5–8.5	2.2–2.4 million
North Africa & Middle East	470,000–730,000	0.2–0.4	35,000–50,000
South & South-East Asia	4.6–8.2 million	0.4–0.8	330,000–590,000
East Asia & Pacific	700,000–1.3 million	0.1–0.1	32,000–58,000
Latin America	1.3–1.9 million	0.5–0.7	49,000–70,000
Caribbean	350,000–590,000	1.9–3.1	30,000–50,000
Eastern Europe & Central Asia	1.2–1.8 million	0.5–0.9	23,000–37,000
Western Europe	520,000–680,000	0.3–0.3	2,600–3,400
North America	790,000–1.2 million	0.5–0.7	12,000–18,000
Australia & New Zealand	12,000–18,000	0.1–0.1	<100
TOTAL	40 million [34–46 million]	1.1 % [0.9–1.3]	3 million [2.5–3.5 million]

Source: UNAIDS and World Health Organization, 2003

Their 34-year-old mother, a domestic worker, died Aug 29; their father died in 2003. Care of the children has fallen to their grandmother, Ester Simelane, 53, who has been jobless for 14 years.

Since the illnesses began, she has sold four of the family's eight goats to raise money for food.

'Wheesh! Now I can feel the hardship,' Nomfundo said. 'Who is going to pay my school fees? Even the clothes. Where am I going to get them?' She tugged at her school uniform skirt, riddled with holes and hemmed several times, to hide tears. 'I feel small,' she said. 'We used to have track suits. Now we no longer have track suits. Other kids say, "Oh, now you don't have a track suit. Not even shoes! Now your are on the same level as us."'

Actually, the two children are headed lower. Unbeknownst to them, their grandmother has tested positive for HIV, apparently contracting the virus while dressing her daughter's bleeding sores. Mrs. Simelane has kept the news from Nomfundo and her brother to spare them further trauma. (Wines and LaFraniere, 2004)

The prevalence of AIDS and the worldwide response to the disease is structured around poverty, global inequality and oppression. With greater education and resources the impact of AIDS in Africa could be seriously addressed. For example, where poverty is prevalent, enhanced by loss of breadwinners, families have to make a choice between buying food or medicine. One political and economic dimension to the problem is illustrated by the refusal of some major pharmaceutical companies in the USA to reduce the cost to less developed countries of anti-retroviral therapies that have a profound effect on the progress of the illness.

The transmission of AIDS varies in different regions. In sub-Saharan Africa it is largely via heterosexual sex; in Western Europe and North America it is primarily via male homosexual sex and drug-users sharing needles. These methods of transmission are implicated in any gender differences in the rates of HIV positive men and women. Thus, in sub-Saharan Africa it is estimated that 55 per cent of women are HIV positive (UNAID, 2000).

Initially believed to be a disease confined to homosexual sexual activity, early responses to the illness tended to apportion blame to those who contracted it. AIDS thus came to be viewed as a moral issue that required individuals to protect themselves against the disease, to avoid infecting others, and to take personal responsibility for failing to do so. Some right-wing political groups in the USA in particular, 'perceiving the issue in terms of guilt or innocence, of morality and immorality' (Almond, 1990: 3), sought to enact legislation to recriminalize homosexuality and to introduce laws of quarantine – typical examples of 'blaming the victim'. Whereas in developing countries AIDS may be perceived as the price for poverty, in the Western context, death from AIDS is commonly perceived as the punishment for immorality. The Western cultural emphasis on HIV/AIDS as a disease associated with gay men has prompted a range of responses from the gay communities in North America, Europe and Australasia. One such reaction has been the resurgence of the use of the memorial quilt. Particularly popular in Europe and the USA throughout the nineteenth century, the quilt was adopted as a means of memorialization. Typically embroidered by a female family member with the name of the deceased and hung in a prominent position in the home, the quilt reminded visitors and marked the life and death of their loved one. The Names Project AIDS Memorial Quilt begun in the USA was a similar attempt to memorialize those who had died of AIDS. Each quilt is produced by family, partners or friends of the deceased and marked with the name of the person who died and often with a message of remembrance. In this way the names of the dead are remembered and their lives and deaths given meaning not only for those close to them but also for the gay community as a whole. The quilt project, a practice that quickly spread to other Western countries, is a good example of the exercise of agency in the face of seemingly insurmountable structural obstacles. As such, it has been successful at a personal level and also as a political mechanism for raising the profile and concerns of gay communities and their struggle with HIV/AIDS.

We will now consider some of the demographics of suicide and the social meanings that are associated with it.

Suicide

Suicide is a growing concern within modern, Western societies. What is especially noticeable about patterns of suicide in these societies is that it is becoming characterized as a category of death that disproportionately singles out young males. Table 2.7 shows the incidence of death from suicide for men and women in selected countries in 1995. Table 2.8 breaks down the suicide rates to reveal the levels of death by suicide according to gender and age. There are a number of observations that invite attention. First, rates of suicide differ dramatically across countries; second, that men and women are affected differentially; and finally, that suicide appears to fall heavily on young males.

Durkheim's classic study, *Suicide* (1951 [1897]), is significant to any discussion of the social meanings of suicide as he was the first sociologist to bring it to our attention. His purpose in studying suicide was to highlight the nature of 'social facts' and to demonstrate that society could be studied in the same way as the natural sciences (Durkheim, 1964 [1895]). He argued that patterns of stability could be discerned from an examination of suicide rates in a range of countries. This stability in the rates led Durkheim to the conclusion that there were social and cultural factors at work here – suicide was not simply the result of individual psychological distress or disordered personalities, but was a consequence of social disorder. For Durkheim, these rates revealed that although suicide might appear to be the most individual of acts, there were underlying 'suicidogenic currents', which stemmed from moral forces in society. These currents determined the levels of suicide. He identified four types of suicide: egoistic (which occurs in social groups that lack strong support mechanisms); anomic (occurs in communities where social regulation has broken down); altruistic (found in strongly unified groups); and fatalistic (in groups with excessive social regulation) (Durkheim, 1951 [1897]). The essence of his thesis was that social regulation constrains individuals to act in particular ways and, therefore, that the extent of suicide in a given society is influenced (if not determined) by moral forces generated by collective life.

Although his work has been heavily criticized for a focus on structural factors relating to suicide, and for neglecting aspects of

Table 2.7 Suicide rates per 100,000 of population in selected countries (1995)

	Men	*Women*
Australia	19.0	5.1
Canada	21.5	5.4
Finland	43.4	11.8
Japan	23.4	11.3
Lithuania	79.1	16.1
Russian Federation	72.9	13.7
United Kingdom	11.7	3.2
United States	19.8	4.4

Source: World Health Organization, Geneva, 2003 (<www.who.int/entity /mental_health/media/en/298.pdf>). Reproduced with kind permission of WHO

agency, his insights into the impact of social change on individuals are relevant to an understanding of the demographic patterns of suicide. Durkheim alerted us to the social consequences of rapid economic change and restructuring. His argument was that one consequence of industrialization was the possibility of anomie. This refers to communities where social regulation has broken down; entailing a breakdown of traditional norms and mores, a tension between expectations and reality, and, as a consequence, an increase in suicide caused by loss of meaning among individuals. Whilst his methods and underlying premise may be criticized, for example, for failing to take account of individual motivation and the socially constructed nature of suicide rates (Atkinson, 1978; Douglas, 1967, Taylor, 1982), it is worth considering the extent to which current suicide rates for men and women in industrialized nations, may be correlated with economic restructuring and globalization.

It is clear from tables 2.7 and 2.8 that suicide rates are much higher for men than for women. To some extent this may reflect cultural expectations of gender differences in suicide. For example, if intention to die is taken as an indicator of suicide (see the discussion in chapter 7), then the type of methods commonly used by males (which tend to be more violent and final than those adopted

Table 2.8 Suicide rates according to gender and age per 100,000 in selected countries (1998–2000)

COUNTRY	M/F	Year	5–14	15–24	25–34	35–44	45–54	55–64	65–74	75+
Australia	M	1999	0.7	22.1	35.4	29.6	24.3	21.3	21.7	30.0
	F		.0.5	5.3	8.1	7.3	7.5	5.5	4.1	3.4
Canada	M	1998	1.5	21.6	22.1	30.3	29.0	25.9	26.7	31.6
	F		0.8	5.1	5.2	7.7	9.2	5.8	6.0	6.9
Finland	M	2000	0.0	31.1	46.5	50.4	49.3	37.3	33.9	42.1
	F		0.6	8.1	12.4	13.6	17.3	17.9	13.1	7.3
Japan	M	1999	0.7	16.5	28.1	37.0	56.9	65.9	46.1	60.7
	F		0.5	7.3	11.6	10.5	15.6	19.5	22.0	34.1
Lithuania	M	2000	2.2	49.0	77.4	98.5	163.8	123.9	96.7	74.1
	F		0.0	9.6	11.3	21.9	25.7	24.6	23.2	28.9
Russian Federation	M	2000	4.0	57.7	86.3	93.1	105.3	90.8	98.1	84.4
	F		1.1	9.1	10.6	11.6	14.2	14.0	19.4	29.2
United Kingdom	M	1999	0.1	10.6	18.1	17.3	15.3	12.8	9.8	15.5
	F		0.0	2.5	3.9	4.7	4.3	4.0	4.2	5.1
United States	M	1999	1.0	17.2	22.2	22.5	22.0	20.2	25.0	41.7
	F		0.3	3.1	4.8	6.4	6.7	5.2	4.2	4.6

Source: Adapted from World Health Organization, Geneva, 2003 (<www.who.int/entity/mental_health/media/en/289.pdf>). Reproduced with kind permission of WHO

by females) are more likely to be identified with suicide attempts rather than accidental death. It is also the case that death caused, for example, by eating disorders such as anorexia (more common in women than in men), are unlikely to be perceived as suicide even though the underlying mental state may be similar. A closer examination of suicide rates by gender and age (table 2.8) reveals that this pattern of high male rates is relatively stable across all the countries considered. What is perhaps most striking is the high rate of suicide among male youth and young to mid-age adults; the high rates in countries such as Lithuania, Finland and the Russian Federation; and the increase in the rate in late old age for both men and women in Japan. Let us briefly consider each in turn.

There has been a growing concern in many Western societies about the rising rates of male youth suicide. In countries such as Australia, New Zealand, the UK and the USA, health promotion and suicide prevention programmes have been developed that attempt to identify those considered to be at risk. From statistical analyses of suicide rates these are usually identified as members of socially excluded and deprived groups, black and ethnic minority groups, those who misuse drugs and/or alcohol, and victims of abuse, including child sexual abuse (De Leo, 2002; Lester, 1994). Campaigns have been launched to curb media reporting of suicide in order to avoid so-called 'copycat' incidents, thought to be especially problematic after cases of celebrity suicide (Phillips, 1974; Phillips and Carstensen, 1986; Hassan, 1995; Pirkis et al., 2001). Although much of the health literature points to risks associated with dysfunctional families, abuse in childhood, and alcohol or drug misuse, other studies have commented on the nature of adolescence in identity formation in Western societies (Gilchrist et al., forthcoming). Difficulties in relationships and failure to meet personal goals may result in young men, in particular, feeling emotionally isolated, lacking meaning in their lives and unable, for reasons associated with prevailing expectations of masculinity, to ask for help and support. Adolescence is often perceived as a period of transition during which individuals move from childhood to adulthood forging a strong sense of personal identity as they do so. For young men there may be cultural expectations related to masculinity that this transition will involve decisions

about a career or apprenticeship often requiring educational qualifications, and securing stable employment and financial
independence. There may also be assumptions of marriage and an
expectation that the male will be able to financially support a family and adopt the role of breadwinner, especially when children are
young and mothers may choose to remain at home as child-carers.
Whilst this traditional notion of male adulthood may be changing,
some studies suggest that it remains largely intact in many
communities (Connell, 1995; Gilchrist et al., forthcoming). Furthermore, in developed societies patterns of employment are
shifting from long-term stable permanent jobs to more short-term
or contract work. In this economic context the goals of young
males may be undermined.

Establishing an identity along the lines of traditional sex roles is
inextricably linked to employment, economic success and individual responsibility. Whilst this may conform to contemporary
cultural expectations in societies increasingly characterized by
individualism, for young people unable to meet these expectations,
for example, due to unemployment, there are few options available
to them. Furthermore, if beliefs about the nature of masculine ways
of coping remain strong and are characterized by a reluctance to
seek help and support, they may well be acting to support suicide as
an option or solution to the problems faced by young men. These
notions of masculinity entail separateness, independence and
reliance on the self (Hallam et al., 1999; Cross and Madson, 1997).
In policy terms, this suggests the need for a fundamental rethink of
suicide prevention strategies. Whilst these continue to focus on specific risk categories associated with marginal groups in society, they
neglect people of all ages and gender who may be struggling to find
meaning in modern societies. This is especially pertinent for countries in Central and Eastern Europe, where the impact of economic
transition has been particularly evident in the rise in mortality.
UNICEF estimated that between 1990 and 1999 there were 3.26
million deaths over and above the levels in 1989. The majority of
these deaths have been associated with men in the 25–60 age group
(Addy and Silný, 2001) and have been attributed to the 'psychosocial stress of economic insecurity'. Other studies have suggested
that high male suicide rates in these countries can be explained by

lack of social inclusiveness, coherence and meaning, and a failure to feel in control of one's life. According to Rutz:

> It is this sense of helplessness and hopelessness, loss of control and identity, loss of coherence and social connectedness which we see today as one of the main causative factors for mental ill health, leading to stress and helplessness – related morbidity and mortality in some European countries of transition. (2001:18)

Whilst there is clearly a role for risk assessment that focuses on particular categories of individuals who suffer mental illness, it is important to recognize that suicide is not simply, or even necessarily primarily, a mental disorder but is fundamentally a social disorder. This is evident in research (for example, that cited above) that links suicide with masculinity, economic restructuring and a sense of lack of meaning in life. It is also demonstrated in studies of aboriginal youth suicide, in countries such as Australia, where suicide has been associated with lack of meaning and loss of control over their destiny (Tatz, 2001).

Turning now to consider suicide at the other end of the life cycle, Japan has a high rate of suicide for men over the age of 75 and is the country with the highest rate of suicide for women in this age category. At 34.1 this compares unfavourably with countries such as the USA (4.6), UK (5.1) and Australia (3.4). Only Lithuania and the Russian Federation (countries undergoing economic and social transition with high suicide rates across all ages and gender) have rates approaching that of Japan. How can such a high suicide rate for older women in Japan be explained? Whilst suicide has always been frowned upon in Western societies (variously viewed as an affront to God who gave life, as a rejection of personal relationships, as an act of loneliness and isolation), in Japan it has been perceived as a noble or honourable act. Indeed, when ritually performed, it results in a good death freed from the impurities of other forms of dying. In this context suicide in late old age may be viewed in a positive way as, with no penalty associated with religion and fate in the afterlife, elderly people release themselves from the trials of old age and ill-health, and their families from the burden of care. Given that women tend to outlive men by an average of 6.5 years, in the light of our earlier discussion of ageing, it is not surprising that the rate for elderly women is so high.

Summary

This chapter has explored some of the demographics of mortality globally. In so doing, it has focused on structural factors that might explain the differences in life expectancy and causes of death both across and within a range of societies. The discussion has considered distinctions in life expectancy, infant and maternal mortality and old age. In examining life expectancy, for example, the increase in life expectancy in Western developed nations was noted against a decrease in some less developed countries. There was found to be a particularly stark contrast between countries such as Japan and the USA when compared with Sierra Leone and Botswana. The social meanings of death and dying were then explored through discussions of AIDS and suicide. The spread and prevalence of AIDS, especially in sub-Saharan Africa, was shown to be a major cause of the fall in life expectancy. Old age is now viewed as the 'right' time to die in Western societies. This condition is not enjoyed globally, as the impact of diseases such as AIDS and tuberculosis and the high rates of infant and maternal mortality in less developed countries continue to decimate populations and account for low life expectancy rates. In this context, the discussion focused on the extent to which mortality is fundamentally associated with poverty and disadvantage.

The chapter then turned to consider suicide, an ever-growing concern of developed societies and those in Eastern and Central Europe undergoing social and economic transition. The high rates of suicide among male youth and, in many societies, those that occur in later life were discussed and shown to be associated with cultural and social factors rather than simply explained in terms of individual mental health. In the context of social policy, this suggests that prevention strategies that target only those thought to be mentally vulnerable effectively marginalize and leave at risk large numbers of suicidal individuals. These tend to be people who may not be able to compete for the social and economic resources that underpin adult, and especially masculine, identities in Western developed societies.

In the next chapter we will further explore the concept of risk in relation to mortality globally.

3

Life and Death in 'Risk Society'

Introduction

At the beginning of the twenty-first century, it is difficult to pass through a day without being reminded that we now live in a global society. In the political arena there may be news that some small nation or dictator is posing a threat to the global order or that one of the larger nations is challenging that leader in an act of so-called 'global protection'. At work and in entertainment, computer and other communication systems allow us almost instant access to people and events around the globe, not only in text but also in reality-enhancing technicolor images. Whilst these may sometimes tempt us to visit faraway places, if we are less inclined or unable to make the journey we can nevertheless enjoy the journeys of others, travelling vicariously, for example, with celebrities such as Michael Palin, to the most remote places on earth. As consumers we can buy goods from all corners of the globe. Indeed, when abroad it is often difficult to find an item that is a speciality of that region of the world – shops everywhere appear to be full of Barbie dolls, PlayStation games and Coca-Cola – so-called cultural McDonaldization.

The notion that we are now living in a global society has important consequences for nations, governments and economies, but also for the way in which lives are shaped and cultures changed. Perhaps one of the most significant impacts of globalization has been the growing perception that we are now confronted by unprecedented global risks. These risks may come in the form of threats to the ecosystem, from natural disasters, environmental pollution, the use of nuclear weapons or the fallout from nuclear accidents. Equally, they may be posed by international terrorism, by unpredictable political regimes, economic instability or the impact of free markets. At a more individual level, health and personal relationships may be undermined, with people less certain about their purpose, direction and identity in societies where familiar structures are undermined and traditional roles open to question. As Beck et al. argue, discussion of risk is coming to dominate public, political and private life: '[e]veryone is caught up in defensive battles of various types, anticipating the hostile substances in one's manner of living and eating' (1994: 45).

All these factors inevitably have significance for the nature of, and experiences associated with, dying and death in contemporary societies. Social and individual perceptions of risk to mortality affect the structural and personal frameworks that are used for understanding and making meaning. For example, if there is a perceived risk of mass death caused by international terrorism, this will impact on government policy and legislation and is also likely to affect the daily activities and choices made by people who live and work in areas where the threat is deemed to be serious. An important question here, however, is whether risks to mortality have fundamentally changed as a consequence of being members of a 'global village', or whether it is only our perception or awareness of risk that has altered. In other words, is the world now a more dangerous place or is it simply that our perceptions of risks have heightened? This chapter will address various aspects of this question in relation to dying and death. It begins with an examination of theoretical approaches to risk and will draw from the work of Ulrich Beck (1992) and Anthony Giddens (1999). We will then consider death risks in terms of individual health and everyday risks, natural and 'man-made' disasters, and threats of violence and international terrorism.

Theories of risk

According to the German sociologist Ulrich Beck (1992), contemporary Western societies are becoming 'risk societies'. Not only do members of these societies have a greater awareness of risk but the nature and extent of risks have been transformed. His position is that risks have increased as a direct consequence of the processes of modernity. One clear example is the risk posed by nuclear activity.

> Take the accident that occurred at Chernobyl on 26 April 1986. As a result of poor management, careless practice and a controlled experiment that went wrong, the inspectors of this nuclear power plant in the Ukraine allowed its fourth reactor to overheat. This caused a meltdown of the core and at 1.23am two explosions blew the top off the reactor building. This had the effect of releasing radioactive clouds of material into the atmosphere, a release that continued for ten days. These clouds blew northward affecting many areas of the world and especially Northern Europe. It has been estimated that 70 per cent of the radiation fell on Belarus and that *'10 years later babies are still being born with no arms, no eyes, or only stumps for limbs'*.[1]
>
> The same source suggests that the accident has affected 15 million people worldwide at a cost of over 60 billion dollars in health care. They also claim that many of the 600,000 people involved in the clean-up are now sick or dead. Furthermore, as Beck argues, it is impossible to calculate the ongoing risks created by this disaster as they are neither local nor bounded in time, for, *'the injured of Chernobyl are today, years after the catastrophe, not even born yet'* (Beck, 1996: 4).

For Beck, risks of this nature and scale are peculiar to contemporary societies and necessarily accompany the production of wealth. Increasingly, the problem faced by societies is not associated with the production and distribution of goods, but the prevention of 'bads'. In making this assertion, Beck outlines three historical periods in which the nature of risk has changed: premodern, early modern, and late modern. Beck's categories are derived from an analysis of European societies and he uses the concept of pre-modern society in a similar manner to Walter (1996a) (discussed in chapter 1). His categories of early and late modern are mechanisms for dividing the period of modernity into two historical periods and as such are similar to Walter's categories of 'modern' and 'postmodern' respectively. For Beck, however, contemporary society or 'late modern' society has become risk society. Let us consider each period in turn.

Pre-modern

According to Beck pre-modern, or pre-industrial, societies are characterized by a lack of control over the hazards and dangers that threaten human existence. Individuals and communities can do little to avoid the, often, great loss of life associated with natural disasters, plagues and famine. These calamities are perceived as ill-luck or fated. It is perhaps the will of the gods that thousands should die in an earthquake or flood, the village punished for immoral behaviour, loss of faith or some other misdemeanour that angered the deities. When individuals suddenly become fatally ill or are accidentally killed, this may be viewed as an act of magic or witchcraft (Evans-Pritchard, 1948). People may also be killed or die as a consequence of wars. All other deaths, are, argued Beck, perceived as being outside of human control. Although people may attempt to assuage the gods or ancestors with sacrifices or other acts, or to seek out and castigate the witch or sorcerer, these dangers are, by and large, assumed to be present in the very nature of existence. If the gods are displeased and determined to punish, there is little that people can do about it. Although they may consult priests or witch doctors to minimize the dangers associated, for example, with travel and hunting, Giddens (1999) suggests that in these pre-modern societies there is no concept of 'risk'. It is only as a consequence of modernization, which generates a concern with profit and loss, that the notion of 'risk' is created. Of special significance here is the idea that in traditional or pre-modern societies dangers are viewed as the result of divine, rather than human intervention.

Early modern

Whereas in pre-modern societies death is represented as fated or the result of chance or luck (Prior and Bloor, 1993), in early modern societies risks become more calculable. In these societies the emphasis is on developing new technologies and mechanisms for enhancing production and profit. Giddens (1999) argues that risk appears as a consequence of attempting to calculate profit and loss, something that became increasingly possible from the fifteenth century in Europe with the development of double-entry bookkeeping. As well as the need to estimate profits, it became possible to assess the impact of industrial processes on the health of the workers. In this respect risks are calculable and largely personal, associated with work and health. They can be detected by the senses in that they can be seen, smelt or tasted. They are, however, limited (in contrast with the global risks of contemporary societies), often localized, and can be controlled.

In order to calculate these risks, Prior (1989) points to the emergence and nature of modern probability statistics and argues that the modern concept of risk can only exist alongside such statistical perceptions. Thus, from the eighteenth and nineteenth centuries European societies began to gather mortality statistics and, as we saw in chapter 2, these were believed to reflect the health of populations.

For Foucauldian scholars such as Armstrong (1983) this emphasis on statistical information, stimulated by new discourses of medicine, led to greater surveillance of populations. Medical discourses of illness and pathology located death and the causes of death within the body. Social medicine recognized the dangerous spaces between bodies and the risk to individuals of proximity to potentially diseased bodies and to material factors (such as poverty and poor sanitation) that might result in ill-health (Armstrong, 1983). This perspective linked social and biomedical approaches to health and facilitated a medicalized society where both the sick and the well were identified as appropriate targets for the 'medical gaze'. A further development in this context is that of health promotion and the emphasis in the early part of the twentieth century on public health – introducing strategies such as vaccination pro-grammes, exercise regimes (especially in large-scale institutions such as schools and the military) and everyday surveillance such as that of the school nurse and health visitor. Utilization of probabil-ity statistics, medicine and public health as mechanisms of surveillance resulted in an understanding of risk factors in modern societies as inherently calculable and largely controllable.

Late modern

Beck (1992) contends that the risks in contemporary societies dif-fer greatly from those of other periods or societies. In late modern societies risks cannot be so easily calculated by utilizing probability, as the dangers posed are frequently on a global scale (for example, nuclear threat or international terrorism). Furthermore, unlike the dangers apparent in earlier modern societies, those we now face are often invisible (such as threats that emanate from air and water pol-lution and the damaging side-effects of the use of modern medicines) and are thus more difficult to quantify, prevent and avoid. In this context, the modern mechanisms for measuring risk are no longer applicable. Moreover, scientists responsible for assess-ing risk are often unable to agree about the nature and the extent of the dangers posed and are increasingly taking the role of protago-nists rather than arbitrators in failing to agree with one another and either playing up or playing down particular risks. Giddens asserts that the upshot of this type of disagreement is that scientists as experts have lost their authority and are ever more searchingly challenged by environmentalists and other political groups:

> Science depends not on the inductive accumulation of proofs, but on the methodological principle of doubt. No matter how cherished, and apparently well established, a given tenet might be, it is open to revision – or might have to be discarded altogether – in the light of new ideas or findings. (Giddens, 1991: 21)

This reflects the process of reflexive modernization (Beck et al., 1994) in which risk society becomes 'world risk society' and, in an environment of scepticism about science, individuals are forced to confront an uncertain and insecure future. Perhaps one of the most disturbing features of these societies is that issues of doubt are not the preserve of the scientists and the philosophers, but are '*existentially troubling* for ordinary individuals' (ibid.: 21).

This assertion is particularly apt to an examination of the threats to mortality posed within late modern societies. In the remainder of this chapter we will consider some of the individual and societal risks associated with the contemporary, global world. The discussion will centre on the themes of the risks to health and everyday life, and those which threaten as a result of natural or 'man-made' disasters.

Health risk

According to Giddens (1991), in late modernity individuals are forced to produce their own biographies because of the decline in fixed norms and certainties such as those associated with gender and social class. In this social environment people are expected to make their own futures and to assess the risks to personal development and health in order to gain control over their lives and lifestyle. Inequalities and differences in risks to the individual are more likely to be perceived in terms of personal or psychological inadequacies rather than the consequence of structural factors. 'Individualisation, therefore, involves a proliferation of new demands upon people at the same time as choices have become more and more complex and difficult' (Lupton, 1999: 70). New ways of thinking about health are the corollaries of this move to individualization.

In a discussion of the relationship between health and dying, Kellehear (1998) observes that by the 1980s Western societies had become obsessed with individual health. People were expected to take responsibility for their own health and thereby avoid behaviour and activities that are detrimental to the aim of living a long and healthy life. Crawford (1980) suggests that in supporting a view of health as responsive to dietary and lifestyle changes, a moral imperative emerged that equated ill-health with poor self-control. People defined as overweight, those who smoke or drink alcohol to excess, and those who fail to take regular exercise are subjected to moral disapproval and, during periods of ill-health they run the risk of having medical treatment withdrawn. In this climate, 'although *control over the production of medical knowledge* remained with the professionals, from now on *control over outcomes* was to be increasingly viewed as the patient's responsibility' (Kellehear, 1998: 293).

This emphasis on individual responsibility is an inevitable outcome of health promotion activities that encourage people to be more concerned about the impact of lifestyle on health. Petersen and Lupton (1996) contend that the new public health model moves away from the biomedical focus on the inner workings of the body and the institutional basis of medicine, and instead turns its attention to social factors by recognizing the multidimensional nature of health problems and solutions. It incorporates strategies of health promotion and education, diagnostic screening, immunization, health economics, epidemiology and so on. The emphasis is on the active involvement (rather than the passive treatment) of individuals, although, as Kellehear notes above, the model continues to privilege professional over lay expertise.

The new public health model can be regarded as a mechanism for health surveillance in contemporary societies:

> With this expansive agenda, involving professional experts, bureaucrats and ordinary citizens, everyone is, to some extent, caught up within what has become an expanding web of power and knowledge around the problem of 'public health'. (Petersen and Lupton, 1996: 5–6)

Whilst one consequence of this may be greater surveillance of members of society, a central concept in the new public health discourse is that of individual empowerment – giving individuals information, education and access to technology in order for them to maintain good health. In so doing, this model of health defines the social in narrow terms – focusing on agency to the exclusion of structure. For example, it neglects structural factors that might inhibit individual participation such as those associated with the differential power relations between, for example, men and women, young and old, dominant and minority ethnic groups. Additionally, although this turn to new public health strategies places emphasis on the voluntary action of citizens, the state may also enact legislation (such as the compulsory wearing of car seat belts and bans on cigarette smoking and advertising) to force people to conform to healthier behaviours, thereby (apparently) reducing the risk of death.

Although dying and death await us all, individuals are given a temporary reprieve, represented in health promotion literature as something that can be avoided through good decision-making and healthy behaviour. For example, in 1999, in a website address entitled, 'Saving Lives: Our Healthier Nation', the UK Chief Medical Officer, Liam Donaldson, provided 'Ten Tips For Better Health'. These are directives for the individual and ranged from exercise and diet plans to road safety and the need to learn the techniques of first aid. Written in language that directly addresses the reader, people are told:

1 Don't smoke. If you can, stop. If you can't, cut down.
2 Follow a balanced diet with plenty of fruit and vegetables.
3 Keep physically active.
4 Manage stress by, for example, talking things through and making time to relax.
5 If you drink alcohol, do so in moderation.
6 Cover up in the sun, and protect children from sunburn.
7 Practise safe sex.
8 Take up cancer screening opportunities.
9 Be safe on the roads: follow the Highway Code.
10 Learn the First Aid ABC – airways, breathing, circulation.[2]

It is clear that in their role as adherents to the new public health model, individuals have a set of rights and a set of responsibilities. Citizens should take responsibility for their health and well-being and on a global level should assist in protecting the planet by changing their behaviour (Petersen and Lupton, 1996). In periods of ill-health, people can expect to receive appropriate medical intervention and treatment.

So, on the one hand it is the duty of the individual to take account of risks to health and to behave in a manner that minimizes these. On the other hand, as Kellehear (1998) argues, the only certain outcome of health is that it will eventually fail and result in death. Viewing dying as the 'final illness is to acknowledge that the dominant framework now, for many people, is a health care one' (Kellehear, 1998: 295). The only remaining question, he asserts, is that concerned with how one is to die.

Let us turn now to consider risks to mortality in the context of large-scale disasters, both 'natural' and, so-called, 'man-made'. The discussion will now explore three examples of death in disasters. The first is the natural disaster of the Asian tsunami in December 2004; next we will consider the disaster caused by the Union Carbide gas emissions at Bhopal in 1984; and finally, the destruction of the World Trade Center in New York in September 2001.

Disasters

Whilst death caused by natural disasters, such as flood, cyclone, fire and drought may be referred to as 'Acts of God', as Parsons and Lidz (1967) argue, in Western societies there tends to be an assumption that the more 'adventitious' aspects of death can be controlled. In terms of natural disasters caused by phenomena such as flood, earthquake, the eruption of volcanoes and bush fires, science works to predict, if not ultimately to control, such events, and disaster management teams of emergency service personnel function to act swiftly to minimize their impact.

The Asian tsunami

At 1am (GMT) on 26 December 2004 a massive earthquake tore through the seabed off the coast of Northwest Sumatra. The earthquake, which measured 9.3 on the Richter scale, lasted for eight minutes as two tectonic plates were forced together – one below the other. There is no estimate of how many people died in the earthquake. The impact of the quake, however, was to set in motion a tsunami – a series of giant waves unleashed across the Indian Ocean. Fifty minutes after the earthquake scientists in the Pacific Tsunami Warning Centre issued a warning of a possible tsunami. This was 20 minutes after the first wave had hit Sumatra, devastating vegetation and buildings and killing thousands of people in minutes. The tsunami continued on its way causing unprecedented damage and killing an estimated 300,000 people in 13 countries around the Indian Ocean, including Sumatra, Indonesia, Thailand, Sri Lanka, India and Somalia. Of this figure, 5,000 were thought to be foreign tourists. It was also estimated that more than 500,000 people sustained injuries, up to 5 million people lost their homes and around 1 million their livelihoods. (Pickerell, 2005)

The Asian tsunami was reported by the media around the globe and images of the devastation were shown on television screens within hours of the disaster. The international response was unprecedented, and even before governments had announced relief programmes, individuals throughout the world were donating aid. This meant that the immediate humanitarian needs were largely met. As David Loyn, the BBC's developing world correspondent, noted, however, it was the poorest people in these countries who suffered most from the impact of the tsunami: 'Living in frail shelters, on marginal land, they were literally swept away by the waves, and the survivors among the poorest communities had less access to medical help than richer people did' (2005). This lack of equity within countries affected by the tsunami was reflected in discussions of the lack of warning of the impending disaster. One of the major concerns following the disaster was that the technology that could have warned of the tsunami (and presumably averted great loss of life) was not in place. Although there had not been a similar disaster in the Indian Ocean since 1945, governments were criticized for their failure to establish an early warning system in the region. The estimated cost of such a system was $20 million, the estimated costs of the disaster (in terms of aid and reconstruction) was $7.5 billion (Pickerell, 2005). This approach assumes that loss of life incurred in natural disasters can, to some extent, be controlled by use of appropriate technology. In those developed societies similarly at risk from such natural phenomena, early warning systems are in use. In the less developed countries affected by the tsunami, where large-scale poverty is a feature of society, risks were taken by governments and blame for the resulting mass death, which might once have been perceived as the 'will of God', was typically viewed as failure to purchase the appropriate technology.

Raphael (1997) considers the consequences of such untimely death caused by disasters in the Australian context and examines the impact they have on the national psyche. She differentiates natural disasters (such as the Darwin cyclone of 1974) from 'man-made' disasters, such as the Granville rail disaster of 1977. After examining an earlier review of Australian disasters (Carroll, 1977), she notes that in reporting deaths in such disasters the deceased become anonymous, referred to as '83 dead' rather than giving any detail of their age, gender or ethnic background. Her conclusion is that it is untimely death that leads to this lack of identity. The sudden and unexpected nature of death threatens our sense of ontological security (well-being in the world) and forces us to acknowledge our own vulnerability. The more anonymous the dead become, the less like us they appear to be. It is perhaps pertinent to note here that after the Asian tsunami the Western media tended to report the names and personalize the stories of foreign (largely Western) tourists killed in the disaster. Similarly, following the attacks on the Twin Towers in New York in September 2001, the names of all the dead were published in the US media. Whilst this was clearly an act of commemoration, according to Raphael's thesis, naming the dead in this way would have added to the shock, horror and the destructive impact of these events. Rather than allowing the dead to be anonymous, identifying or making them similar to us would have enhanced the individual's empathy with them and their families.

Raphael also discusses the impact of the media in providing us with texts and images of the disaster areas, the dead and the grieving families. In these descriptions, emergency service workers are often prominent, emphasizing, she suggests, 'their potency as defeaters of death' (Raphael, 1997: 75–6). We might add here, that these workers are also cast in the role of 'hero', as was clearly evident after the destruction of the World Trade Center in New York – a subject that we will return to shortly. By providing pictures and descriptions of the events and the aftermath of violent and traumatic death, the media have played a significant role in raising awareness of the nature and extent of death from such disasters. They have also been influential in encouraging individuals and governments to establish organized responses to disasters. On a more negative note, she points out that the regular coverage of such traumatic events may result in individuals becoming desensitized to the issues and experiencing 'compassion fatigue' in the face of such crises. This may have explained the relative lack of Western aid donated after the Pakistan earthquake in October 2005.

We will return to a discussion of the media in chapter 5. Let us now consider 'man-made' disasters.

Bhopal

On 3 December 1984 there was an accidental emission of gases into the surrounding neighbourhood of the Union Carbide chemical plant located in Bhopal, India, killing more than 2,000 people and injuring many more. Although the exact cause of this leak is unknown, a combination of equipment failure at the plant was responsible. Carbaryl, the chemical being produced, was used worldwide as an insecticide with low toxicity for humans, although most of the chemicals that go into its production are toxic (Boyne, 2003). This chemical was manufactured in the USA, but in 1975 the company acquired a licence to produce the insecticide in Bhopal. This new location was particularly attractive to the manufacturers as it provided them with the benefits of being situated in a relatively low-cost service centre in the less developed world. By the early 1980s, however, it became clear that the market for pesticides in India was unstable because of agricultural problems and competition from other brands. In attempting to avoid economic losses, the company introduced measures to make the plant more economically viable. The most significant of these was to manufacture on site some of the primary toxic chemicals that are used in the production of carbaryl. This would inevitably lead to greater hazards, but local objections were overruled at state and national level. As Boyne remarks, 'Union Carbide India were one of the biggest employers, paying well, and it was important to embrace the modern industrial project' (2003: 18).

In an old plant that was not geared up to cope with such demands, the ensuing disaster was almost inevitable, yet the potential risk to the health and safety of the workers and neighbouring population appears to have been largely ignored. Workers were insufficiently trained, the infrastructure was old and deteriorating and there had been several breakdowns and accidents. On the day of the disaster safety mechanisms that might have averted such a great loss of life failed. For instance, the caustic soda shower that could have neutralized the gases was not working, the flare tower was similarly out of order and the alarms that might have alerted local people were inadequate (Boyne, 2003). The majority of victims were poor, shantytown dwellers living close to the plant.

Whilst the responsibility for this disaster cannot be placed solely at the door of the US company, it is clear, according to Boyne (2003) that the desire to maximize economic returns on the investment resulted in a lowering of safety standards. Union Carbide Corporation (the US arm of the company) had effectively handed over control of the plant in 1982. When it did so, it cited a number of areas that required urgent attention, some of which actively contributed to the disaster in 1984. It would seem that there was no attempt to estimate the risks to the population around the plant, and, as Boyne argues, '[w]e can infer that UCC did not carry out a state-of-the-art risk estimation with respect to the plant handover' (2003: 21). In this way, the company passed responsibility for the plant to Union Carbide India Ltd, and with that the attendant risk. Despite relinquishing control, the closure report and the full handover of the facilities suggested that the parent company were either satisfied that the plant was relatively safe, or, more likely, that as entrepreneurs they were willing to accept the risk. Clearly, this approach to risk cannot be defended given that those with no knowledge of the dangers where the ones who experienced the risk to life. Indeed, this corporate negligence has been identified with white-collar crime (Mars, 1982) and, in the UK, as corporate manslaughter (Slapper, 1993).

Beck (1992) argues that in contemporary 'world risk society' social class is no longer an adequate indicator of risk; that wealthy and poor alike are subjected to the risks involved in air and water pollution, nuclear annihilation, radiation and deforestation. He does, however, concede that as less developed societies become the dumping grounds for the chemical plants and toxic waste of the developed world, the poor in those societies have less opportunity to avoid risk. He points to new forms of social inequality where class positions and risk positions overlap as the 'proletariat of the global risk society settles beneath the smokestacks, next to the refineries and chemical factories in the industrial centres of the Third World' (1992: 41). Although those responsible in Western developed countries are undoubtedly aware of the hazards to health of their economic activities in less developed societies, they, and the governments and populations of those societies, may consider the risks to be offset by the material relief created by industry and employment. This, Beck suggests, is in part due to the fact that industrial complexes stand as measures of success, the risks they contain are largely invisible and the benefits in production of food and access to material goods are viewed as paramount: 'In the competition between the visible threat of death from hunger and the invisible threat of death from toxic chemicals, the evident fight against material misery is victorious' (1992: 42).

The threat from terrorism: 9/11

In stark contrast with the seemingly unremitting death tolls in less developed societies caused by industrial negligence, wars, drought, famine, flood and other natural disasters, many wealthy Western developed countries appear to have been shielded from the risk of large-scale violent death. In the USA in particular, a country protected by the army and air defences of the sole remaining superpower, the events of 11 September 2001 that led to the death of more than 3,000 people were extraordinarily shocking.

On 11 September 2001 two aeroplanes were flown into the twin towers of the World Trade Center in New York by Al Qaida supporters, killing everyone on board and many more in the offices of the Center. The attack was totally unexpected and led to tremendous loss of life as well as the total destruction of the site that has since become known as 'Ground Zero'. The city authorities were ill-prepared and ill-equipped to deal with such a tragedy, and emergency service personnel battled for days to find survivors in the rubble. The event was televised by news networks live throughout the world, and millions watched as the second plane flew into the building and listened to recordings of final messages from the passengers to their loved ones. As one commentator observed as she watched the events unfold, it was a day of unprecedented horror.

> Chaos and terror had exploded into everyday normalcy, in a magnitude far beyond any nightmare we might ever have envisaged. What could be more unimaginable than a bright fall day when, within hours, three thousand innocent people were killed, millions of lives shattered, and a significant part of New York's economy destroyed. The analogy was drawn to the shattering attack on Pearl Harbor but we – and the TV networks – saw it that day as if it were the eruption of atomic war, the beginning of the Apocalypse. (Cohen, 2002: 114)

There was a sense, continually repeated within the media, that the world had fundamentally changed as a consequence of this attack and that the risk to the security of all Western nations was now dramatically heightened as a result of the threat of terrorism. Some international security analysts were almost mournful of the Cold War era when US–Soviet superpower gridlock kept the lid on respective spheres of influence.

In many respects the events of 9/11 conform to Beck's criteria for 'world risk society' in that, whilst the threat of terrorism is now considered to be 'real', the enemy in this new form of war is, for the most part, invisible and eludes capture. Western governments, following the lead of the USA, are at pains to convince, and continually remind their populations that the activists of the Al Qaida network (more a state of being than a membership group) pose a permanent threat to their national security and may strike at any time. Continued vigilance by, and surveillance of, the populace raises the sinister spectre that death could be around every corner, may come when least expected, may strike at anyone, and that everyone may be suspected. This inevitably leads to greater surveillance of the public and is particularly visible in airport terminals and train stations. The more recent bombing of trains in Madrid in March 2004, with the loss of 200 lives, and in London in July 2005, now thought to be the work of an Al Qaida cell, is used as evidence that no one is safe in this new world of political terror.

Whilst no one would want to underestimate the trauma and grief that has resulted from the loss of the lives of people from many countries, ethnic backgrounds and religious faiths caught up in the fundamentalist war on the West, it should be pointed out that this form of political violence is neither new nor restricted to Islamic movements. Many countries in Europe and the Middle East have existed against a backdrop of violent political resistance to established states and governments. In the UK, for example, the war of the Republican movement in Northern Ireland not only killed many in the Provinces but was for intensive periods carried to mainland Britain, causing deaths in railway stations and shopping malls. Similarly, having experienced the violence of ETA (the Basque separatist group) for many years, the bombings in Madrid in March 2004, whilst devastating, were not a new phenomenon, as is evidenced by the fact that the government of Spain initially attributed the outrage to ETA. It seems, therefore, that it is the international basis of such violent political acts, and the fact that these have spilt over into countries once secure from them, that create this impression of a new, and extremely hazardous, risk for contemporary societies. As Morgan contends, 'The murder exists. The fear exists. The grief exists. But, yes, the terrorist *is* a figment of our imagination – and more, a figment of our lack of imagination' (1989: 3).

To extend this existential metaphor further, it has been argued that in identifying such political violence as 'international terrorism' we, in the West, have constructed a demon that fires our imagination to new levels of horror and sees new risks at every turn. This demon is conceived of as 'pure evil' and, as Dr Zimbardo, then President-elect of the American Psychological Association, described it, this 'creative evil' flourishes 'throughout the world with nameless conductors orchestrating ever-new violence' (cited in Cohen, 2002: 115). The inevitable consequence of this perception of an unpredictable and uncontrollable force of potential devastation is a loss of ontological security, a sense of utter meaninglessness, and a failure to recognize the underlying political struggles that might lead to such activity.

Whilst it is not the purpose of our discussion here to examine the conflict between East and West, or Christian and Islamic fundamentalism, any attempt to make sense of such political violence requires in-depth scrutiny of the ideological causes associated with each side of the 'terrorist' war. As Woolacott protests:

> Any understanding of terrorism that pictures governments as completely legitimate and rational and 'terrorists' as completely illegitimate and irrational must be flawed. Governors and terrorists are both involved in the pathology of societies that have broken down to the point where politics has been wholly or partly replaced by violent action. (1995: 20)

In the context of global society, this conflict could be framed in terms of tradition versus modernization. As the late modern world becomes a global society, traditions continue to exist. Giddens (1994) suggests these may be respected as having value in a pluralist world. To realize this value they must form part of a dialogue with other value systems and be 'discoursively articulated and defended' (1994: 100). In a modernist world comprising perpetual radical doubt, traditional value systems can mutate into forms of fundamentalism, asserting grand truths about the nature of the world and refusing to enter into dialogue with other beliefs. Fundamentalist beliefs or traditions can provide security in a world otherwise perceived in terms of risk. This desire for safety is not confined to the Islamic world or the world of the 'alien other' but may also be found within Christian fundamentalism which, like its counterpart in non-Western societies constructs unbelievers as alien and other. Wherever it is found, whether in the forum of religion, nationalism or ethnic identity, fundamentalism is characterized by an unwillingness to enter into dialogue, yet, 'is nothing more or less than 'tradition in its traditional sense', although today embattled rather than in the ascendant. Fundamentalism may be understood as an assertion of formulaic truth without regard to consequences' (Giddens, 1994: 100).

Summary

To conclude, let us return to the question, posed at the start of this chapter, about the nature of risk in contemporary societies and the impact that perceptions of risk have on our understanding of mortality. Have risks to mortality fundamentally changed as a consequence of being members of a global village, or is it merely our perception or awareness of risk that has altered? It seems clear from the preceding discussion that whilst dangers and risks to life do exist, the manner in which they are constructed has changed transhistorically and cross-culturally. In the early modern period, for example, in Western societies risk was often associated with work and illness and was perceived as quantifiable. These risks have now been minimized with more sophisticated technology, more emphasis on health and safety at work, and the developing partnership between professionals and lay people in the project of better individual health. At the same time, threats to national security and concerns about the risks of international and national travel have heightened, although against a background of relatively few incidents of political violence (albeit involving substantial loss of life and associated trauma). The media have played an important role in increasing awareness of such risks and in posing them, with encouragement from governments, as major threats to the lives of each individual.

If we consider the concept of risk in the less-developed nations of our so-called global society, it would appear that there is great inequity between their experience of risk and those of the West. Not only are people in those societies more susceptible to the dangers associated with natural disasters (and phenomena such as tsunamis and earthquakes kill thousands, and sometimes hundreds of thousands, of people) but they are also more likely to take risks associated with employment in industries that handle hazardous materials, or to be located in neighbourhoods adjacent to such businesses. Two important considerations here are, first, that individuals taking risks may lack knowledge of the hazards they hold and, second, that even with some awareness of the dangers, people in less developed societies may, when facing poverty as the alternative, accept these risks or regard themselves as effectively having no choice.

Whilst life in Western societies may have become less risky (despite the views of those who currently perceive the West as engaged in a 'war on terrorism'), this may be regarded as a consequence of the unequal distribution of risks around the world, with the poor in less developed countries in the world facing substantial threats to mortality. For although Beck (1992) argued that some of the risks in contemporary global society are 'democratic' (for example, pollution), poverty remains as the greatest source of risk of death in the global world.

4

Death, Religion and Spirituality

Introduction

The social diversity noted in chapter 1 and the demographic and risk factors discussed in chapters 2 and 3 underscore differential social relationships and experiences of mortality. These relationships and experiences are also strongly influenced by social beliefs about the nature and status of death in society, in other words by cultural approaches within each society.

Attitudes to death and dying are sometimes perceived as a reflection of culture in society and, for some, the very basis on which culture is founded (Bauman, 1992). Many studies of the changing nature of culture in societies, however, have identified an overarching trend that has occurred as a consequence of modernity, and that is a move from collectivist to individualist cultural frameworks (Beck, 1992; Giddens, 1990; Triandis, 1990). According to this view, the actions of people in traditional or less developed societies are characterized by a concern with collective norms and expectations and are heavily influenced by the needs and interests of the social group. In contrast, people in modern developed societies are perceived as being more concerned with personal goals that override those of the social group. There is much debate amongst scholars as to the utility of such a dichotomy. Some authors note that cultural diversity both across and within societies challenges the value of identifying a society as either collectivist or individualist and the dynamic nature of societies suggests that such absolute categories are unhelpful (Matsumoto, 1999; Reykowski, 1994; Allik and Realo, 2004; Sinha et al., 2001). For example, most Western societies are now increasingly multicultural and this presents a serious challenge to the idea that any one society can be identified as either collectivist or individualist. Others, however, point to the negative and positive connotations of collectivism and individualism; for example, collectivist societies are (from the perspective of Western, modernist thinkers) rather negatively associated with cultures of dependence, and individualistic societies with independence and autonomy (Tripathi and Leviatan, 2003).

Notwithstanding these criticisms of identifying societies as either collectivistic or individualistic, this theoretical framework is useful for an enquiry into popular culture and death. In examining the place of death in the popular cultures of Western societies, it is necessary to place this study in the context of contemporary dominant discourses. In Western consumer societies these tend to privilege individualism over collectivism, with each of us forging our own identity and making meaning in our own lives (Giddens, 1991; Howarth, 2000b). By thinking about death, people are also making sense of life. The manner in which understandings of mortality are constructed will vary according to social factors and individual experiences. Two significant features of these constructions will be the relationship with spiritual matters and the role of the media in representing aspects of mortality.[1] Whilst spirituality and the media are not signifiers of cultural attitudes to death, they are spheres of influence that offer a narrative, or a series of narratives, about the nature and meanings of dying, death and loss, and also about relationships with the dead. Walter (2004), drawing from the work of Berger (1969) and from Giddens's concept of 'fateful moments' (1991), has argued that the media have, to some extent, replaced the role of religion in repairing the damage that death inflicts on the social fabric. This, he asserts, is particularly significant in media constructions of disasters in which social values are first threatened, and then reaffirmed.

For this reason the following two chapters will explore, first, in this chapter, some of the religious and spiritual dimensions of understandings of mortality and then, in the following chapter, the way in which the media portray death. The focus, once again, will be on contemporary Western societies where it is important to remember that attitudes to mortality – whether religious, spiritual or lay representations in the media – are dynamic and diverse, responding to social, cultural, economic and political changes and events that inevitably frame individual perceptions.

This chapter, on religion and spirituality, will examine significant changes in spiritual behaviour, firstly in the context of religious beliefs, and also by looking at alternative forms of spirituality. The importance of spiritual matters in the context of dying will also be considered. The following chapter will examine some of the more material aspects of popular culture via a discussion of death in the media and entertainments industry. It will conclude with an examination of Walter's thesis that the news media have recently usurped the role of religion in taking responsibility for offering salvation following major disasters.

Religion and spirituality

We have already observed in chapter 1 that the growth in secularization has been a notable feature of modern Western societies. This should not, however, be taken to imply that the majority of people are no longer concerned with spiritual matters or that they deny death. Employing the collectivist–individualist dichotomy suggests that secularization may more accurately refer to a trend away from collectivist forms of spirituality (for example, those of the established Western religions of Catholicism[2] and Protestantism) to individual or 'alternative' spiritual and ecological movements which do not require communal rituals of worship. We have already acknowledged that religion has been perceived as important in helping individuals and societies to make sense of mortality. Indeed, Berger (1969) has referred to religion as a 'sacred canopy' under which humans shelter from the terrors of death and meaninglessness. In the light of our discussion of spirituality and the decline of established religion (to which we will shortly return), it might be more appropriate in contemporary Western societies to speak of spirituality as the sacred canopy. Let us further explore this suggestion in relation to established religions and new age forms of spirituality.

Traditionally, discussions of spirituality have focused on religious beliefs and practices. These have tended to examine a range of belief systems to show how each can help people to make sense of death, dying and grief. More recent definitions of spirituality have contextualized life and death in notions of a 'soul', 'spirit' or 'self'. These concepts may not be defined strictly in religious terms but they nevertheless rely on an all-encompassing belief system such as those incorporated in 'new age' thinking or psychological perceptions of an 'essential self'. Broader and less clearly defined approaches take spirituality to refer to the way in which individuals make meaning in their lives and, in so doing, seek to transcend the mundane world. Whichever of these approaches is adopted, there is recognition that spiritual and related experiences are not solely features of dying and grief, nor are they exclusively associated with religion. Whilst experiences of loss may result in greater spiritual needs for individuals (whether or not these are religious in nature), spiritual issues are confronted throughout our everyday lives.

At the beginning of the twenty-first century there is mounting popular concern with issues of environmental damage and the need for greater recognition of cultural diversity. Whilst religious orthodoxy continues to thrive, environmental concerns have become intensified and, as we noted in chapter 3, have impacted on the concept of risk in contemporary society. Although some argue that the decline in orthodox Christian traditions is a consequence of growing individualism, greater cultural diversity within societies has undoubtedly played a part with the adoption in Western societies of religions such as Judaism, Buddhism and Islam. Whereas for centuries in the West, Christianity has imposed itself on the cultures of nations (for example, through the oppression and rooting out of earlier traditions such as paganism), as we reach into the new century there is increasing awareness of, and tolerance towards, not only non-Western religions and ways of thinking, but also a resurgence (albeit in new forms) of 'alternative' forms of spirituality.

Western religions

Christianity

Much of the study of the establishment and development of Christianity within Western Europe advises us that this once new religion was established at great social cost and that privileging Christianity as the dominant, indeed sole, religion was achieved in a conscious and ruthless fashion. Prior to the introduction of Christianity in the West, forms of pagan beliefs existed. These religions worshipped nature and the power of the sun and the moon; and natural phenomena were believed to influence everyday life. When Christianity was brought to Europe this new religion mapped its rituals onto those of pagan traditions in just the same way as it did centuries later when carried by missionaries to South America, parts of Asia and Africa. In Europe, traditional festivals and ceremonies were absorbed into Christian practice. Yule, the time when the moon goddess gave birth to a son (who was himself a god), became the birth of Christ and Christmas was born. Ostara, the spring equinox, was celebrated as Easter. Samhain, celebrated in the autumn at a time of reflection on death as people prepared themselves for the long winter, is marked in the Christian calendar by All Souls' Day. It is argued that in this way, those who followed the monotheistic Christian religion that worshipped only one 'true God' were able to blend their beliefs and rituals with those of a previous era. The continued respect for the power of nature was accepted as nature came to be perceived as the mirror image of the Christian God. Thus, for a time at least, in the Western world the rituals of Christianity and paganism existed side by side. Although Christianity dominated as a form of explanation and source of understanding of the meaning of life and death, by allowing pagan practices to continue, the conjunction of these two belief systems became seamless.

During the early Middle Ages in Western Europe, Catholicism, although based on the belief of the one true God, called into use a range of significant holy entities and objects through which the populace could worship. Many of the earlier ritual practices continued, and popular worship of the deity incorporated the worship of saints, statues, relics and such like. It was not until the later Middle Ages that the Christian authorities attempted to outlaw these practices and to rid the religion of its pagan roots. Whilst many practices remained in Catholic worship, in Protestant liturgy the worship of images and reliquary became outlawed and associated with devil worship and witchcraft. As the power of the Christian Church grew, the desire to establish Christianity as the dominant religion brought with it a prohibition on religious dissent and, with that, a rejection of cultural diversity. The persecution of witchcraft throughout Europe and North America was a fundamental aspect of this religious revolution. The so-called Holy Wars against the 'infidels' of the East were a pronounced form of Christian imperialism. From the Middle Ages, right through to the twentieth century, these attempts at religious colonization continued in the form of missionary work across the globe. Indeed, these movements highlight the links between religious and political persuasion that continue into the twenty-first century.

Following the European Enlightenment and the advent of science came a sense that science was integrally connected with nature and that one of the pure goals of modern humankind was to discover the laws of God's natural world. As science has progressed throughout the twentieth century and attained a heightened profile in modernist and individualistic interpretations of nature and attempts to exert control over death, the grip of religion and the belief in God as omnipotent has declined.[3] More recently, however, there has arisen a general sense of disappointment with the promise of science, and individuals have become aware of the failed expectations of science, and the problems of worshipping the god of scientific progress. Governments and environmental activists now keep a close eye on environmental damage caused in part by the unremitting emphasis on scientific progress and discovery. Similarly, there is also recognition of the negative impact that modern living has on the environment. These concurrent features have led to broader social concern with the need to live in a 'more natural' and more environmentally responsible world.

Coupled with these concerns has been the sense of a loss of meaning. This has come in a variety forms. First, there is a popular perception of a loss of community that has occurred in societies with an increased division of labour (see Durkheim, 1964a [1893]), in which people live in often large, urban, anonymous areas with little meaningful contact with those around them. Second has been the sense of discomfort at the dominance of expertise in all forms of life and this is part of a wider unease with modernity and, some would argue, with a move to postmodernity (Baudrillard, 1993; Bauman, 1992). In the context of death and dying, this disquiet with forms of expertise has been especially noticeable in terms of the medicalization of dying (Elias, 1985; Illich, 1976; Ariès, 1981), and as a corollary of that, the medicalization of life itself (Zola, 1972). We will encounter the debate on the medicalization of death in chapter 6. Here we consider the impact of disillusionment with both Christianity and science with respect to popular aspects of spirituality.

The above account has provided a broad and somewhat popularistic version of the establishment of Christianity with its collectivist approach and its constraint on cultural diversity. Whatever the historical accuracy of such narratives – and there is much debate on these matters (see for example, Hutton, 2000) they have informed many popular religious movements seeking to find what they perceive as more individually fulfilling belief systems. This is in keeping with the assertion that modern societies have become more individualistic.

These new or regenerated religious movements in Western societies take a number of forms. Some individuals have retained a Christian framework whilst choosing to emphasize the re-establishment of relationships with the dead, relationships proscribed in early modernity in many Western European societies. For others, the quest for the meaning of life and death and the striving for lifestyles more in harmony with nature can be found by turning to traditional Eastern religions, such as Buddhism. We will consider these shortly when we return to our discussion of established religions. Yet others have sought fulfilment in what they perceive to be a return to forms of paganism.

Pagan religions

A general dissatisfaction with the modern world and disillusionment with mainstream religion and materialism has, according to Hardman, resulted in the development of a new form of paganism, where people, 'see they can change the world by changing themselves and following one of the spiritual paths that form what is essentially a kind of nature religion' (2000: x). Some modern pagan practitioners argue that we are witnessing a resurgence of a very old form of religion. Others claim that contemporary paganism is a new age religion that has its roots in nineteenth- and early twentieth-century ritual magic practised by societies such as the Freemasons, Friendly Societies and The Order of Woodcraft Chivalry (Hutton, 2000). In the English context, according to Hutton, it is nostalgia for the English rural lifestyle that has led to an idealization of the natural world and this new form of 'nature religion'. Whatever the source of contemporary paganism, the proliferation of goods and services that accompany it demonstrate its increasing popular attraction for individuals in Western societies. The individualistic elements of new paganism are to be found in the belief that people can effect change to their own lives and to their environment. Science and technology may be seen as harming the world and the ecosystem, but individuals can use forms of magic to harness natural forces and reassert control over their lives. This is not undertaken in the same manner that science attempts to control nature. It is, rather, by utilizing nature, by respecting and worshipping the sun, moon, trees and water, and by performing specific rituals at the right time in the year, that new pagans seek to transform their world. They argue that by respecting and recognizing the power of nature, societies (through the actions of individuals within those societies) can avoid damaging the environment. In addition to changing lifestyles, many also subscribe to the performance of magic and rituals that they believe can help to improve their quality of life. In so doing, there is a general principle that this 'white' magic should have at its core the rule to 'do no harm' and to be 'non-manipulative' of the will of another. Whilst there is a range of beliefs with regard to death and dying, most pagans adhere to some form of reincarnation (Phoenix, 1997) and, like many Eastern religions, the idea that everything, including life, death and rebirth, are interrelated.

Eastern religions

It is often said that one of the consequences of the Second World War was that it gave 'ordinary people' access to worlds that would normally have been beyond their experience. So, for example, young working-class men fighting in parts of Africa and India would have come into contact with forms of religious and spiritual practices that were quite alien to their own, broadly Western Christian belief systems. This meant that Westerners caught a glimpse of polytheistic beliefs, beliefs in reincarnation, and a view of religions that enjoyed greater connection with an afterlife than that experienced in modern Western, individualized and commodified societies.

One such religion was Buddhism. In Western societies Buddhism is a belief system that is not to be found solely among minority ethnic groups, but is also now increasingly adopted by those who seek solutions to the problem of loss of meaning in life and death.

Buddhism

Taking Buddhism as an example of an Eastern religion that is becoming more significant in the West, it is easy to see the popular attraction of a system that ties deeds in this life to the next. According to Buddhist traditions, after death the spirit is continually reborn until it reaches a stage of enlightenment. During each incarnation, the behaviour and thoughts of the individual determine their 'karma'. Karma is an inventory of good and bad deeds that remains with the individual throughout life and impacts on the nature of the next life. 'Impure acts defile a person; stinginess defiles an offering; so evil acts defile not only this life but also the following lives' (Kyokai, 1996). In thinking about the next life, there are six realms of existence and good karma will result in movement from a lesser to a higher stage of existence; bad karma, the reverse. An especially important distinction between Western Christianity and Buddhism is that life, death and rebirth are seen as a continuum. The notion of the life cycle clearly has more meaning in this context than in contemporary Western societies where the concept of life cycle with its emphasis on rebirth has been largely discarded in favour of a life course that stresses beginnings and ends.

Islam, Hinduism and Sikhism

A further factor of relevance to the dynamic nature of religious practice in Western societies was the extent of migration to Western countries during the twentieth century. Some countries, such as Australia, Canada and the USA, are essentially migrant communities, their populations made up of indigenous peoples and those who have migrated from other lands to the New Worlds. Migration was initially from European countries, where many people practised Christianity or Judaism, and later, particularly after the Second World War, from countries in Asia. In Europe a similar pattern emerged with increasing migration from the 1950s from countries such as India, Pakistan, Bangladesh, Jamaica and countries in Africa. Migrants brought with them a range of religious beliefs and practices, many of which were unfamiliar to European populations. For example, Hinduism and Sikhism, religions largely found in India, Southern Asia and Africa, adhere to a belief in reincarnation. Sikhs differ from Hindus in that they reject the caste system (a central feature of Hindu belief based on the notion of karma [4]) and instead aim to develop unity with God through the many cycles of birth and rebirth.

An increasingly significant religion practised by around one-fifth of the world's population is Islam. Islam is currently one of the fastest growing religions across the globe and Muslims derive from all races and ethnic groups. Muslims believe that there is only one God and that the Prophet Muhammad is his Messenger. They do not believe in reincarnation but that actions in this life will be used to determine one's destiny in the next life. Thus a belief in life after death is fundamental and the soul is held to be indestructible. The ultimate fate of the soul – heaven or hell – is determined after death. At death a person is transferred from the material to the spiritual world where the journey of the return to God begins. This is a purification process whereby the soul is cleansed of sin through suffering. The extent of suffering is determined by the extent of sin and is assessed immediately after death and again on the Day of Judgement.

Spirituality and dying

Whatever religious belief or lack of belief, the issue of spirituality has attracted a great deal of attention from researchers concerned with the nature of dying and with attempts to understand the individual response to dying. In his review of spirituality, Walter (1997) has identified a number of distinct approaches to the concept of spirituality. For example, traditional discussions of spirituality have focused on religious beliefs and practices (Rumbold, 2002). These have tended to examine a range of belief systems to show how each can help people to make sense of death, dying and grief. Alternative approaches to spirituality have placed it in the context of notions of a 'soul', 'spirit' or 'self'. These concepts may not be defined in strictly religious terms but they nevertheless rely on an all-encompassing belief system such as 'new age' thinking or psychological perceptions of an 'essential self'. Broader and less clearly defined approaches take spirituality to refer to the way in which individuals make meaning in their lives and, in so doing, attempt to transcend the mundane world. Further attempts to define and understand the concept have focused specifically on dying people and the professionals who work with them (Barnard, 1988; Doka and Morgan, 1993; Heyse-Moore, 1996; McGrath, 1999; McSherry and Draper, 1998; Martsolf and Mickley, 1998).

Whichever of these approaches is adopted, there is recognition that spiritual and related experiences are not features solely of dying and grief. Whilst experiences of loss may result in greater spiritual needs for individuals, spiritual issues are confronted throughout our everyday lives. As Kellehear argues, at base spirituality is about the human 'desire to transcend hardship and suffering' (2000: 150). Thus, whilst questions of spirituality become fore-grounded during periods of crisis, they also need to be, and are, addressed throughout the life course.

Kellehear (2000) has developed a model of spiritual needs in the context of palliative care. He bases his discussion on an understanding of spirituality as taking many forms but that essentially it is about meaning making and transcendence. His framework has three constituents: *situational needs, moral and biographical needs* and *religious needs.*

Situational needs derive from the individual's 'need to question and reflect about suffering and life changes' (Kellehear, 2000: 151). These are directly related to the circumstances of the illness and lead people to reflect on hope, to find purpose and meaning and to connect with others.

Moral and biographical needs arise from the direct situation of the individual. Once situational needs have been met, individuals are able to focus on moral or biographical requirements such as the desire to negotiate forgiveness, to deal with feelings such as vulnerability and isolation, and to search for resolution and peace. These needs are not overtly religious but may lead the individual to ask religious questions.

Religious needs may emerge from moral and biographical reflections. In the context of dying, these may encompass concerns about the nature of God, the possibilities of an afterlife and religious reconciliation.

By distinguishing these three dimensions of spirituality, Kellehear helps us to think more clearly about the spiritual needs of dying people. In this way he suggests some theoretical, research and practice implications for professionals working in palliative care. This model of spiritual needs may also bring greater clarity to an understanding of spiritual needs at other times during the life course. Whilst the circumstances surrounding dying are likely to demand an unprecedented concern with the spiritual dimensions of life, other experiences can have a similarly profound impact on meaning making. For example, grief and a resulting loss of ontological security (ability to make meaning) may leave individuals with spiritual needs similar to those identified in Kellehear's model.

Summary

Whilst this discussion has presented only a brief foray into some of the religions currently practised in Western societies, what seems clear is that many individuals in contemporary Western societies are searching for new (or sometimes established) forms of spiritual meaning which are not based on the materialism of science and the commodification of society. There is a move in the early twenty-first century to re-establish a connection with nature and, in some realms, with the supernatural, in order to assert greater control over the environment and to rekindle the relationship between life and death. This is often defined as an individual search for meaning that rejects the collectivist and prescriptive structures of established religions. For example, in reporting the reasons for this turn to new forms of spirituality Midgley cites people as saying: 'We are not affiliated to any religion and there is no belief system imposed on anybody here';'I don't want to be preached at any more. I'm sick of being made to feel guilty. I don't need to be told how to live my life'; I didn't find any help in the churches. I found it in a 12-step programme. That was the start of my personal journey' (2004: 12).

Of course, this is not to suggest that established religions have lost their importance. Although there are many studies that point to increased secularization (see for example, Bruce, 1992), it is important to recognize that in some cultural and national contexts there is a significant resurgence of orthodox beliefs. This is especially true of Christian and Islamic fundamentalism. It could, however, be argued that this is itself a further attempt to reach beyond the purely material world of modern industrial and technological

society and to revisit a more meaningful, and individual relationship with God and the afterlife. Such relationships may become
paramount when the individual is faced with death and the final
section of the chapter considered a more social model of spirituality that focused on the situational, moral and biographical, and the
religious needs of dying people.

In the next chapter we will examine the role of the media in the
construction of popular representations of mortality.

5

Death and the Media

In this chapter we will continue with the theme of cultural approaches to death and dying. The focus will be on the role of the media, as it is here that we find representations and images of mortality that reflect the beliefs, values and attitudes inherent within society.

Some theorists argue that the media fundamentally shape popular attitudes and beliefs and act as a determining structural constraint that moulds the lives of the audience as they absorb the images and messages with which they are confronted. Others contend that the media merely reflect the values found in society. Yet the media is neither a shaper nor a mere mirror image of attitudes; rather, there is a symbiotic relationship between society and the media (Blumer and Katz, 1974; McQuail, 1994). Using Giddens's structuration thesis (1984) to better understand this relationship, the media can be viewed as a resource that may be used in everyday narratives of culture and self-identity. The media present cultural scripts that are themselves then adopted selectively and adapted to the social context and lifeworld of the individual. Whatever the relationship between society and the individual, the media is significant as a marker of popular cultures and social mores surrounding death and dying.

Research by Goldberg (1998) suggests that in Western societies there has been an increase in images of death at a time when direct contact with death has decreased. In this section we will consider some of these images in cinema, news and documentary media and will examine them as a means of tapping into popular perceptions of death and dying and theories that identify Western societies as individualistic. Let us begin this exploration by examining cinematic representations.

Cinema

Death has been a hallmark of cinema since its inception and, together with sex, has commonly been regarded as one element to guarantee a box-office success. Whereas in the early days of film-making death may have been represented from a more factual perspective, from the mid-twentieth century, fictional violence has proliferated and the act of killing has been portrayed as easier. This is in keeping with Gorer's (1955) thesis that the media has become obsessed with violent and horrific death that bears little resemblance to the realities of death and dying in contemporary societies. According to Gorer, death is the taboo of modern society, having replaced sex as a source of pornographic entertainment. He contended that whilst in the Victorian period sexual pornography was produced, in the twentieth century the silence around mortality has led to a pornography of death. These pornographic images, he argued, have resulted in unrealistic and sensational representations of death and dying in the media. For example, in so-called 'westerns' of the 1950s, cowboys, and in greater numbers 'Indians', were killed with ease on cinema and television screens. Gangster movies and some 'tongue in cheek' films, such as the James Bond spy series, were equally able to kill vast numbers of people with little effort or remorse. As the century progressed and visual effects became more sophisticated, these killings became bloodier and more realistic. Films such as *Pulp Fiction*, for example, were box-office successes as much for their depiction and deft handling of violence and death as for the storylines and dialogue.

One particularly notable feature of these types of film is that although death is present, it is distanced from the audience and bears little resemblance to the everyday experience of dying. In these cinematic depictions the deaths that occur are accompanied by little or no dying – a single bullet, the swift removal of a head with a sword. They may be violent, but these deaths are not the ones that happen to 'us'. They are not deaths that follow protracted periods of illness – they happen to cartoon characters, criminals or members of gangster organizations, people from the distant past with whom we can no longer identify and those from alien worlds or non-Western cultures. Death is 'othered' and as such, although it may be horrific and violent, people in the developed world can watch without too much anxiety as it is not the type of death that they expect for themselves.

Although the subject of death may not always have been explicit in filmmaking, a cursory glimpse at some of the genres of the last century – the cinema age – amply demonstrates its significance. Whilst there are many distinct narratives of death in cinema, the discussion here will consider three major themes that have permeated Western cinema during the twentieth century. These are war death, horror and, towards the end of the century, individual loss and bereavement.

War death

War and the threat of war have stimulated a great deal of film-making. Many of the early films, produced during the first decades of the twentieth century, concentrated on bringing news and images of events to the populace. As Clark (2001) notes, these were frequently records of natural disasters and the death and funerals of notable figures (such as that of Queen Victoria). Many of these images, however, related to conflict and were used as tools for propaganda. For example, the Russian Revolution sparked a wealth of images of revolutionary events and the First World War was the first such conflict to be filmed on a large scale and from the propaganda perspectives of opposing forces. Subsequent wars in which Western countries have been involved have been recorded on film, to the extent that some of the most recent military activities have been regarded as something of a media festival. In addition to documentary or news reporting of war, fictional accounts and feature length films have been produced – particularly by Hollywood – often as either pro- or anti-war statements. US involvement in the wars in Vietnam and Korea, for example, acted as the stimulus for a growing number of films, such as *Apocalypse Now* (1979), *Good Morning Vietnam* (1987) and *Mash* (1970), producing powerful images of the horrors of death in war and the moral conflicts that war creates. Much of the symbolism in these films portrays death in war as a waste of the lives of young men. In some cases, these deaths are justified by reference to the notion of a 'just war' in which heroic combatants fight against tyranny and believe that they have God on their side. Some deaths are represented as 'worthy' or 'heroic' according to the political prescriptions of culture: dying for nation or for an ideal. In other films, the deaths are depicted simply as a waste of life. Films of this type commonly focus on the meaninglessness of war, the lack of moral justification, and often (as in many of the films depicting the First World War, the Vietnam or Korean conflicts), the sense that the soldiers are being used as 'cannon fodder' by powerful regimes. In these representations, life is cheap and easily replaced as national leaders trade for power using soldiers' lives as their currency.

This cinematic portrayal of war as the immoral power games of the ruling elite began during the late 1960s and '70s, a time of popular protest against conflict, when the peace movement and anti-nuclear campaigns were increasingly significant. Following the Second World War, the outbreak of the Cold War and the fear of nuclear weapons (which had been used at the end of the Second World War) had resulted in growing popular anxieties about the fate of the globe and for some time this fuelled cinematic images of global annihilation as a consequence of the use of nuclear weapons (see, for example, *Dr No*). The Cuban missile crisis in 1962, which was reported around the clock by media across the world, exacerbated these fears. People watched the events unfold daily on their television screens and held their breath in anticipation of the outbreak of a war fought with nuclear weapons that could bring about the end of the world.

Horror movies

The genre of the horror movie can be dated back to the 1920s and '30s when filmmakers released the first screenings of movies such as *Nosferatu, Dracula* and *Frankenstein*. These were based on popular Victorian novels that raised questions about the boundaries between life and death and were to mark an ongoing concern. Some theorists have argued that the film *Dracula* explores the relationship between Christianity and superstition. In this way the symbolic significance of defilement and blood and the magical power of the crucifix and holy water reflect 'an ideology of the violent purification of society from the influence of enemies of religion' (Herbert, 2002: 100). It could also be argued that it was a concern with secularization and the failure of established religion that gave rise to this exploration of the boundaries between holy and unholy, the sacred dead and the impure undead.

This theme of the undead has continued to be popular. Although vampires, werewolves, zombies and such like have taken many guises, they have been central to popular culture in blurring the boundaries of mortality. In recent film media in particular, the boundaries between the living and the dead are portrayed as fragile. There is less reliance on the connection between 'this life' and 'the next' and more emphasis on multidimensional realities where, if the dimensions begin to break down, the dead and the undead come to live amongst us. The undead are usually recognizable as such when they appear in the guise of vampire, werewolf and so on. Others of the 'undead' may not only look like us, but may also become our heroes; like the living, they may even possess a soul – albeit a tortured one – as is the case with the characters of Angel and later Spike, in the popular *Buffy* and *Angel* television series.

In much of this debate there is recognition of the link between death and sex and the risks inherent therein. In the late twentieth and early twenty-first centuries there has been a proliferation of media that recruit the vampire in particular as a mechanism for exploring the boundaries and also for the gendering of sexual relationships. For example, whilst some authors have argued that the vampire reflects a fascination with the proximity of death (Wing, 1996), others have related the character to the behaviour of women and the romanticization of abuse (Beres, 1999), to ideologies of love and sex (Burr, 2003), and to the gendered experiences of young women in school (Jarvis, 2001). A further explanation derives from the AIDS epidemic in the West during the 1980s. The risk of contracting AIDS during sexual activity was associated with the transfer of body fluids, especially blood. The vampire's association with blood and sexual lust could thus be viewed as symbolic of the moral panic of the period when both blood and sex were associated with death.

Individual loss and bereavement

Over the last twenty years the media and entertainment industries appear to have rediscovered personal loss and bereavement as issues for popular consumption. This is not to suggest that loss and grief were totally neglected earlier in the century, but that their visibility was often shrouded by other concerns. During, and immediately after the Second World War, for example, there were a number of television programmes and feature films produced in which loss as a consequence of war clearly played a prominent role. These, however, were largely constructed around the practice, realities and effects of war rather than being centred on issues of grief and bereavement. Of course, there were exceptions to this rule, and the classic film, *A Matter of Life and Death* (1946), in which an airman is killed and his death accidentally overlooked by the gatekeepers of heaven, is clearly a film about love, death, grief and near-death experiences.

It was not until the 1970s and 1980s that the cinema industry began to recognize and embrace a market in films that identified the trauma of loss, popular beliefs in the supernatural, and continuing relationships with the dead. In this genre we can place films such as *Love Story* (1970) in which terminal leukaemia destroys a young couple's hopes for the future. This film clearly taps into the popular understanding of cancer as a modern killer disease. During the 1990s the question of whether death resulted in a final separation from loved ones with the consequent loss of intimate relationships was revisited in films such as *Ghost* (1990) and *Truly,*

Madly, Deeply (1991). Films of this nature suggest that life and death are becoming indistinguishable and that relationships between the living and the dead can continue – albeit bringing with them the inherent problems associated with lovers who exist in different dimensions. What is especially interesting about this cinematic theme is its overlap with the academic literature and with personal testimony literature of the time. This literature suggests that there may be a 'continuing bond' between the living and the dead (Klass et al., 1996) and that relationships continue beyond the boundaries of the material world. This thesis will be discussed in greater depth in chapters 10 and 13. It is also worthy of note that roles given to the dead in many recent films have shifted from those designed to terrify the living to those that act as guardians or negotiators – see, for example, *Meet Joe Black* (1998). This, again, suggests a blurring of the boundaries between life and death and a rejection of the idea of death and its associations as forbidden and necessarily terrifying.

Television soaps and shows

Television drama that utilizes issues of death as a central theme is ever more popular. Moreover, soaps, such as the highly popular US *Six Feet Under*, are now framed by the theme of mortality – this particular series being set around the lives of a family of dysfunctional funeral directors. A raft of medical soaps now exists that, rather than emphasizing the 'cure-all' power of medical science, regularly plays out the drama and trauma of life and death in the lives of the protagonists.

The popularity of such television viewing suggests that dying, death and grief are ever more visible in Western societies and that there has been an increase in demand for programmes which provide information and allow the audience to explore the complexities of life–death imagery and morality. Furthermore, with advanced technology such as digital, on-line and interactive television, and with the proliferation of channels, audiences are now able to access a wide range of programmes that not only allow them greater viewing choice, but also offer the opportunity to engage and interact with others from the comfort of the lounge. So, for example, they can observe the distress and pain of people 'confessing' the intricate details of loss. They are also able to observe, and at times participate, in shows such as the US programmes on spiritual mediums (for example, John Edward's *Crossing Over*). These replicate the sort of performances previously found in spiritualist churches which people attend in order to make contact with the dead. This suggests that Church communities and spiritualist movements are changing, as people no longer need to subscribe to them. A television studio audience of individuals all hoping to be chosen for contact with the dead has replaced the Church. An even larger television audience viewing from the comfort of their own homes could replace the Church community.

Documentaries and news media

In the world of the television documentary, aside from features that focus on violent death, much of the media dealing with dying and death now concentrates on professional practice (such as that of funeral directors) and new movements (such as the natural death movement and the debate on euthanasia). Most of these documentaries are devoted to debating the moral imperatives and ethical implications of birth, life and death. From the late twentieth century onwards there appears to have been an increasing fascination with the subject of mortality. Documentaries abound that have considered a raft of issues as they relate to contemporary narratives of death and risk (for example, workplace death, youth suicide and the nature of sudden, accidental death). Indeed, as Walter pointed out in his 1991 article entitled, 'Modern death – taboo or not taboo?', if we look at the media, the idea that death is a taboo subject in contemporary modern societies is absurd. A popular fascination with all aspects of mortality has stimulated the production of thousands of hours of documentary airtime, much of which draws from interviews with people who have experience of life-threatening illness, near-death events, grief and bereavement. What is distinct about this portrayal of death is that it has resonance with our own experiences of dying and death and might offer insights into our futures.

The visual, audio and printed news media are a further significant resource for information and cultural understandings of mortality. As Merrin observes, news reports produce 'specific forms of consciousness and modes of knowledge that affect our experience and interpretation of the world' (1999: 42). Furthermore, we do not receive this knowledge directly; it is interpreted and moderated by the media. This means that the form that reporting takes is inevitably bound up within the event itself. 'Hence today, the event and its broadcast have become a single phenomenon: *the media event*' (ibid.). What makes news is determined by what the media consider to be 'newsworthy' and by the way in which they investigate and construct their reports. As we have earlier noted, the proliferation of news media around death events challenges the view that death has been banished from public discourse (Walter, 1991, 2004; Giddens, 1991; Mellor and Shilling, 1993).

There is now considerable research that examines the social construction of emotion in media reporting of death and dying (particularly in the context of the death of celebrities such as Diana, Princess of Wales) and this is pertinent to both news and documentary media (Walter et al., 1995; Merrin, 1999; Parrott and Harré, 2001). As Walter et al. assert, this category of coverage provides cues to the appropriateness of grieving behaviour and underscores the contemporary trend in the 'psychologization' of grief and individualization of mourning styles. Walter (2006) goes on to theorize the role of the media in the reaffirmation of social ties and repair of the social fabric following mass death. He employs a number of examples of disasters to illustrate his thesis. For example, reporting of tragedies such as the school massacres in Dunblane, Scotland (1996) and Columbine High School (1999), the Oklahoma City bombing (1995) and the destruction of the World Trade Center in New York in 2001 fill us not only with horror, but also with hope. He notes that the news media graphically represent the 'meaningless' or 'evil' nature of these disasters, but that alongside these depictions we are offered affirmation of the, 'ordinary, and sometimes extraordinary, goodness of the local community' (2006: 275). His conclusion is that the mass media have taken a social role formerly assumed by religion:

> Like churches that preach hell-fire and damnation, the media first scare us to death and then offer salvation and comfort. This formula has traditionally been the terrain of religion, and just as its use can reinforce the power of religion so it is effective in selling newspapers. (2006: 277)

A further concern with media reporting of death is demonstrated by the assertion that coverage of death by suicide may lead to further suicides. This claim was the result of research into the nature and extent of reporting of celebrity suicide. Studies appeared to show that if suicide was given high profile in news media, with details of the person, their psychological condition and the methods they used, further 'copycat' suicides were likely to result (Phillips, 1974; Pirkis and Blood, 2001; Hassan, 1995). The assumption was that reporting such events would be likely to encourage psychologically vulnerable people to repeat the act. Data was drawn from a study of the Viennese rail network where it was allegedly shown that front-page newspaper reporting of suicide events led to an increase in the number of suicides on the rail network. Guidelines were subsequently introduced that discouraged journalists from reporting such suicides with an apparent reduction in the overall numbers of suicide. Assuming the success of this policy, similar guidelines were introduced in countries such as the USA, Canada and Australia in order to tackle the problem of so-called 'copycat' suicide. Although the research on which these guidelines are based has been heavily criticized for lacking scientific rigour (Hittner, 2005; Sullivan et al., forthcoming), the guidelines remain in place and this is a reflection of the assumption of the power of the media.

Summary

This chapter has continued the theme of the last chapter, that of exploring popular or cultural attitudes to death, dying and loss. The media have been portrayed as significant in their role as markers of popular culture and as representing social values surrounding mortality. Focusing on Western societies, it has examined media images of death through a number of distinct genres – cinema, television broadcasting and news reporting. Chapter 4 suggested that contemporary Western societies might be identified as individualistic rather than collectivist in that they are more concerned with the goals of the individual than with the collective good of society. To some extent the media support this stance in that portrayals of death and loss frequently privilege individual relationships. In contrast, however, media representations and reporting of death in war and large-scale disasters commonly remind us of the importance of society and of collective values associated with moral rightness and the need to care for those who are suffering. It is this collective approach that Walter (2004) identifies when he argues that the media may be taking on roles previously performed by religion. In so doing, they report the horror of events but are ultimately able to provide hope by pointing us to the fundamental collective goodness inherent in society and humankind more generally.

Part II
Social Structures and
Individual Experiences of Dying

6

Dying: Institutionalization and Medicalization

Introduction

We have so far considered death in a global context and have explored the changing nature of death and dying in modern Western societies. We have observed that in these societies science has largely replaced religion as the dominant mode of understanding mortality. We now turn to a discussion of dying and the ways in which this is socially managed. This chapter is the first of three that will examine some of the structural and individual aspects of dying and of sudden death. It will look more closely at the institutional management of death and dying and will consider the way in which institutionalization has, from the nineteenth century, been utilized as a strategy for dealing with social problems. We will then examine the concept of medicalization as it has been used by social theorists to understand medicine and medical science generally, as a form of social control. These theorists suggest that as society has become ever more medicalized, dying, like living, has been firmly located within the domain of the expert doctor and medical science. From around the middle of the twentieth century, research and theoretical approaches have critiqued institutionalized and medicalized forms of dying and have instead argued for the establishment of more 'natural' ways of dying. In this context the chapter will also introduce the notions of demedicalization and deinstitutionalization. These movements broadly fall within the auspices of the concept of the 'good death'. This concept will be explored in greater depth in the next chapter and will ask the question 'for whom is the death good?'. The third chapter in this section will consider the notion of the 'bad death'. This will be examined primarily in relation to sudden, unexpected and violent death and will discuss the role of emergency service personnel and the coroner (or medical examiner) in the social management of such death. Let us now begin by looking at the institutional management of death and dying.

The institutional management of death and dying

Historically, in Western societies, death has occurred in the home. Indeed, until early in the twentieth century it was assumed that, barring accidents, people would usually die at home. Prior to this, hospitals were largely institutions dedicated to providing care for travellers, the destitute, the orphaned and the poor. These institutions were commonly run by religious orders, although from around the twelfth century secular hospitals – sometimes linked with universities – began to appear. During the seventeenth century hospitals came to be associated with the growing discipline of medicine, and institutions for medical research and teaching were established. Eighteenth-century Europe and North America also witnessed the development of military medicine and the growth in numbers of hospitals dedicated to caring for those sick and wounded in war.

It was during the nineteenth century, however, that the modern hospital emerged as an institutional response to the problem of sickness in society. This was at a time when institutions were emerging to deal with all forms of social problems – prisons to separate the criminal from the law-abiding, asylums to separate the mad from the sane, cemeteries (as we shall see in chapter 12) to separate the dead from the living, and hospitals to separate the sick from the well.

The nineteenth-century hospital, though, continued to be an unpopular institution, as there was limited medical knowledge of the nature of infection and little to offer by way of pain relief or anaesthesia. Consequently, hospitals were not typically identified as places where people would wish to die and they remained in the public perception as places to be avoided if at all possible – if people died in hospital it was not because it was the preferred place but, rather, because these institutions were fatally injurious to health.

Care of the dying continued to take place in the home and was usually undertaken by the women in the extended family. When a person died it was the female members of the family who would wash and lay out the body and prepare it for visits from friends, relatives and neighbours paying their last respects. Since the middle of the twentieth century, however, the hospital has come to be identified as a place to die, with about 60 per cent of people in modern societies dying in a hospital. There are four primary reasons for this major shift in place of death.

Firstly, there have been significant advances in medical technology that have resulted in most sick and dying people receiving hospital-based care and treatment. This has meant that people suffering from both acute and chronic illnesses are now drawn to the hospital setting. Some may die shortly after admission (for example, following cardiac arrest); others may die following treatment for serious illnesses that have necessitated hospitalization. Yet others, although they do not die in the hospital, may be taken to the hospital to access life-saving medicine but may die on the way and be announced 'dead on arrival'.

Second, the twentieth century has been a time of greater urbanization and, coupled with this, there has been an increasing professionalization of skills and services. In the realm of medical science, medics and the services of other health care professionals have been located within the hospital. This is often seen as the most efficient use of resources – co-locating professional services and medical technology within the hospital.

Third, until the 1970s, institutionalization was perceived as the most efficient approach to dealing with social problems. If sickness is viewed as a social problem, then placing services and users together in one geographical location was viewed as an efficient and cost-effective use of resources. Some theorists, such as Foucault (1973), have argued that this developed as part of the sophistication of discourses of medicine. One consequence of this institutionalization of the sick has been the more general rise in surveillance of the population. We will return to this thesis below when we consider medicalization.

Finally, the changing role of women in modern Western societies has meant that they are no longer as available to perform informal caring tasks that would once have been expected of them. The number of women in paid work has markedly increased since the turn of the twentieth century, and this has forced families and governments to rethink the nature of care in society. In any case, the skills and expertise amongst women to perform this role have all but disappeared through disuse. This is not to suggest that women have entirely relinquished their role as informal carers. Indeed, studies have shown that they continue to be the primary carers for sick, elderly and dying family members. The greater emphasis on so-called 'care in the community', established in many Western societies in the 1970s and 1980s, has reinforced this role and resulted in many women leaving the labour market in order to perform the tasks associated with care. Furthermore, at the same time as women gave up responsibility for much of the informal care of dying people, their numbers increased in the formal care sector. The majority of hospital nurses are female, as are care workers in residential homes for the elderly. The hospice movement (to which we will turn in chapter 7), devoted to the care of dying people, has been described by Klass (1981) as a 'female sphere of influence'.

The removal of the sick and dying from the home to the hospital has stimulated a great deal of criticism. In the context of dying, many commentators have argued that in removing dying from the wider community to an institution, people have become distanced from, and unfamiliar with, death and that this has negatively impacted on the dying individual (Ariès, 1981; Elias, 1985; Illich, 1976; Becker, 1973). Physical death in institutions, particularly for elderly people who may die in nursing or care homes, is often preceded by social death (Sudnow, 1967; Mulkay, 1993). This refers to a process whereby dying people are marginalized and separated from mainstream society and, depending on how long dying takes, may see less and less of their relatives and friends. Prior to examining these claims in more detail, familiarization with the concept of medicalization will aid our enquiry.

What is medicalization?

Medicalization is a sociological concept that essentially refers to the process by which social life comes to be seen through a medical framework (Zola, 1972; Illich, 1976). Although he resisted being linked with any specific academic discipline, Michel Foucault (1973) provided an important way of thinking about medicalization. Foucault was a post-structuralist. This means that he did not use a traditional structural analysis to help him understand the functioning of society. So, for example, he did not focus on the impact that institutions such as the family or education might have on social life. Nor can Foucault be associated with theorists who emphasize agency, as he was not concerned with the individual experience. Foucault's argument is that in order to make sense of societies we need to analyse discourses, as it is these that frame and give meaning to society. A discourse can be defined as anything that is written, spoken or thought. Foucault argued that societies are organized around discursive frameworks that represent particular forms of knowledge. These frameworks of knowledge do not equate to some absolute truth about the world, but, rather, to a way of seeing or making sense of it in a particular era. Medicine is one such discursive framework that, according to Foucault, effectively determines the way in which we perceive health and illness in society.

It was Foucault who alerted us to the relationship between power and knowledge, asserting that the two are inextricably linked. Put simply, in terms of medicine this means that those with medical knowledge are able to exert power over those without it. According to the medicalization thesis, medicine, with its emphasis on the biomedical model, has become a dominant discourse in our understanding of social life and is, therefore, able to define health and illness. The biomedical model relies on the idea of the body as a source of knowledge; the greater the knowledge of the body, the greater the power over individuals. According to Foucault, from around the eighteenth century the human body came to be treated 'as something docile that could be subject, used, transformed and improved' (1973: 56). With this perception of the ability to work on and improve the body came a range of techniques to assess and enhance its functioning. Within medicine, disease and sickness came to be seen as the product of abnormal bodily functions and, thus, health was regarded primarily in mechanical terms as a state of 'lack of illness'. The greater the claims of the medical profession to the 'truth' about illness, and the more societies came to rely on their expert knowledge, the more power they had to define the nature of social reality. Foucault speaks of the way in which dominant discourses engender the monitoring and surveillance of individuals in society. This is able to occur because of a perceived need to deal with defective or pathological functioning. In the context of medicine, he refers to this as the 'clinical gaze'. Although the initial focus of the clinical gaze may be on illness, once it is set in motion surveillance is extended to the whole of the population.

Zola (1972) takes this analysis further by arguing that medicalization results in the medical profession determining what is healthy and normal in society, and, in this way, medicine has become a mechanism of social control. In other words, it is the process by which more and more areas of social life and human experience come to be framed in biomedical terms. Illich (1976) used the term 'medicalization' to refer to the process by which aspects of social life come to be seen in biomedical terms, and hence as the rightful domain of the medical profession. He introduced the concept of 'social iatrogenesis', which refers to harm caused when,

> health care is turned into a standardized item, a staple; when all suffering is 'hospitalised' and homes become inhospitable to birth, sickness and death; when the language in which people could experience their bodies is turned into bureaucratic gobbledegook; or when suffering, mourning, and healing outside the patient role are labelled a form of deviance. (1976: 41)

It is important to note, however, that whilst most commentaries on medicalization have perceived of this process as necessarily negative, there is an argument that it is not medicalization per se that is negative, but 'over-medicalization'. According to this perspective, it is the degree of medicalization that is important in assessing its benefits. For example, fostering institutions that focus on developing medical knowledge and technology has resulted in the destigmatizing of certain conditions and in extending lives by pursuing the search for effective treatments. There are few among us who would refuse the assistance offered by medical professionals in the face of serious illness. However, when medicine becomes too pervasive and threatens to invade all aspects of our lives, it can foster more problems than it solves; taking unnecessary risks with little concern for the psychological or emotional impact on lives. It is the latter that is referred to as 'over-medicalization' and it is this that Illich, in particular, rails against, claiming that '[t]he medical establishment has become a major threat to health' (1976: 3).

Let us now consider how medicalization has affected dying.

Medicalization and dying

As indicated in chapter 1, in modern societies the doctor has replaced the role of the priest at the deathbed. Rather than preparing a person for death, the doctor's concern is to provide pain relief and, if at all possible, to extend the life trajectory. In other words, where once death was explained via religious discourses and viewed as natural and inexorable, in modern societies it has largely come to be perceived as a challenge for science, a scientific problem that might be 'solved' by appropriate intervention and medical technology.

There are three important developments to consider in understanding this remarkable shift in emphasis. These are the introduction of anatomy, pathology and probability statistics (Prior, 1989). We will look at each in turn.

The discipline of anatomy is concerned with understanding the structures of organisms. Anatomy schools were established in

Europe from the sixteenth century, but it was during the eighteenth century that surgeons came to view dissection of the human corpse as a mechanism for furthering understanding of illness and death. Indeed, according to Richardson and Hurwitz, '[t]he medical school curriculum still starts with the dead and moves slowly towards the living patient'. Indeed, they argue that this reflects the fact that medicine is preoccupied with death and that '[m]edical endeavour takes place in death's shadow' (1997: 6). The point here is that medical science has set itself the challenge of defeating death by predicting its approach and by developing strategies and technologies for its avoidance. One of the key mechanisms for achieving this has been the science of anatomy, whose aim is to attain a thorough understanding of the human body.

The second significant development that has contributed to the medicalization of society is the science of pathology. This is linked with anatomy in its pursuit of a detailed exploration and knowledge of the inner workings of the body. A central feature of the discipline of pathology is the attempt to understand death by locating its causes within the structures and tissues of the human body. Thus, as Armstrong argues (1983), through the discipline of pathology the causes of death came to be perceived as lying within the human body.

It was the two disciplines of anatomy and pathology that paved the way for an analysis of life and death based on probability. As discussed in chapter 3, Giddens (1984) claims that probability analysis developed in part as a response to more sophisticated understandings of risk. In terms of death and dying, explanations of the causes of death enabled analysts to generate mortality statistics to predict the incidence, occurrence and likelihood of death according to age, gender, ethnicity, location, social class group and so on.

All these factors have been significant in the increased medicalization of dying in modern societies in that they have resulted in a view of mortality as a phenomenon that can, to some degree, be controlled by medical science. The emphasis on professional expertise, some argue, has resulted in death becoming the exclusive preserve of the medical profession. Consequently, dying has been dehumanized, and dying people are isolated and disempowered (Illich, 1976; Elias, 1985). Furthermore, because death is seen as a failure of medicine (Feinberg, 1997), dying people are subjected to a range of indignities in attempts to keep them alive. So, for Illich, 'natural' death has disappeared to be replaced by a form of techno-logical dying which is determined by the exigencies of medical technology:

> The medicalization of society has brought the epoch of natural death to an end. Western man has lost the right to preside over his act of dying. Health, or the autonomous power to cope, has been expropriated down to the last breath. Technical death has won its victory over dying. Mechanical death has conquered and destroyed all other death. (1976: 207–8)

For sociologists such as Elias, this dramatic structural shift in the management of dying has not only deprived individuals of their own deaths but has done so in an institutional setting that gives rise to isolation: 'Never before have people died as noiselessly and hygienically as today in these societies, and never in social condi-tions so much fostering solitude' (1985: 85). Furthermore, he asserts that whether in an institutional setting or at home, dying has now become a private event, framed by the relationship between the dying person and the doctor, and usually confined within the fam-ily. The aftermath of death and the pain of grief are again dealt with, whether through medical or counselling therapy, using an individual systems model, confined to the immediate family (Gorer, 1965). According to such critiques of medicalization, there is a resounding conspiracy of silence in the public domain, one that has effectively hidden death from the public gaze.

In contrast to these writers, Armstrong (1987) argued that death has not been privatized or silenced; quite the reverse. The discipline of pathology, which looked to the human body for the causes of death, together with the introduction of death certification in the nineteenth century, has transformed death from a private to a public event:

> In the old regime the patterns of ceremony, speech and silence had existed in a context demarcated by the domestic, the family and the neighbour; in the new it was the administrative author-ities, particularly in the form of medicine, which demanded the

ritual of death certification and registration, and speech and/or silence from the protagonists involved. The death of a body was thereby removed from its private domestic setting and exposed to a truly public visibility. . . . But the new silence at the end of life was matched by a hubbub of voices after life, as clinicians, pathologists and coroners subjected the corpse to a detailed scrutiny to establish the true cause of death. (1987: 652)

We will address the treatment of the body after death in chapter 9. For Armstrong, this trend toward the 'confessional' is simply a mechanism for relocating the public discourse of the powerful, seeking the truth about death from those closest to it. It may have shifted slightly, but only from one centre of the medical world to another.

Nevertheless, during the 1960s and 1970s a number of disturbing accounts appeared in both academic literature and the popular media of the impact of the medicalization of dying (Glaser and Strauss, 1965; Sudnow, 1967; Kübler-Ross, 1970). For example, in a moving autobiographical account, Simone de Beauvoir (1973) allowed us an insight into her mother's death. Her dying was clearly prolonged by the use of invasive technology with apparently little or no concern for the physical and emotional well-being of the patient and her family. The work of sociologists such as Glaser and Strauss and Sudnow (who adopt a theoretical perspective that focuses on agency and interaction among individuals) highlighted the problems of dying in a hospital setting. The work of medical professionals as structured by the hospital setting is framed within a discourse of treatment and cure. The role of doctors is to cure illness and save lives, whilst the largely female nursing profession focuses on caring for patients and restoring them to good health. Within this discourse, death is perceived as failure and people dying in hospitals may be marginalized and feared – consigned to the dying rooms of the ward. When death occurs in hospitals, it is likely to be hidden as the beds of dying people are commonly surrounded by screens and dead bodies are removed rapidly in covered and often disguised trolleys to the hospital mortuary. The latter is usually hidden away in the basement or other inaccessible location, away from the public gaze (Sudnow,

1967). Thus, the hospital has been identified as an institutional setting that is particularly inhospitable for dying people and their families.

The medicalization of society can also be understood using the theoretical framework adopted by Habermas (1987). Like Giddens and Bourdieu, Habermas rejects the dualisms inherent in traditional approaches to structure and agency and argues instead for a balance between the social system and the lifeworld of individuals. The two are interdependent, as the system or social structure needs properly socialized individuals and the lifeworld relies on structure for the efficient use of resources and government of organizations. However, as society becomes more complex subsystems of expertise develop and these detach themselves from the lifeworld. Once uncoupled, these expert subsystems come back into the lifeworld as dominant, colonizing forces. Once this has occurred, only a new social movement (NSM) may be able to eject the expert subsystem from the lifeworld. Medicine may be understood as one such expert subsystem. Once uncoupled from the lifeworld and the everyday experiences of individuals, medicine is professionalized and medical knowledge becomes largely inaccessible to lay people. In this context, alternative medicine may be viewed as a NSM that will force the expert subsystem of orthodox medicine out of the lifeworld.[1]

Much of the criticism of medicalization has been important in stimulating changes in practice. Yet, the relationship between the dying person and the medical profession is not always one of conflict. Medical science has engendered significant advances in the treatment of illness and the control of pain. It is the experience of medicine as the dominant discourse in dying that is problematic. In this respect, the work of Glaser and Strauss (1965), in their ethnographic study of the experience of dying in hospitals in the USA, has been especially significant. One aspect of their study that had a resounding impact on the practice of medical professionals was the question of whether patients knew that they were dying. Glaser and Strauss drew attention to the fact that in an institution that regards death as failure, medical personnel may try to hide a terminal diagnosis, at least from the patient if not from the family. Glaser and Strauss developed a typology of awareness contexts:

closed awareness, suspicion awareness, mutual pretence and open awareness.

Closed awareness

Closed awareness occurs when staff and relatives are aware that the patient is dying but the patient does not know. Patients are not usually able to recognize the signs of impending death, are given no access to information that might alert them to it and therefore remain unaware of the prognosis. Glaser and Strauss pointed out that, whether by accident or design, hospitals are easily able to hide information from their patients:

> Records are kept out of reach. Staff are skilled at withholding information. Medical talk about patients generally occurs in far-removed places, and if it occurs nearby, it is couched in medical jargon. Staff members are trained to discuss with patients only the surface aspects of their illness and . . . they are accustomed to acting collusively around patients so as not to disclose medical secrets. (1965: 31)

Despite this, the researchers found that, depending on how long it took to die, patients were likely to move to a state where they either suspected or became aware of their terminal status.

Suspicion awareness

Bodily changes and lack of healing can provide the patient with clues that death may be a possible outcome of their illness. Furthermore, staff, relatives and friends may begin to change their behaviour towards the patient and to avoid certain topics of discussion, for example, talk of the future. In this awareness state, the patient may suspect a terminal diagnosis but there is no confirmation of this from others. Glaser and Strauss viewed this as being particularly destructive for relationships, as patients became engaged in behaviour that was designed to trap others into confirming their suspicions.

Mutual pretence

In this awareness state, staff, patients, family and friends have knowledge of the prognosis but refrain from discussions of death. In this
context the interactional problems of closed and suspicion awareness are solved as each party tries to save others from the potentially
unpleasant confrontation associated with discussions of imminent
death. It does not, however, allow patients to explore their dying
with those close to them.

Open awareness

This is a state where all are aware of a terminal diagnosis and there
is no pretence or hiding.

Glaser and Strauss noted that there may, of course, be different
awareness states presented to different people, in different roles and
at different times. In general, however, since the 1970s there has
been an assumption in modern Western societies that 'open awareness' should be the preferred state for both patients and staff
(Field, 1995). If this were the case, it would facilitate patient and
family involvement in end-of-life decision-making, in the management of care and in the practical arrangements for death. As a
consequence of the work of Glaser and Strauss and others – for
example, the psychologist Elisabeth Kübler-Ross (1970) – there
has been a principled move from closed to open awareness in the
disclosure of terminal diagnoses. This is especially true within the
USA (Novack et al., 1979). However, it is worth bearing in mind
that not all cultural scripts are predisposed to open awareness in
dying. For example, Seale argues that disclosure may be more
appropriate to Anglo-American cultures which are more individualistic and where there is a commitment to the 'reflexive formation
of self-identity' (1998: 110). He points to studies that reveal that a
desire for open awareness is culturally inappropriate in countries
such as Japan (Ohnuki-Tierney, 1984), Uganda (Goodgame, 1990),
Spain (Centeno-Cortes and Nunez-Olarte, 1994) and Italy (Surbone, 1992). MacConville (2004) notes that the same is true of

Ireland, where in a survey of elderly patients and their relatives the principle reason given for not wanting to be told of a terminal diagnosis was that it would cause anxiety or depression. In Western societies, with increased cultural diversity, it is important that account is taken of cultural preferences that might impact on individuals' desire to know.

In the UK, Field and Copp have argued that although there has been an ideological commitment to open awareness, this seems to have partially reverted to a state of 'conditional awareness', whereby full information is available but patients and their families do not want to be continually reminded of the proximity to death. They point out that this inevitably creates difficulties for professionals trying to facilitate patient choice (1999: 467). Disclosing a terminal diagnosis to patients may also depend on age, with older people less likely to be told. For example, in my own study of ageing and dying, many of the elderly people interviewed reported that although the doctors had told them of the diagnosis, their dying spouse had been unaware that death was close (Howarth, 1998).

Glaser and Strauss alert us to a further significant element of awareness contexts within an institutional setting. That is, the extent to which the degree of awareness is related to retaining order and routine in the hospital. They refer to hospital care as a 'negotiated sentimental order' (Glaser and Strauss, 1967) in which threats to the orderly routine need to be averted by avoiding any behaviour that might lead to disruption. It is easy to see how managing open awareness could be perceived as potentially threatening to the emotional order of the hospital ward. This might be especially problematic for hospital nurses whose work is essentially task-oriented and for whom there is little time to devote to the emotional labour (Hochschild, 1983), energy, or companionship that might result from the disclosure of terminal diagnoses to patients (Field, 1996).

A further form of institutionalization that is relevant here are nursing or residential homes for elderly people, referred to in North America as long-term care facilities. In the UK between 12 and 15 per cent of deaths occur in nursing or residential homes (Cartwright, 1991). Unlike hospitals, medicalization tends not to present the same manner of problems for elderly institutional care as the majority of residential homes do not have medical facilities to care for terminally ill residents. Although these institutions have a doctor who visits regularly and is available for call-out, it is usually the case that if a resident requires medical treatment over and above that offered by the home, they will be transferred to a hospital. As Katz (2001) has argued, in the UK at least, care has focused on attempts to improve quality of life for residents rather than quality of dying. For the majority of residents, however, care at the end of life may simply comprise a greater quantity of the care usually provided rather than something qualitatively distinct. This means that dying residents may spend more time in single rooms and receive more visits from staff. Due to the long-term nature of the relationship between residents and carers, when a resident becomes terminally ill and subsequently dies, carers may grieve and need time before they can resume their normal duties within the home.

Deinstitutionalization and demedicalization

Since the 1970s, in many fields of health and disability, there have been moves away from institutionalization and towards care in the community. This deinstitutionalization movement has largely occurred in the areas of mental and physical disability where people who would once have been institutionalized are now, as far as possible, provided with resources to allow them to remain within the community. In caring for the sick, the elderly and the dying, however, trends towards deinstitutionalization are not so pronounced. Whilst general practitioners are now encouraged to carry out small-scale surgery themselves, the majority of serious illness is still referred to the hospital. The hospital continues to be the location for the majority of deaths of terminally ill people, accounting for roughly 60 per cent in countries such as the USA, UK and Australia; nursing and residential homes account for around 12 per cent, hospice (mainly for cancer patients) 5 per cent, with the remainder dying at home. Whilst many studies have shown that people would prefer to die at home (Lynn et al., 1997; Field and James, 1993; Parkes, 1985), those able to realize this goal usually spent some part of their terminal illness in either a hospital or a hospice, and their care at home is often primarily undertaken by unpaid lay, and often female, carers (Field and James, 1993). So, although there has been much criticism of terminal care in the hospital, this has not resulted in any significant attempt at deinstitutionalization. Rather, attempts to improve care for dying people have centred on alternative forms of residential provision. These alternatives have usually come in the shape of the residential or nursing home for the elderly, or the hospice, which, in its early form at least, presented a serious challenge to medicalization.

Much of the literature discussed above has been significant in respect to the rise of professional and lay attempts to demedicalize dying. The hospice movement can be seen as part of the resistance to medicalization. Although hospices have been identified as existing in the medieval period in Europe, these were essentially places of shelter for travellers and, later, for the sick. The modern hospice is dated, organizationally, to the opening of St Christopher's Hospice in London in 1967 (Small, 2001b). Its aim was to provide 'total care' to both the patient and their family and this required a multi-disciplinary approach, which, initially at least, was not dominated by the medical profession. We will discuss hospice care in more detail in the next chapter.

Homecare programmes are further examples of attempts to, at least partially, demedicalize dying. Here, terminally ill people may be offered a wide range of medical, personal, domestic, spiritual and counselling services to enable them to live and die in their own homes. These and other examples, such as the natural death movement (Alberry et al., 1993) and 'health promoting palliative care' (Kellehear, 1999a; 1999b) represent attempts to resist the power of the medical profession and to reclaim the experience of dying and death as the rightful domain of dying people and their families. These will also be considered in more detail in the next chapter, which focuses on the concept of the 'good death'.

Summary

This chapter has explored the nature of medicalization and some of the theoretical approaches that help us to understand the place of medicine and medical discourses in modern societies. The dominance of medicine in the care of dying people has been discussed and the significance of critiques in highlighting the problems associated with 'technological dying' has been noted. The work of Glaser and Strauss, in particular, has been influential in changing practice in relation to awareness of dying. David Sudnow's ethnographic study of hospital dying in the USA in the 1960s and Elisabeth Kübler-Ross's (1970) work with dying patients have similarly raised levels of understanding of the problems of dying in modern, medically focused institutions. These, together with the pioneering work of Cicely Saunders (1996) in the UK, have been fundamental to change in practice and to attempts to demedicalize and deinstitutionalize dying in modern societies. The creation of the modern hospice movement and attempts to introduce palliative care into hospitals are part of this process.

The chapter has also raised questions about the appropriateness of assuming that models of care and practice can be utilized for all dying people and has suggested, for example, that whilst open awareness in dying may be best practice for some people, cultural diversity needs to be respected when considering whether it is suitable for everyone. Furthermore, the model may not be easily utilized in settings other than the hospice, where patients are fully aware of the terminal status of their illness.

The next chapter will consider the concept of the 'good death' in modern societies, especially as discussed in the works of Kübler-Ross and Saunders.

7

The Good Death

Introduction

In the last chapter we considered the institutional management of death and the idea that death, like life itself, has been medicalized. This chapter will explore notions of the 'good death' and what this concept alludes to in contemporary Western societies. The next chapter will then complement this one by considering 'bad death' and how this is socially organized and managed.

This chapter begins by noting historical perspectives on the good death and then asks whether there can be a 'good death' in modern societies and, if so, what this might entail, and for whom it is good – the dying person, the family or the professional carers? The discussion will look at the timing, location and 'acceptance' of death and will focus on dying in a hospice. The concept of 'health promoting palliative care' will be discussed as a new way of thinking about the nature of dying. The final section will briefly consider the phenomenon of euthanasia in the context of its original definition as a 'good death'.

The good death in pre-modern societies

In chapter 1 we noted that, according to Ariès (1981), dying in pre-modern European societies entailed being prepared for death. Knowing that death was imminent enabled people to complete their business in the world and to prepare themselves for the life to come. Ariès refers to this as the 'tame death' because individuals had some measure of control in terms of knowledge and preparation and this is what signified a good death. This required the services of a priest, who would guide the dying person through the appropriate religious rituals to ensure a safe passage into the afterlife. Furthermore, in the medieval period, for those able to access the literature, there existed a range of Christian texts that provided information on the art of dying or 'Ars moriendi'.[1] These texts were particularly significant during the fourteenth and fifteenth centuries when, according to Bartley (2001) there was a general anxiety fomented by religious crises of the time. Perhaps the most important stimulus for the proliferation of the genre was that, at the time, divine judgement was coming to be seen less in terms of the salvation of mankind, and more in terms of a 'theology in which the solitary individual is alone before God, with critical responsibility for his or her own choices' (Bartley, 2001: 31).

Gittings (1999) contends that in England, from the early modern period (mid-sixteenth century), the deathbed came to be concerned more with material than with spiritual matters. Hallam (1996) concurs with this assertion in her analysis of gender issues surrounding the deathbed during this period. She claims, for example, that the deathbed was constructed as a place where, amongst other things, wills could be made and instructions given as to the disposal of material objects. Whilst material concerns were afforded greater emphasis in Protestant practice, in Catholic cultures the care of the soul continued to be the primary concern of the Catholic good death in nineteenth-century rural France (Ariès, 1974: 7). It was still important, however, to check that temporal matters were in good order, as Lysaght (1995) asserts of Irish deathbeds, where it was important to ensure that a priest was present at the bedside to administer last rites.

The good death in modern societies

We have already observed in our discussion of institutionalization and medicalization in the previous chapter that it has been argued that control over dying and death has been removed from the individual. This shifted into the hands of the medical profession, with people not always even aware that they were dying. Ariès (1981) conceives of this as the 'wild death', often characterized by the 'lie' that death is not close (as Glaser and Strauss (1965) note in their discussion of awareness contexts); and that it is usually hidden away in institutions.

It has been argued that the modern good death entails some degree of control over death in terms of both its location and timing (Bloch and Parry, 1982; Howarth, 1996) but it is unclear for whom this is a good death. For example, in contemporary Western societies there is an assumption that death occurring in later life is more likely to be constructed as a good death and that elderly people are ready to accept death as an inevitable and natural event (Stedeford, 1984). This emphasis on death in old age as being 'good' may more accurately be associated with the views of younger generations who prefer to view death in later life as more acceptable and in so doing tend to marginalize older people and avoid contemplation of death (Howarth, 1998; Hallam et al., 1999). This is in sharp contrast to earlier periods in history where death in childhood may have been viewed as a more 'natural' time to die (Walvin, 1982). Indeed, as was noted in chapter 2, with high infant mortality rates (IMR), it was not until the end of the nineteenth century and the early decades of the twentieth century that adults in Western societies might expect their children to outlive them (Mitchison, 1977). In contemporary developing societies, IMRs continue to be high.

There are many definitions of the good death in contemporary Western societies (Kellehear, 1990; Seale, 1998; Hart et al., 1998). According to Bradbury (1999), good deaths are not easily, nor objectively, defined but are constructed through a process of cultural negotiation. So, for example, death in war may be conceived as either good (a noble death) or bad (a waste of life) depending on the manner in which it is represented. These representations are essentially, 'culturally prescribed ways of viewing death which serve to delineate the social order' (Bradbury, 1999: 144). Kellehear (2000) suggests that there are two primary approaches to the understanding of a good death. The first is linked with the notion of dying well and this is manifested through a concern with the physical quality of the end of life. The second is to 'die nobly' and is much more a social concern with preparations for the end of life. In practice, he argued, the two converge, with dying people and their carers concerned with both elements. From his own study of people dying of cancer, he observed that, '[p]aramount for the dying person is the experience of adjusting to the different cycles of illness and treatment; the various preparations for death such as in legal, financial or religious matters; the engagement or disengagement from work, paid or unpaid; and the bidding of farewells' (Kellehear, 2000: 210). For caregivers (whether formal or informal) the focus tended to be upon the need for the dying person to be as comfortable and pain-free as possible (and this resulted in emphasis on pain and symptom control); and psychological and social adjustment to loss. For caregivers, definitions of good death incorporated assessment of the quality of the care they had provided.

Bradbury argued that it was during the eighteenth and nineteenth centuries, with the advent of modern medicine, that conceptual understandings of the good death changed and concern for the fate of the soul was replaced by anxieties about the nature of the physical event (1999: 192). An increasing trust in medical expertise in relieving pain and curing illness was fundamental to establishing the hospital as the place of death in modern societies. We have already acknowledged the problems associated with the hospitalization and accompanying medicalization of dying. Further, it has been suggested that studies such as those of Glaser and Strauss (1965) were instrumental in stimulating change from what eventually came to be seen as a 'bad' rather than a 'good' death and this may reflect a change in emphasis from attempts to cure to concern with the quality of the experience of dying.

Elisabeth Kübler-Ross (1970) presented a further significant study in the critique of modern, scientific dying in her research with people dying in hospitals. She depicted hospitalized death as lonely, undignified and medicalized. From her analysis of observations in a hospital setting, she asserted that people passed through five psychological or emotional stages as they approached death: denial, anger, bargaining, depression and, finally, acceptance. Each stage was characterized by specific emotions and behaviours. It was only when people reached the final stage of acceptance, that death could be classified as good.

> *Denial*, according to Kübler-Ross, is the first reaction to news of a terminal diagnosis. This cannot be happening to me; there has been a terrible mistake. From here, once it is clear that there is no doubt that the diagnosis is accurate, *anger* sets in. The primary feature of this stage is rage. Someone or something must be to blame as the person views death as an undeserved punishment. *Bargaining* is identified by Kübler-Ross as the next stage. 'What can I do to prevent this?', or at least, 'How can I avoid dying before a particular event or until I have finished a special task?' *Depression* is the fourth stage. This is the time when hope is lost and the full impact of impending death is faced. At this point she observed that people might deteriorate physically and that fear of death may be acute, bringing with it anguish, guilt, helplessness and despair. According to Kübler-Ross, the final stage, of *acceptance*, characterizes the good death and is defined as the time when the individual is able to give up the struggle to live and be ready to let go of life. This, she claimed, although it may not be a happy period, and, indeed, may be characterized by a deadening or lack of emotion, nevertheless brought relief (Katz and Sidell, 1994: 18).

Reaching Kübler-Ross's final state of *acceptance* can be likened to Ariès's (1981) notion of the 'tame death', where people have put their affairs in order, have made their farewells, and are ready to die peacefully. Kübler-Ross's five-stage theory has been extremely influential in lay and professional understandings of dying (and, as we will see in chapter 10, has also been adapted to create stages of grief). It has given voice to the concerns of dying people and has stood as an important critique of medicalization. As Hart et al. concede, 'her stage theory gave a tangible script for dying and death that in many ways assisted them [professionals] to make sense of interactions and behaviours' (1998: 68) and has forced recognition of a wider need to reflect on the treatment of people dying in hospitals. Charmaz (1980), however, contends that the methodology on which Kübler-Ross's study was based was fundamentally flawed. The research was undertaken solely in a hospital setting and did not recognize individual diversity. As such, the theory was at best only applicable to people dying in hospitals. Despite this failing, Kübler-Ross's study was ground-breaking and her theory has been widely utilized by professionals working with dying people. They embraced the stage model as a strategy for understanding their patients in an otherwise confusing, contradictory and chaotic area of practice. In many respects it was this wholesale adoption by professionals that led to the model being interpreted too rigidly, as a prescription for dying. With this came the assumption that in order to achieve a 'good death', individuals must necessarily pass, in an orderly fashion, through the emotions and behaviours ascribed to each stage. As Hart et al. contend, this has resulted in the development of a dominant ideology of the contemporary good death as centred around the 'ideal of dying with dignity, peacefulness, preparedness, awareness, adjustment and acceptance' (1998: 65). Furthermore, they assert that this ideology has come to dominate the social management of dying within the hospice movement. In this respect it has become a model of good death for professional carers rather than for the dying person. One consequence of this is the failure to recognize cultural diversity among patient groups and to assume that this 'ideal', modern Western death is suitable for all.

It is to the hospice that we now turn, as, with growing concern during the 1960s that medicalized dying was a 'bad' rather than 'good' death, this institution has been held up as the ideal location for the good death in modern societies.

The modern hospice movement

Although the term has a long history, the modern hospice has been identified as dating from after the Second World War and developing in response to the powerful critiques of hospital dying. The hospice movement was created to challenge the growing culture of medicalization by developing a 'practical and theoretical commitment to holistic care, defined as physical, psychological, social and spiritual care' (James and Field, 1992). Hospice refers not only to a place but also to a philosophy of care that incorporates the notion of palliative care. The latter concept has been defined by the World Health Organization as:

> the active total care of patients at a time when their disease is no longer responsive to curative measures and when control of pain and other symptoms and of psychological, social and spiritual problems is paramount. The goal of palliative care is the highest possible quality of life for the patient and family. (WHO, 1990)

The pioneering St Christopher's Hospice, which opened in Sydenham, London, in 1967 (its home care team in 1969), established a model for hospice care. According to Clark (1998), this was the outcome of 'ideas, strategies, alliances and teambuilding undertaken by Dame Cicely Saunders in the years after 1948' (quoted in Small, 2001b: 245). Saunders, who is generally perceived as the charismatic leader of the movement (James and Field, 1992), documents her interest in developing a better way of dying as stemming from her relationship with a dying patient:

> As a social worker and former nurse I met David Tasma, a young patient from Warsaw, in 1947. I think of him as the real founder of St Christopher's Hospice. When he approached death some months later, he said to me, 'I want what is in your mind and in your heart'. This commission led, on reflection, to the realization that patients facing the end of life as he was would need all the skills that could be developed, researched and taught, together with the friendship and care of the heart. He felt that he had done nothing in his life for the world to remember, but his gesture in leaving me £500 in his will 'to be a window in your Home' was the beginning of this worldwide movement. The 'Home' he referred to was something we had discussed together, where people would have the space and openness so hard to

come by in the busy surgical ward in which he was dying.
(Saunders, 1996: 318–19)

Since 1967 the hospice movement has spread worldwide and in
1998 there were estimated to be 1,400 hospice or palliative care
units in Europe, 600 in Canada, more than 240 in Australia and
around 3,000 in the USA (Hospice Information Service, 1998).
From its inception, hospice was founded on Christian religious
beliefs. As Small notes of St Christopher's Hospice, it was designed
as a community 'inspired and informed by Christianity' (1998:
170). Whilst hospices have sprung up all over the world, the majority continue to adhere to Christian traditions and this has been
interpreted as problematic in relation to caring for dying people of
non-Christian faiths and for those from minority ethnic communities (Clark, 1993). (We will return to this criticism shortly) A
further significant feature of hospice has been its emphasis on caring for people who are dying of cancer. One justification of this
specialization has been that, in contrast with many other terminal
illnesses, cancer is more clearly diagnosable and prognoses tend to
be more accurate (Field, 1996). Harris (1990), however, has suggested that this focus has created an 'underclass' of dying people
who are starved of the resources otherwise concentrated on those
dying of cancer.

Hospice developed in response to recognition of the poor quality of care for people who were dying. Dying was not being
managed adequately and, it was argued, this new model would
develop ideas through research and practice and spread these
through greater social education. The hospice movement was to
devote itself purely to the care of dying people and in this respect
having a narrow focus was, therefore, able to provide better quality
of care than other institutions such as the hospital or residential and
nursing homes. Furthermore, as noted in the discussion above, the
ethos was dedicated to facilitating a good death.

Hospice philosophy and the relief of 'total pain'

The hospice was instituted as a fundamental critique of modern hospitals with their emphasis on increasing technological intervention, intrusive procedures and the prolongation of life. The hospice model of care is founded on the principle of facilitating a good death for dying people and as such has six basic tenets:

- that it provides *holistic* care;
- that it involves *interdisciplinary* teams;
- that it is *non-hierarchical*;
- that it is *not rule-bound*;
- that hospice work should be viewed as *vocational*; and
- that it should be committed to *research and education*.

As is clear from this basic philosophy, the founders of hospice believed that hospitals, with their technological intervention and intrusive procedures, constructed dying patients as mere onlookers in their own death, often not even given information about their diagnosis and prognosis (Glaser and Strauss, 1965).

Briefly, the original ideals of the hospice movement were to establish a form of extended family that could care for the needs of both the dying person and his or her family (DuBois, 1980). In this way, communication and disclosure of diagnosis and prognosis were central to the hospice philosophy; only through good communication could the goal of high quality of life be achieved for dying people. Interdisciplinary teamwork was core to the hospice and staff; both professionals and volunteers were expected to be able to talk with patients and their families about dying and death. The emphasis on holistic care meant combining attention given to physical and other distress and this led to the development of the concept of 'total pain' (Clark, 1999). Patients were encouraged to talk about physical, social, emotional and spiritual pain, and staff were assured that their own pain, engendered by their emotional involvement with dying people, would be supported. In keeping with the idea of a familial approach, the hospice saw the patient's family as part of the unit of care and they were encouraged, alongside the patient, to be involved in decision-making, and supported through bereavement. Unpaid volunteers were welcomed and they provided a range of services, such as driving patients to and from the hospice (Field and James, 1993).

The focus in hospice and palliative care on the notion of relief of 'total pain' is based on the idea that, in dying, pain may be present on four levels or dimensions – physical, emotional, social and spiritual. There is an assumption, however, that physical pain may mask other forms of pain, and equally that emotional or social pain may exacerbate physical pain (Baines, 1990: 28). In attempting to relieve total pain, hospice has produced a model of care that assumes that the reduction of physical pain will assist in alleviating the distress of other symptoms of pain. In other words, if physical pain can be controlled, this will reduce emotional and spiritual suffering and, therefore, improve quality of life for dying people. Thus, one of the fundamental tenets of the hospice movement is pain management. Saunders remarks, for example, on:

> the unceasing need to influence the education of physicians and the nursing profession and, indeed, to enlighten the general public of the fact that morphine and often other opioids properly used do not lead to drug dependence and addiction. These fears often deny relief and have been shown to be unfounded. (1996: 321)

Whilst this is an admirable intention, it has been argued that placing social, emotional and spiritual pain within the remit of medicine (that in practice they are treated as secondary symptoms of physical pain) is effectively a mechanism for extending medical control over dying (Arney and Bergen, 1984). As Clark (1999) asserts, one consequence of 'total care' may be 'total control'. Although the concept of total pain recognizes that pain may refer to something more than physical symptoms, treating people with such pain may in effect be a form of medical imperialism, utilizing physical distress as a tool for searching deeper into the individual psyche (Armstrong, 1987). This manner of approach is reminiscent of Foucault's work on surveillance (1973) that constructs the extension of medicine into the field of social aspects of health and illness as the 'clinical gaze'. According to this thesis, the holistic model of care (fundamental to

hospice and palliative care) results in professional power and knowledge directing its gaze inwards, constructing the individual as
subject rather than object, and, in so doing, gaining knowledge and
control over the consciousness (Foucault, 1982: 214).

Notwithstanding these criticisms, it has been argued that the
hospice movement has in recent years begun to move away from its
early ideals and that it is now embracing, and being incorporated
into, mainstream health care provision (Abel, 1986; Ashby, 2001;
Clark, 1993; Finn Paradis and Cummings, 1986; Higginson, 1993;
James and Field, 1992). Indeed, Ashby contends that the increased
use of the term 'palliative care' as an alternative to 'hospice' is a
change in terminology that reflects the increasing embedding of
hospice into mainstream health care systems (2001: 343). James and
Field (1992) have identified problems associated with growing
'routinization' and bureaucratization. They focus on five primary
aspects of change within the hospice: spheres of authority, hierarchy, training, separation of official duties and rules. We will briefly
consider each in turn.

Spheres of authority

One of the original ideals of the hospice was that they should not
be rule-bound. In accordance with the remit, James and Field
(1992) argue, hospices tended to be places where there were no
rules to follow and no established authorities or organizations to set
standards. More recently, pressure groups have begun to respond to
this lacuna by defining aspects of good practice and establishing
professional standards of care. For example, in the UK there is now
a new authority, the National Hospice Council, with regional and
national health authorities also involved in setting and enforcing
standards and procedures.

Hierarchy

The early hospice deliberately blurred or challenged traditional
patterns of hierarchy. So, for example, nurses were able to diagnose

and prescribe medication, and volunteers allowed to participate in activities from reception duties to counselling. With the move towards greater incorporation into mainstream health care systems, there has been a return to traditional hierarchical structures and clearer job demarcation.

Training

Hospice was created with a philosophy of interdisciplinary team-work and the provision of holistic care. One consequence of this was the blurring of boundaries between tasks and the nature of care undertaken. James and Field argue that the increase in training and specialization in terminal care that is available for professional staff has resulted in the reinforcement of mainstream divisions of labour with their traditional specializations. Hospice is now less reliant on the work of volunteers, and where these are employed they are usually given less responsibility and are, therefore, less central to care.

Separation of official duties

Cicely Saunders's model of the hospice entailed a perception of the care of dying people as a vocation or calling. For some it continues to be a vocation, with staff devoting body and soul to the work of the hospice. However, long hours and stressful demands on staff have worked to undermine this vision. Furthermore, recruitment patterns have changed, and there has been an increase in the number of staff entering hospice as part of their career development. This means that much of the vocational ethos of hospice care has disappeared and given way to more pragmatic approaches to the work.

Rules

All the elements discussed above have led to hospices becoming increasingly rule-bound places that are very different from the early institutions, where a fundamental aspect of the role of hospice was perceived as the breaking of rules in order to provide more appropriate care.

A further critique of the contemporary hospice is offered by Clark (1993) who argues that the ever growing involvement of career specialists in palliative care is leading to the remedicalization of dying and to greater emphasis being placed on physical rather than psychosocial aspects of care. This raises the question as to whether hospice death continues to be the good death for dying people or if it has become managed in such a way as to conform more closely to professional ideals of the good death.

These criticisms suggest that whilst the early ideals of hospice and palliative care may have provided a significant alternative to the technological intervention characteristic of hospital death, hospice care is now reverting to more mainstream medical structures. Indeed, Sinclair (2004) asserts in his analysis of the devaluation of dying people that it is extraordinary that in countries such as the UK and Australia the hospice opted for an institutional response to dying. Thus, whilst the care of physically and mentally disabled people has increasingly adopted the tenets of community care, the care of dying people has simply been relocated from one institutional setting (the hospital) to another (the hospice). This critique is sustained in the work of Lawton (2000). In her ethnography of in-patient hospice provision she found that with increasing pressure on beds and a concomitant reduction in resources (inevitably consequences of the competing demands of other health services), in-patient hospices may become places where people go to die because their bodies are so uncontrolled that either they, or their families, cannot bear death at home. Whilst most hospice units are able to offer home and community care, being allocated to 'at home care' does not ensure that the person will eventually die at home (Grande, 1999).

In modern Western societies, as suggested by Hart et al. (1998), the contemporary good death has become established as one in which dying people conform to the model that dominates within the hospice and palliative care movements. This has occurred to such an extent that there have been calls for palliative care to be extended to people dying from conditions other than cancer. For example, there are now hospices for those dying with AIDS and for children dying from a range of illnesses. Furthermore, some have argued, for example, that palliative care should be provided for elderly people (Rumbold, 1998) and for people dying from other diseases such as dementia (Parker and Aranda, 1998). However, although the hospice way of dying may be an attractive alternative to the hospital death, it is important to acknowledge that it may not be appropriate for all. For example, for some people the experience of pain is a significant feature of dying and, therefore, the hospice emphasis on pain relief may be inappropriate. A further example stems from Kübler-Ross's position that death is the final stage of growth and therefore is something to be embraced. This has been described by Lofland (1978) as the 'happy death movement'. This approach assumes that 'adjustment and acceptance' is the correct manner in which to confront death. It also allows little voice to those whose cultural traditions do not conform to this approach, for those who may want to 'rage against the dying of the light' (Dylan Thomas) or, as Walter (1996) asserts, those who want to construct their own pathways through dying. Indeed, one definition of the 'good death' that is frequently perceived as the antithesis of palliative care is euthanasia. We will consider this shortly.

This discussion leads us to the question, posed, amongst others, by Clark, of the 'extent to which the hospice model is taking account of a range of social differences relating to gender, age, sexuality, family circumstances, religion and ethnicity' (1993: 172). Furthermore, Clark asserts: '[t]oo often hospices appear as white, middle class, Christian institutions serving a carefully selected group of patients, which the "odour of goodness" (Smith, 1984) surrounding them cannot fail to disguise' (1993: 172). There have been several attempts to redress this situation and to move away from the Christian, ethnocentric ethos.

As we saw in the Introduction and chapter 1 of this book there are a number of sociological theories that might help us to understand the significance of social and cultural diversity in relation to experiences of mortality. These range from theories that focus on social structures in societies (and neglect the role of the individual) to those that privilege agency, yet fail to take account of the

structures of power within society. In attempting to provide services for dying people that take account of social and cultural
diversity, it is important to recognize both structural and individual
factors and, furthermore, to acknowledge that simply understanding a range of cultural belief systems is insufficient for meeting the
needs of dying people. There have, for example, been moves to provide hospice personnel with something akin to a 'factfile' of beliefs
and rituals associated with a range of ethnic and religious groups.
There are many factfiles now available, providing guidance for professionals (see for example, Neuberger, 1987; Henley, 1982, 1987;
Green and Green, 1992; Noggle, 1995). Factfiles typically produce
accounts of cultural and religious beliefs and rituals surrounding
death. For example, following two sections on general information
concerning legal aspects of death, care of the living and dying, and
death with dignity, Green and Green (1992) divide Part Three of
their book into short chapters that provide information on fifteen
different churches and religious and ethnic persuasions. Each chapter includes 'facts' on 'the dying patient', 'diet', 'at death', 'post
mortem examinations', 'blood transfusion', 'organ transplantation',
'body for research', 'abortion' and 'funerals'. As Gunaratnam (1997)
explains, factfiles stem from recognition within palliative care services of the desire to identify ' "culturally sensitive" services in
relation to the "spiritual, language and dietary" needs of Black and
ethnic minority services users' (1997: 166). Whilst she acknowledges that this is in general a positive move, she argues further
that the 'factfile' provides professionals with models for service
provision that are essentially task-oriented and assume cultural
homogeneity and constancy. The dynamic nature of culture is neglected in favour of a set of guidelines for practice. This approach
assumes that people from particular ethnic groups are homogenous
and fully share sets of values and beliefs. It takes no account of
change, nor does it recognize that different social circumstances
(such as those associated with income and housing), social structures and power relations (for example, those associated with racial
inequalities) and other identities (such as gender, sexuality, age and
disability) impact on the experience of dying and the construction
of a 'good death'. An approach is, therefore, required that combines
knowledge of cultural systems with 'a dynamic and politicised

conceptual framework' (Gunaratnam, 1997: 184). The concept of 'health promoting palliative care', which places more emphasis on social care and communication with the individual, may provide a context for developing such an approach to supporting dying people to achieve a good death.

Health promoting palliative care

In part as an attempt to return to the philosophical ideals of the hospice movement and to address the need to communicate and respect social and cultural diversity, Kellehear (1999a, 1999b) has developed the concept of health promoting palliative care. His aim was to put social aspects of the care of dying people firmly on the palliative care agenda as a mechanism for emphasizing heterogeneity and as a way of re-empowering dying individuals.

Health promoting palliative care (HPPC) focuses on post-diagnosis chronic care and concentrates on assisting people to live with a terminal illness rather than primarily providing essentially medical care in the final three to six months of life. As such, the emphasis of HPPC is on social care. Kellehear has argued that health promotion and palliative care are commonly viewed as contradictory approaches to health care. Whilst palliative care has tended to focus its resources on individuals close to the end of life, health promotion, in neglecting the needs of people with chronic terminal illnesses, has become 'death-denying' in its framework, perceiving death as failure. In establishing a case for HPPC, Kellehear argues for a radical reappraisal both of health promotion and palliative care in order to:

> enhance a sense of control and support for those living with a serious life-threatening illness. It is not about 'denying' that death is a serious prospect for those under palliative care but rather recognition that the prospect of death is shared by all of us all of the time too. In this way, death is not the central psychological fact of care but rather the day-to-day quality of life issue for everyone. (1999a: 77)

The fundamental elements of HPPC are:

- providing information and education in health, dying and death, and informed consent in decision-making;

- providing social support to individuals and the community;

- interpersonal reorientation to help adjust to life and lifestyle changes;

- political exchanges and collaboration between health professionals working in public health and palliative care;

- to address wider community issues such as those related to the association of stigma and prejudice with dying (e.g., cancer, HIV/AIDS).

In arguing for further collaboration between health promotion and palliative care professionals, Kellehear states that HPPC, 'is not simply service provision but research, community development and policy criticism and development with and toward those who are normally associated with palliative care – everyone in the community' (1999a: 78).

Let us now conclude our discussion of the nature of 'good death' in modern societies by examining strategies that people might adopt to ensure greater control over their dying: living wills and euthanasia.

Living wills

The increasing popularity of the living will and the debates that surround its legality reflect common concern about the over-medicalization of dying and the desire to avoid 'bad death'. If good death might be defined as having some control over the physical quality of dying and the social preparedness for death, the living will is designed to facilitate both.

A living will is a document that an individual draws up that takes the form of an advanced directive. The purpose of the will is to provide information and directives about the person's wishes as to the nature of medical intervention should they become unable through illness or injury to indicate this themselves. Living wills usually indicate the extent of medical treatment and when this should be curtailed if the illness is incurable and will result in death – this may include ventilation, antibiotics, resuscitation, nutritional support and hydration. There are two major types of living will. The first is a directive for the physician and the second a document which gives a named person (for example, a close relative) the power to make decisions on their behalf. In some societies, such as certain states in the USA, the living will is a legally binding document.

The efficacy of the living will is open to debate, particularly in respect of wills that name a close friend or relative as the surrogate decision-maker. Where documents are drawn up stating wishes regarding the specifics of medical treatment, these are more likely to be honoured. For example, in a study of living wills, Hammes and Rooney (1998) found that in La Crosse, Wisconsin, USA the majority of living wills were respected by medical practitioners when making end-of-life decisions. When a person is asked to act as decision-maker the dying person's wishes are less likely to be respected. Bendiksen (2001b) cites a study by Hare et al. (1992), who found that surrogates' treatment decisions agreed with those of the will-maker in only 70 per cent of cases. This was largely due to the fact that whilst surrogates were focusing their decisions on the person's pain, will-makers were considering factors such as 'time to live' and 'burden on family'. The latter is a theme that is also significant in decisions around euthanasia.

Euthanasia – the good death?

Euthanasia refers to the hastening or causing of death. The term itself derives from the Greek meaning 'good death'. Debates over the use of euthanasia usually centre on attempts to alleviate the suffering of someone who is terminally ill. Although both are relevant to the discussion here, euthanasia should be distinguished from physician-assisted suicide. Euthanasia assumes action on the part of a medical professional. This can take many forms and may be either active (such as administering a lethal injection) or passive (an act of omission, such as the withholding of antibiotics or hydration). In physician–assisted suicide, the fatal act is performed by the individual, with the doctor being the agent who supplies the means. In cases of assisted suicide the physician is usually responding to the repeated requests of a patient considered to be mentally competent for technical assistance to commit suicide. The distinction lies in the action of the physician: in euthanasia the person dies as a result of the actions of the physician; in cases of assisted suicide it is the patient who undertakes the fatal action (Bendiksen, 2001a: 38) It is important also to recognize that euthanasia can be voluntary (at the suggestion of the patient) and non–voluntary (without consent, for example, in cases of persistent vegetative state). However, as we are currently considering euthanasia in the context of definitions of good death that presume the dying patient is able to exert control over the circumstances of death, non–voluntary euthanasia will not be examined in this chapter.

Debates over euthanasia and physician–assisted suicide have become common in Western societies and have largely focused on ethical, religious and political issues and have been driven by members of interest groups hoping to shape legislation. There are, however, relatively few countries that have introduced laws that allow this form of dying. In Europe, in the Netherlands, euthanasia has been decriminalized following legislation implemented on 1 April 2002 in the form of the Termination of Life on Request and Assisted Suicide (Review Procedures) Act. Similar legislation is in force in Belgium (following an Act passed on 28 May 2002 and implemented on 20 September of that year). Assisted suicide is accepted in Switzerland, although euthanasia continues to be illegal (Hurst and Mauron, 2003). Oregon is the only state in the USA with legislation, introduced in 1999, that allows doctors actively to help patients who wish to end their life.

Groups who oppose euthanasia do so for a range of reasons. Religious adherents, particularly those of the Christian faith, may oppose euthanasia on the grounds that life is the gift of God and it is, therefore, only God who may take it away. Medics and health care professionals may reject it on the Hippocratic grounds that they have a duty to care for and preserve, rather than to end, life.

Furthermore, many argue that the adequate provision of palliative care, with its objective of relieving total pain, should enhance quality of life for dying people and reduce the attraction of euthanasia (Saunders, 1988). Those in favour of euthanasia primarily emphasize the need to address suffering and to put an end to physical and emotional pain and distress. For them, the issue rests on the rights of the individual to take control over their dying and to enable them to die with dignity (Kennedy, 1994; Singer, 1993; Kuhse and Singer, 1997).

Whilst it is clearly the case that those who oppose euthanasia regard it as a 'bad death', those who favour euthanasia do so on grounds that are compatible with the critiques of the modern way of dying that we have been examining. Indeed, contemporary movements for euthanasia can be viewed as a response to the medicalization of dying and the propensity for medical science to perform life-saving 'miracles' that result in 'bad death' by keeping people alive only with superior technology. The upshot of this has been that some people are able to survive with extremely debilitating, chronic conditions that inevitably lead to a deteriorating quality of life. The pro-euthanasia lobby is concerned about the quality of life experienced by such people and also by people surviving into late old age with incapacitating chronic illnesses. As one of the movement's chief proponents has argued, these advances in medicine have 'resulted in prolonged and contented living for some and prolonged and miserable dying for others' (Kennedy, 1994: 4).

Many research studies have demonstrated that dying people frequently consider ways to end their suffering and that some terminally ill people and their families would welcome euthanasia (Seale and Addington-Hall, 1994; Howarth, 1998; Young and Cullen, 1996). In a study of factors that might lead to requests for euthanasia, Seale and Addington-Hall (1995) discovered that pain relief was less important than loss of independence and that women were more likely than men to have asked for help in dying. This they suggest, is because, due to differences in age at mortality (see the discussion in chapter 2), women are particularly vulnerable in the final years of life and are less likely than men to have people emotionally close to them. This finding led Seale to argue that social structure 'exercises a profound influence on the experience of ageing and dying' (1998: 46).

Young and Cullen (1996) undertook research into the nature of the good death. Their qualitative study produced sensitive and in-depth insights into the lifeworlds of fourteen dying people in the East End of London. The authors disclosed, however, that they had not expected euthanasia to become an issue in their study. Yet, one of their informants, Harold, forced them to address it. For him, the fact that the hospice could control his physical pain was insufficient, and this had clearly not fully alleviated other distresses including breathlessness, loss of faculties and his sense of becoming a burden on his wife and family. He reported that his attempts to discuss his desire for euthanasia with his doctor and home care nurse were unhelpful.

Organizations that promote euthanasia, such as the Voluntary Euthanasia Society, may be viewed as part of a new social movement (McInerney, 2000) that has developed as a direct conse-quence of the concern to achieve a 'dignified' death. Furthermore, as Howarth and Jefferys (1996) have argued, the pro-euthanasia lobby has strengthened at a time of growing individualism in West-ern societies. This is reflected in the turn from welfare and paternalistic government systems towards an enterprise culture based on individual rights and responsibilities such as those entailed in the new public health agenda (Petersen and Lupton, 1996; see the discussion on the new public health model above, pp.75–7). According to this, health and the management of illness has become a partnership between the individual and the health care profes-sions: people are responsible for behaviours (such as controlling diet and exercise) that maintain good health and have the right to expect that health professionals will care for them in times of illness. As Kellehear (1998) contends, in Western societies, where sickness appears to have replaced death and dying is regarded as the final ill-ness, euthanasia, and more specifically, physician–assisted suicide, might be regarded as an extension of the public health partnership (see also Riley, 1989).

A further impetus for the trend towards demands for assisted dying can be identified as the secularization of Western societies. In societies where established religions have lost much of their power there is less emphasis on the care of the soul and its passage to the next life and more concern with the nature and quality of life and dying in this life.

Bob Dent was the first person to utilize the Rights of the Terminally Ill Act in the Northern Territory of Australia. This Act provided medical assistance for terminally ill people who wished to die.[2] In a final statement and open letter to Federal Parliamentarians, dictated on 21 September 1996, Mr Dent described his illness, his quality of life and his reasons for requesting euthanasia. In one section of the statement he expressed his belief that the relief of physical pain was insufficient to improve his quality of life; that religious groups and medics should not be allowed to determine life and death choices; and that he should have the right to end his life if he so chose:

I have always been an active, outgoing person, and being unable to live a normal life causes much mental and psychological pain, which can never be relieved by medication. I read with increasing horror newspaper stories of Kevin Andrew's attempt to overturn the most compassionate piece of legislation in the world. (Actually, my wife has to read the newspaper stories to me as I can no longer focus my eyes.) The Church and State must remain separate. What right has anyone, because of their own religious faith (to which I don't subscribe), to demand that I behave according to their rules until some omniscient doctor decides that I must have had enough and goes ahead and increases my morphine until I die? If you disagree with voluntary euthanasia, then don't use it, but don't deny me the right to use it if and when I want to.

I am immensely grateful that I have had the opportunity to use the 'Rights of the Terminally Ill Act' to ask my doctor Philip Nitschke to assist me to relieve this interminable suffering and to end my life in a dignified and compassionate manner.

Summary

This chapter has explored the concept of the 'good death'. It began by locating the notion of good death within the discourse of pre-modern societies and then examined the nature of good dying for the modern world. The discussion considered Kübler-Ross's critique of dying in the hospital setting and her five-stage model of dying. This asserts that 'successful' dying is a staged process whereby the individual eventually comes to accept death as inevitable and is able to let go of life. This 'final stage of growth' can be likened to Ariès's concept of the 'tame death' in pre-modern societies.

The philosophy of the hospice movement was then examined, together with its emphasis on the relief of 'total pain'. Critiques of the movement were considered. These included a growing concern that hospice and palliative care are moving away from an earlier understanding of the nature of the good death as non-medical and reverting to adopting mainstream medical frameworks. The discussion also addressed the need for greater understanding of social and cultural diversity within terminal care provision. The notion of health promoting palliative care was considered as a development that attempts to restate the importance of social perspectives in the provision of palliative care. The chapter concluded with an examination of living wills, euthanasia and physician–assisted suicide as approaches to a 'good death' in modern societies.

In the next chapter we will explore the concept of 'bad death', particularly in relation to sudden, unexpected death and the role of those professionals who manage such death.

8

The Social Organization of Sudden Death

Introduction

Although individuals differ in their response to sudden death, research on bereavement has shown that the lack of preparation, and the often violent nature of sudden death, exacerbate the trauma for bereaved people (Lindemann, 1944; Bowlby, 1981; Lundin, 1984; Murphy, 1988; Wright, 1991; Yates et al., 1993). The loss of a close relative or friend can threaten ontological security and leave survivors with a sense of personal meaninglessness. This is particularly the case when people have gone through what are commonly perceived to be bad deaths – violent deaths, such as victims of car crashes, homicide, manslaughter, large-scale disasters and suicide. When death is sudden or unexpected there is a special need to understand what caused a precious life to be extinguished without warning. Indeed, it is the apparent senselessness of the loss that is so much at odds with the assumptions that underpin Western social life. In daily existence there is an expectation that the world we inhabit is regulated, controllable, that we have responsibilities and choices, that life is ordered and framed by birth, and death, the latter coming at the end of a long life and by 'natural' means. In contradiction to these expectations, sudden death strikes in various guises and, like the Grim Reaper of the medieval woodcuts, randomly claims young and old, male and female, wealthy and poor.

In the majority of cases of sudden death, the professionals whose work it is to deal with the aftermath have no previous knowledge of the deceased. Although this means that they do not experience a personal sense of loss, the threat of emotional trauma and sense of meaninglessness are nonetheless present. Thus, for emergency service personnel and for coroners and their officers, this face-to-face contact with unexpected, untimely and often distressing death poses problems for their sense of well-being and ontological security.

In this chapter we will consider the way in which sudden death, or bad death, is socially organized and managed; in other words, how is sudden death made sense of by those who encounter it? In this context the discussion will explore the role of emergency service workers such as the police, fire service and ambulance workers and hospital personnel, and their organizational and personal encounters with sudden and often violent death events. We will then consider the medical and legal management of sudden death through an examination of the office of the coroner or medical examiner which is responsible for investigating individual deaths. The reasons why some cases of sudden death are pursued and others halted in the early stages of investigation are considered. The discussion raises questions about the distinction between 'natural' and 'unnatural' death and the way in which these categories are constructed and utilized in the medical and legal structures surrounding sudden death. The final section of the chapter will engage with some of the problems bereaved people experience when a loved one has died and the difficulties they face in making sense of their loss. This will incorporate an examination of professional and lay discourses and will note the implicit assumptions, structures and procedures adopted by each. Tensions which exist between the public management and the private experience of death will be highlighted.

Let us begin with a brief look at the work of emergency service personnel.

The work of emergency service personnel

When a death occurs suddenly, workers from the emergency services are often the first on the scene. This may occur at the public site of a road traffic or other transport fatality (such as a rail or aircraft crash or incident at sea), or it may be a death that has taken place unexpectedly in the home – encompassing anything from the sudden heart attack of an elderly person to a suicide or murder scene. The police are often the first officials to arrive and, depending on the nature of the death, they may be followed by fire fighters or ambulance workers. It is the job of the emergency workers to rescue anyone injured in the incident and to make the area safe. In cases where there have been a number of people involved, some of whom may be dead and others still alive, although possibly injured, the emergency workers will ascertain the condition of the injured and focus their energies on those whose lives may be saved.

When death occurs in the home, assuming there are no suspicious circumstances (such as possible homicide), the number of professionals involved will be kept to a minimum. The occurrence of death at home is common and will frequently require only input from the police. When a death happens, people are often unsure as to which professional bodies they should contact. In cases of sudden death, it is the police who are usually alerted. Thus a police officer may attend the home of an elderly person who has died unexpectedly even when there are no suspicious circumstances, and especially if that the person has been dead for some time. A sudden or unexpected death will also require input from the coroner's office or medical examiner. Once the site has been made safe, the coroner's office will take responsibility for transferring the dead person to the public mortuary from where the investigation into the cause of death will begin. We will return to the work of the coroner shortly.

Emergency service personnel are trained to deal with sudden death and this usually includes training in offering sympathetic assistance to the bereaved and to others who may have witnessed the death. For their own part, whilst some may attend numerous instances of sudden or violent death, others may encounter such deaths only infrequently. The emotional impact of death on these workers may be significant and there is now a nascent body of literature which addresses the coping strategies needed to help them when confronted with violent death. It also identifies the available support services (including bereavement counselling) to assist them to overcome any resulting post-traumatic stress. Emergency service personnel work within a wider social framework in which sudden or violent death is perceived as 'untimely', abnormal and inappropriate. Furthermore, confronting and handling the bodies of people who have died violently can be especially damaging to individual sense of well-being.

We have already noted, in chapter 3, the perception of fire service personnel as 'heroes' who put their own lives at risk and battle against the odds to save the lives of others – overwhelmingly strangers. Whether such workers place their own life at risk or not, the impact of dealing with unpleasant incidents *in extremis*, in which people may have died violently, has been noted as potentially harmful for these workers (Mitchell and Munro, 1996). In studying the coping mechanisms used by emergency service workers, research has revealed the use of 'gallows' or 'grave' humour and centred on the way this form of relief is used as a strategy for managing anxiety and stress when confronted with sudden death (Moran and Massam, 1997; Scott, 2003). It has been suggested that gallows humour has been associated with 'hardiness' – the ability to continue to function effectively in an environment of multiple exposure to traumatic events. Whilst Mitchell (1996), in her study of strategies adopted by police officers, argues that gallows humour may not be as prevalent or efficacious as previous studies suggest, she acknowledges that there may be considerable peer pressure from colleagues to engage in such humour.

Other studies have pointed to the debilitating effect of multiple exposures, and this has led to the development of techniques for crisis intervention such as 'critical incidence debriefing' (Mitchell, 1993). It has been argued that contrary to expectations, continued exposure to sudden and traumatic death may result in prolonged personal trauma for emergency service workers. Although there is relatively little research directly concerned with the long-term impact of this form of deathwork, that which exists has tended to derive from psychological theorizing which views contact with the aftermath of violent death as precipitating post-traumatic stress disorder (PTSD) when coping mechanisms fail to alleviate the pain and distress of the confrontation with mortality (Mitchell, 1996). Mitchell highlights the need for more research that focuses on the effect of large-scale disasters, such as the Lockerbie aeroplane bomb in 1988, on the psychological well-being of those involved in the 'clear-up' operation. By acknowledging that emergency service work can cause distress, 'critical incident debriefing' has been developed. It was originally designed as a form of crisis intervention for emergency service personnel. Its purpose is to support professionals following a disaster or other stressful incident. The intervention involves working with a trained facilitator to debrief individuals as soon as possible after the event – usually two to three days (Rowling, 2001). However, although techniques such as critical incident debriefing have been adopted by a number of organizations (including the World Health Organization (1992)), there is still debate over the scientific nature and efficacy of such approaches. For example, Raphael et al. (1995) question its effectiveness as a general principle. They note that there is no 'scientific' evidence to demonstrate the effectiveness of debriefing, arguing that this will largely depend on the quality of those who carry it out. Furthermore, the way emergency personnel respond to death is influenced by their own circumstances, by the nature of the event and the meaning it has for them; in other words, by the subjective context. This is also true of those who work within the coroner's office, and, moreover, of bereaved people themselves. Different forms of death elicit diverse reactions. Individuals experience death in varying ways according to the nature and circumstances of the loss and of their relationship with the deceased. If, as is the case with emergency service workers, there was no relationship with the deceased, the death may still be poignant in terms of their own lives or systems of personal meaning.

Let us return now to examine the coroner's role in relation to sudden death.

The role of the coroner or medical examiner

If we remind ourselves of the definition of the good death used in the last chapter – the physical quality of dying and the social preparedness for death – sudden death, particularly violent death, is the antithesis. Death is commonly viewed in a linear fashion, encountered at the end of the road of life. Sudden death, however, is perceived as death out of time and out of place, that disrupts both the individual and social biography. In social or public terms, the medical examiner or coroner system plays a pivotal role in constructing a narrative of life which places the deceased person on a unique and inexorable trajectory towards their death. Sudden death threatens chaos and the notion that death may be random suggests lack of control. The ordered public ritual of the inquest, with its aim of classifying and explaining mortality, attempts to give it a more predictable veneer.

It is the duty of the coroner to conduct an investigation and to hold an inquest into cases of sudden death. The limit of the inquiry is laid down in statute and is to identify the deceased and decide how, when and where they died. As a government service, the coroner's work is now primarily geared to the needs of the death certification system with its foremost aim of determining the medical causes of death. In this role coroners can be perceived as policing the boundaries between life and death – explaining the nature of sudden death and ensuring that its management is kept within specific institutions, spatial boundaries, and defined according to specific verdicts.

Within this system the emphasis is on the need to understand mortality and to identify potential hazards or risks inherent in society that might result in the unexpected deaths of individuals. This role reflects the coroner's connection with national death registration systems and the requirement for nations to measure and classify death. In pursuit of these aims, coroners or medical examiners rely on expert and lay narratives of the legal, medical and social circumstances of individual deaths. The mortality statistics generated by coroners are employed in analyses of the health of the nation, in identifying causes of death and as mechanisms for maintaining and improving public health and safety. The narrative constructions of individual deaths (produced at inquest in the courtroom) provide information for families and friends and media images or representations of death events. A central element of these purposes is the classification and differentiation between 'natural' and 'unnatural' death.

Before examining the social role of coroners we will begin with a brief outline of the history of the coroner's office in the UK; an office that was the precursor to many similar systems throughout Europe and the modern world. We will then scrutinize the aims of the coroner system in relation to the delineation of the nature of death, the construction of death as either natural or unnatural, and the medical, legal and social discourses that accompany it.

Background to the coroner system in the UK

The office of the coroner in the UK is an ancient one, established in 1194 under the Articles of Eyre (Matthews and Foreman, 1993). At that time the coroner was the 'keeper of plees of the Crown' and as such was responsible for protecting the interests of the monarch in respect of revenues owed, and for the administration of criminal justice. It was also the role of the incumbent to investigate and hold inquests into cases of sudden death. From around the sixteenth century, however, with the development of the criminal justice system, coroners lost their powers associated with criminal work (these were transferred to the justices of the peace) but retained their role in the examination of sudden death. As Matthews and Foreman observe, '[t]he only important duty that coroners retained was that of holding inquests into cases of violent or unnatural death' (1993: 5). An established principle here was that coroners were able to indict people suspected of homicide, manslaughter or infanticide. It is worthy of note that during the medieval and early modern period, although people may have stood trial for murder or similar crimes, these were commonly explained in terms of religion and fate, with the hand of God or the devil clearly visible in court accounts. As a consequence of Enlightenment thinking, these supernatural elements were gradually superseded, and death became seen as more controllable and predictable, with the introduction of modern, rational explanations and procedures, such as the generation of mortality statistics via the death certification system (Prior, 1997).

Among other innovations, the development of public health policy and factory legislation in the nineteenth century radically affected the nature of the coroner's work and the manner in which sudden death was construed and investigated. The changing industrial environment altered the nature of sudden death itself. As discussed in chapter 3, there was a new perception of the quantifiability of industrial risk. Factory machinery and industrial diseases became major causes of mortality and, in the twentieth century, automobiles claimed lives that had once been lost, in smaller numbers, to the horse-drawn cart. The state requirement to monitor the risks inherent in the rapidly developing urban centres changed the role of the coroner and demanded that the office become more accountable to government systems, prioritizing the coroner's role vis-à-vis the death certification process.

The development of disciplines of anatomy and pathology (as discussed in chapter 6) were crucial to the refinement and focus for the investigation and management of sudden death, in that the causes of death came to be located within the human body rather than external to it. According to Prior (1989), this 'pathological vision of mortality' held important long-term consequences for the coroner system:

> It justified the autopsy as a method of inquiry; it generated the need for the mortuary as a site of investigation; it structured the language of causation which was to be inscribed on the medical certificates of causes of death; and it justified an understanding of death and disease in terms of anatomical sub-systems. (1989: 10)

In keeping with coroner systems in Europe, USA and Australia, this new perspective enshrined the importance of medicine within the system. The most significant legal ruling in the UK was established in 1977 when the coroner's office was formally separated from the criminal justice system. Before this, coroners were entitled, and usually expected in cases of murder, manslaughter or infanticide, to name those considered responsible for a death and to commit them for trial. This power, a residue from earlier centuries, was considered irregular and the Broderick Report of 1971 (which conducted a major investigation into the role of the coroners) recommended it be revoked. The last person to be indicted in this way was Lord Lucan, who in 1975 was named by a coroner's court as the murderer of his children's nanny.

The modern coroner system

The coroner or medical examiner is tasked with investigating sudden or unexpected death. This may be death that results from road, rail, sea or air fatalities; death at work or caused by industrial diseases; death in custody; large-scale disasters; homicide, manslaughter, infanticide and suicide. Additionally, all other unexpected deaths – defined according to whether the deceased has seen a medical doctor within a short period prior to death – must also be scrutinized. In addition to determining the identity of the deceased and when, were and how the person came to die, one of the key aims of the modern coroner system is to decide whether a death was due to natural or unnatural causes. The verdicts available to coroners reflects this distinction. Verdicts include death from natural causes, industrial disease, lack of attention at birth, the result of an accident or misadventure, suicide, unlawful killing (murder, manslaughter or infanticide) or open verdicts (to reflect the difficulty in ascertaining the exact cause of death). According to the Liberty Guide to Human Rights (2002), 'An unnatural death has been defined as one where there is suspicion of foul play, wrongdoing such as negligence, or some other peculiarity.'

The definition used by coroners, however, is not entirely clear. Indeed, Prior argues that coroners themselves are not always able discursively to define each category, but nevertheless have a 'practical consciousness' (Giddens, 1979) or unconscious under-standing of the distinction between the two categories which they utilize in making judgements of the nature of death (Prior, 1989: 60). For Prior, the distinction hinges on (1) the presence or absence of disease within the body and (2) the presence or absence of agency and intention in any actions surrounding death. Utilizing Prior's analysis, let us now consider how each of these categories are constructed in the social management of sudden death.

Natural death

Prior cites Goffman (1974) as identifying two types of framework that distinguish natural from unnatural events. Natural events are 'seen as the result of unguided, unmotivated and purely physical processes' (Prior, 1989: 61). Unnatural events have human agency and motivation embedded within them. If we apply these frame-works to the definitions of natural and unnatural death, natural death is that which is caused by disease or illness found within the body. Unnatural death requires an element of agency, whether or not intention was present. We will develop this latter point shortly when we consider the way in which accidental death is framed. For the moment it is sufficient to note that deaths resulting from human action (or inaction in cases of death caused by neglect) are perceived as unnatural. Where intention is clearly present, these may generate verdicts such as unlawful killing or suicide. The natu-ralness or otherwise of the death will be determined at autopsy through a detailed examination of the body of the deceased.

In the coroner system the body is central to the narrative recon-struction of life; it is from 'readings' of the corpse that the reconstruction begins. Pathology, developed in the nineteenth cen-tury during a time of increasing concern with public health, demonstrated a link between death and disease, scientifically locat-ing the causal sequence for death within the human body. Through pathology the body became a source of knowledge, allowing med-ical experts to locate it in time and space, pinpointing the moment of death and its physiological causes. The locus of this knowledge is central to the coroner's investigation, for without a body an inquest cannot take place. It is during autopsy that the pathologist will be able to ascertain the presence or absence of disease within the body. If disease is found to be present and, more importantly, to be the cause of death, the verdict will be one of natural causes. That is, the cause of death is located within the body and was not a result of human agency. 'Where disease exists, motives, will, purpose and agency are held to be absent, and this decontextualisation or dethematisation of disease marks death as natural' (Prior, 1989: 61). Indeed, it is sometimes the case that if death is thought to have been caused by disease the investigation may go no further than the initial notification and may not even require a post-mortem (autopsy). This may occur, for example, in cases where the deceased had not seen a doctor for a number of weeks but had a chronic illness, or disease that was expected to lead to death. Although these deaths are reported to the coroner, the general practitioner or physician caring for the person would be notified and asked if they were able to issue a death certificate without further investigation.

If the causes of death are not deemed to be disease-related and there is no diagnosis of terminal illness, the post-mortem examination of the body will identify the physical injuries that brought about the death. It is the purpose of the ensuing investigation and the inquest to scrutinize the social circumstances of the death, to ascertain how the deceased came about those injuries and to map human agency in relation to them. In order to highlight some of the principles used in defining unnatural death we will focus now on the way in which accidents and suicides are constructed within the coroner system.

The accident: an unnatural natural death

The *Oxford English Dictionary* defines 'accident' as an 'event that is without apparent cause or unexpected' and notes further senses in which it can be understood as an 'unlucky event', 'chance', 'misfortune' or an 'unintended act'. According to the UK coroners' handbook, *Jervis*, an accident is defined as something over which there is 'no human control, or an unintended act' (Matthews and Foreman, 1993: 250). What these definitions have in common is the notion of accidents as chance or unintended events where blame cannot be apportioned. Thus, although some deaths deemed to be unnatural do involve human agency, the lack of intention identifies them as uncontrolled. This use of accidental death, however, is relatively recent. As noted earlier, during the medieval and early modern period in Europe, what we might now define as an accidental death would then more likely have been identified with the work of God: 'The 19-century Coroner ... maintained a further source of naturalness, namely, God. "Visitation of God" was a common cause and mode of death prior to the 1887 reforms, and such visitations covered all kinds of death where human agency was apparently absent from the causal process' (Prior, 1989: 61). Prior goes on to argue that with the decline in religious belief, we have witnessed the rise of the 'accident'. The definition of accident, with its chance and unintended nature, is now used by coroners to distinguish deaths which are both unnatural yet unintended.

Prior goes on to argue that in modern societies the verdict of 'accidental death' is serving to disguise death which is linked to social action or structures that might have been part of the causal sequence. In this context he suggests that a verdict of accident 'serves to garb the death in a false cloak of naturalness' (1989: 62), thus removing the 'guided quality' of certain human actions. See, for example, the discussion of the Bhopal disaster in chapter 3 where what was defined as an 'industrial accident' was clearly a consequence of corporate negligence. To further complicate this framework of accidents, coroners are increasingly linking the verdict of 'misadventure' with that of accident. Misadventure, 'indicates some deliberate (but lawful) human act which has unexpectedly taken a turn that led to death' (Matthews and Foreman, 1993: 250). One effect of this practice is that it enables the coroner to bring a verdict of accident in cases where the death was the 'unexpected result of a deliberate act' (ibid.). Thus, although human action is clearly visible, intention has been removed. If human intention is eliminated and we can no longer rely on God to take the responsibility for such deaths, accidental death attains an aura of naturalness, and deaths, such as those associated with occupational diseases, disappear into this broad category. As Prior insists, death which might be, 'due to industrial processes, lack of warmth, activity of the police, or negligent (drunken) driving' (1989:62), may be masked by the adoption of such verdicts. As I have argued elsewhere (Howarth, 1997c), as long as we continue to define such fatalities as 'accidents' and to deal with them as though they were 'acts of God', any corporate or individual responsibility for such deaths will continue to be hidden.

Suicide: an unnatural and intended death

Prior (1989) focuses on the work of sociologists such as Durkheim (see the discussion in chapter 2) to show how the study of suicide has helped to clarify the distinction between natural and unnatural death. He notes that since its creation as a distinct discipline, and for most of the twentieth century, sociologists have studied suicide as a marker of sudden, unnatural and intended death. This has led to the assumption (which has become ingrained in society) that 'unnatural' death is associated with disorganization, whether social or personal. Durkheim (1951) used suicide rates as a measure of weakness, particularly of the moral forces in society – as a product of a weak social system that lacks social and moral integration. As Prior notes, Durkheim linked high suicide rates with marriage, divorce rates, single status, urban living and social and religious integration. Thus, Durkheim showed, for example, that suicide rates are higher in countries with weaker religious and social integration, and among single rather than married people. Prior convincingly goes on to argue that factors such as age, sex, rural or urban living and marital status have thus come to be constructed as causal elements rather than indicators of suicide:

> [T]he kind of evidence which the suicide researchers amassed . . . tempts one into the belief that among those deemed to have died unnaturally one would expect to find a preponderance of people in socially marginal positions; that is, for the single and widowed to appear more frequently than the married, for the unemployed to appear with greater regularity than the employed, vagabonds and hawkers to appear more frequently than accountants and priests, and altogether those

who lived in peripheral social roles to be overrepresented compared to those who, in Durkheimian terms, could be considered
as being well integrated into social life. (1989: 55)

However, although as a consequence of this research we would
expect an overrepresentation of unnatural death among those in
socially marginal positions, Prior's own study of death in Belfast
reveals that this is not the case. On the contrary, it would appear that
it is the more socially valued members of society – members of
socially dominant groups, such as males and the economically
active – who are more likely to have their sudden deaths investigated. This is, however, in keeping with the likely direction of
the coroner's investigation into death that might have been the
result of suicide, and could, in part, help to explain suicide rates
that show a preponderance of such deaths among males in the
18–45 age group.

In their investigation, coroners look to a number of factors to
help determine whether the deceased intended to kill themselves.
The necessity to prove intention 'beyond reasonable doubt'
requires evidence of motivation. Intention and motivation are
examined in tandem in the gathering of information of the circumstances. Factors which point to the presence of both these
elements have been identified by various researchers as including
suicide notes, methods used, mental and physical health, location
and circumstances of death (Atkinson, 1978; Linsley et al., 2001;
Taylor, 1982). Indeed, Atkinson and Taylor have pointed to the
manner in which intention is imputed according to individualistic
and subjective criteria. So, for example, if a suicide note is absent,
but hanging or shooting rather than a drug overdose brought
about death, it is more likely to be interpreted as intentional. If the
deceased was a young, unemployed male who had undergone
treatment for mental health problems, this combination is likely to
be perceived as grounds for motivation. In cases where intention
and motivation may not be so clearly delineated, the coroner's
inquest may return an 'open' verdict, suggesting that the criteria
for 'suicide' could not be proved beyond reasonable doubt. However, Linsley et al., in their study of the distinction between 'open'
and 'suicide' verdicts, suggest that the similarities in the cases were

such that for purposes of research, the two should be studied together.

In this discussion of the three categories of sudden death – natural, unnatural natural, and unnatural intended – it is clear that sudden, unexpected death is categorized according to (1) whether it is perceived as natural or unnatural and (2) whether it is affected by the role of human agency. In determining the status of death, medical expertise will be utilized to identify the presence or absence of disease within the body. If disease is shown to be absent, and thus the death considered unnatural, professional expertise (for example, the police, psychiatrists, social workers) and lay narratives of social circumstances will be employed to construct explanations of the death that highlight the impact of human action and produce insights into questions of motivation and intention. It is to these lay perceptions that we now turn in order to progress our discussion of the way in which bereaved people make sense of sudden death.

Bereaved people's experiences of the sudden death 'system'

On a private or individual level, sudden death is traumatic not only because it truncates the life of the deceased but because it also damages the self-identity of survivors (Riches and Dawson, 2000). A sense of self is constructed in relation to the identity of others; death of a significant other results in the loss of a substantial element of the self (Howarth, 2000b). By reconstructing the last moments or hours of life, survivors are completing the dead person's biography and in so doing they are creating a continuity that will be so central to their own self-identity. Taylor (1989) argues that in 'order to have a sense of who we are, we have to have a notion of how we have become, and of where we are going' (1989: 54). In the context of sudden death, survivors often require the information produced by the coroner's inquest in order to make sense of their own future. That is, they need to know how, when and where the deceased died. What the inquest may not provide, however, and what is often central to a bereaved person's sense of biographical continuity, is the knowledge of 'why' their loved one died. If, as we have suggested, the key characteristic of the coroner's role is to distinguish between natural and unnatural death, this does not entail an understanding of why the person died, nor does it apportion blame – a further area of tension between legal require- ments and expectations of the bereaved. Let us now consider how this tension is manifested in the relationship between coroners and the bereaved.

The coroner's office and the public mortuary

When a person dies suddenly or unexpectedly, as we have noted above, the coroner is required to investigate the circumstances of death. The coroner's officer is the pivot around which the work of the coroner and the public mortuary revolve. Dealing with the dead and their relatives presents difficulties for these officials. Immediate loss of their rights over the body, which is relinquished to a government agency then compounded by restricted access, tends to exacerbate a sense of alienation and heightens relatives' dis- tress. Indeed, coroners' officers, often police officers by profession, have been criticized for their close links with the police service. This exposes them to allegations of bias, for example, in dealing with deaths in custody. It is this officer who controls the day-to-day running of the office and the procedures for the inquiry, com- municating with doctors, pathologists, hospital administrators, undertakers, the police, relatives of the deceased and witnesses to the circumstances of the death. The officer is responsible for keep- ing all parties informed of the progress of the investigation and for preparing a report for the coroner. This report is constructed from the results of the post-mortem and from the statements and testimonies of expert and lay witnesses, significant relatives and friends. The report forms the basis of the coroner's proceedings and judgement in the courtroom.

The investigation on which the inquest report is based begins with an examination of the body of the deceased. As noted above, if death was found to be due to natural causes, an autopsy may not be

required. However, if further investigation is thought to be necessary, the coroner will require an autopsy because the body is central
to the narrative reconstruction of death and to the categorization
of death as natural or unnatural. Although there can be no owner-
ship of a dead body, in these circumstances coroners have legal
jurisdiction over the corpse. This can be traumatic for the bereaved
family, for whilst the coroner, pathologist and mortuary technicians
view the corpse as an objective source of knowledge, for the
bereaved it is not simply a body but a person, albeit a dead person.
The objectification of the corpse and the coroner's jurisdiction
over its fate may cause them great distress. This distress is exacerbated for people of Muslim, Sikh or Hindu faiths whose religious
or cultural beliefs determine that the body of the deceased should
be cared for in a specific way and buried or cremated within a certain number of days of death. For Muslims, a post-mortem is
especially problematic because it is forbidden in their faith for a
body to be cut or harmed in any way, as it is believed to belong to
God.

The next-of-kin is commonly required to identify the body, and
this legal identification usually takes place at the public mortuary.
Identification procedures may vary across geographical regions. In
most cases the police or the coroner's officer conducts the identification process and guides the bereaved relative through the
mortuary. In recognition of the distress this may cause, some public
mortuaries (frequently located in hospitals) set aside space for
grieving relatives and may adopt a sympathetic approach. In other
districts the families may be treated in a perfunctory manner, as
their presence within the mortuary is seen merely as an unfortu-
nate, if necessary, function of legal requirements. Whether
sympathetic or otherwise, there are bureaucratic procedures that
have to be followed. Sheila Awoonor-Renner described her own
experience of these procedures:

> Recently my child was killed in a road accident. He was 17 . . .
> On arrival at the hospital just after 10.15 pm no one was expect-
> ing us . . . Eventually the system assembled itself again. It seemed
> that I had not after all come to see my son but to identify him . . .
> But it was explained that I couldn't see him until I had been

interviewed by the coroner's officer, who, not knowing I was to arrive, was somewhere else. Eventually he arrived. By now I was getting nicely institutionalised. I was behaving myself. I put him at his ease when he asked his questions – well, I tried to . . . He knew what to do with grieving relatives. He knew the formula, so he did it – to the end. He had no idea who, in reality, I was. I said that I wanted to see my son alone – no, I asked permission to see my son alone. Permission was granted on condition that I 'didn't do anything silly'. (1991: 302, 356)

From these extracts, it is clear that whilst Sheila wished to see her son, and to reaffirm her connection with him in some way, for the professionals the purpose of her visit to the mortuary was only to identify the body. Thus, on the one hand we see a grieving mother come to see her son and, on the other, we see a group of professionals attempting to complete a series of bureaucratic procedures in relation to a corpse. This situation is undoubtedly problematic for both relatives and professionals and each symbolically negotiates the interaction and performs emotional labour in relation to it. It is worth noting, however, that next-of-kin who may be shocked and traumatized are vulnerable and relatively powerless in contrast to the professionals, who not only control the ritual but for whom the grief of others is an everyday encounter.

The inquest

It is during the inquest that the public ritual of the reconstruction of death takes place. If the case has not been taken up by the criminal justice system, the inquest may be the sole remaining forum where bereaved people can ask questions about how their relatives died. For the coroner, the purpose of the court is to promote an understanding of the medical cause of death and to reach a legal verdict. To do so the coroner calls two distinct types of witness: expert and lay. The testimonies of expert witnesses are based on the narrative of their expert reports – documents that adopt the jargon of their respective disciplines and are perceived by the court as inherently objective, professional and scientific. In contrast, the social discourse of lay witnesses is replete with subjective observations and common-sense knowledge. It is in the courtroom that these diverse accounts are interwoven to produce a narrative of death, and here where tensions between professional and lay accounts may struggle with one another to create, or recreate, a social being recognizable to all. When the reconstruction is complete, the coroner must reach a decision about the nature of death, or, if a jury is sitting, must guide them to do so. In order to achieve this, expert and lay accounts must fuse together and translate into knowledge about the death befitting the legal confines of the verdict. In this way, as we noted earlier in cases of suicide, expert testimonies such as that of the pathologist and psychiatrists will be placed alongside information from family and friends about the deceased's mental and emotional health and any other social circumstances that might be relevant to ascertaining intention and motive.

It is the official interpretation of the medical, legal and social discourse of the courtroom, culminating as it does with the coroner passing a verdict, which can result in a gulf between the official purpose of the inquest and the expectations of the bereaved. The aftermath of the inquest for bereaved families is frequently characterized by bewilderment as they are left nonplussed by the implications of the verdict and are left with questions such as, 'Is that all?' and, 'What was the point?' (Howarth, 1997c). This can largely be attributed to the common assumption that 'something' will come out of the inquest. It is implicitly assumed that this will entail an explanation of the social causes of death and, in many cases, an assignation of blame. Whilst the official purposes of inquests can be fulfilled by understanding the medical causes of death and by reaching a legal verdict, bereaved people need to construct a narrative of death which explains its occurrence in the midst of life. In making the death ineluctable, the question of causation is frequently linked to the concept of blame. Although often confused and untutored about the task of the coroner's inquest, families tend to see this legal procedure as part of the criminal justice system and have expectations of the court's ability to bring about justice. If dissatisfaction with the outcome of the inquest derives from a feeling that 'justice has not been done' because no one is being blamed, then this is in large part due to the separation of the coroner system from that of the criminal justice system and the abrogation of power to name persons responsible for death. It is also, fundamentally, a consequence of a system geared to the death certification process which requires a mapping of the causes of death according to natural and unnatural classifications.

Frustration with the aims and functioning of the coroner's system has, in the United Kingdom at least, led to increasing demand for public accountability. This is demonstrated in the proliferation of campaigning groups whose purpose it is to increase public awareness of their plight, to gain compensation for their loss, and to challenge government procedures for processing sudden death which currently privilege legal and medical requirements over the needs of bereaved individuals. These campaigning organizations address both 'accidental' and 'unnatural' death, and groups have been formed to draw attention to the dissatisfactions of people bereaved across a range of causes, from road death (RoadPeace, Campaign Against Drinking and Driving – CADD) to deaths in custody (INQUEST). Coroners have made no consistent response to their critics. For example, the coroner in one district in the UK insisted that it is not their role to hold an inquest for the 'delectation of the relatives of the deceased'. At the other extreme, there are coroners keen to provide a service which is more sensitive to the needs of bereaved people. At inquest, some coroners allow families a higher profile, encouraging them to ask questions of witnesses and providing contact with counsellors in its aftermath. What is notable in this communication between state systems and personal experience, between public and private, is the extent to which this dualism is being challenged.

Although currently under review,[1] the coroner system in England, Wales and Northern Ireland remains largely unchanged since the 1970s. Since then, however, there has been rising tension between the public coroner system and the private needs of bereaved individuals. Sudden death threatens ontological security; it can also threaten the stability of society. The management of sudden death, therefore, needs to be explored at two levels: as a system of symbolic management at the structural or public level and as the private experiences of bereaved people, where issues of agency are paramount. These twin spheres are encapsulated in the coroner system that primarily exists to investigate and distinguish between natural and unnatural sudden death. This currently meets the needs of government agencies, for example, by gathering information about risks to society and how they might be avoided in the future and, perhaps more mundanely, to enable them to complete mortality statistics. On an individual level, however, suddenly bereaved families require information about the nature of death and, more often than not, in needing to understand why the death occurred they want to be able to apportion blame. In its remit to thoroughly investigate sudden or unexpected death, the office of the coroner would appear to be in harmony with the public interest. However, it is as a consequence of the aims of the system and its separation from the criminal justice system, with the resulting inability to apportion blame, particularly for deaths defined as 'accidental', that tensions arise between the official task of the coroner's office and the needs of bereaved people. Moreover, government requirements to classify and categorize death are at odds with the private grief-work of bereaved individuals. (See chapter 10 for a discussion on the concept of 'grief-work'.) The office of coroner or medical examiner is an ancient one that has mutated many times in different countries over the last 800 years. The nature of its future role may depend on how adaptable and responsive to perceived needs it proves to be.

Summary

This chapter has drawn together different aspects of the social organization of sudden death and has sought to address the question of how individuals and social institutions make sense of death. In so doing, the discussion has ranged from the experiences of emergency service workers and the role of professionals associated with the coroner's office, through to the private experiences of bereaved people. Sudden or unexpected death can threaten both individual and social stability. It is often the untimely nature of death and the need, in contemporary societies, to feel that we are able to exert some measure of control over mortality that makes this form of dying particularly problematic. In pre-modern societies individuals may be charged with the responsibility for unexpected death, construed as a consequence of evil acts or witchcraft (Malinowski, 1954). Modern societies have created and used a system for defining the nature of sudden death which differentiates between the 'natural' and the 'unnatural', locating the former in the physical structures of diseases within the body and the latter according to a narrow set of criteria for determining human agency, intent and motivation. This has resulted in decontexualization, in which interpretations of sudden death have been removed from their social, political and economic context. This has led in turn to a greater reliance on categories such as 'accidental' death that acknowledge 'unnatural' elements yet imply a lack of human responsibility, and, ultimately, a lack of human control.

9

The Dying and the Dead Body

Introduction

In previous chapters in this section we have examined dying in contemporary Western societies and have explored notions of good and bad deaths. This chapter will consider the material reality of both dying and death through a discussion of embodiment. Sociologists have been challenging the orthodoxy that has assumed a separation between mind and body, with the mind as the source of social being and the body as a mere container. One of the pioneers of this challenge was Turner (1984, 1996), who argued for a sociology that recognized the centrality of the body in social experience. Rather than simply being a vehicle for the mind, the body both shapes and is influenced by the self. Thus, our bodies, and the way in which we develop them, are crucial to self-identity and are significant markers of values in society.

Moreover, we both 'are' and 'have' bodies and, as Seale (1998) asserts, our material bodies have been represented as demonstrating the limits to life. Thus, bodies are subject to change throughout the life course, and the death of the body appears to point to the inevitable foundering of the self. As Mulkay (1993) argues and Lawton, in her research in a hospice (2000), demonstrates, bodies that become unkempt and disordered through illness, ageing and dying are perceived as unmanageable and can become 'socially dead'.[1] Youthful bodies come under threat from the processes of ageing, and dying is represented as the loss of agency and social identity.

This chapter will begin with a brief exposition of some of the theoretical work that has taken place in relation to the body and society. It will then explore the assumptions of the connection between the body and the self and will raise questions about the impact of illness and dying for the construction of self-identity. It will also problematize the social perception of death as the final separation and loss of self and, following the theoretical perspective of Hallam et al. (1999), will argue that theories of embodiment need to be placed alongside theories of disembodiment in order to make sense of experiences of dying and death. The chapter will also address concerns about the boundaries between life and death, self and other, and will question theories that construct the body as a bounded entity, separate from the bodies and selves of others.

Some theoretical approaches to a sociology of the body

Sociological theories of the body have tended to emphasize the importance of either social structures or agency. Whilst for theorists such as Foucault the body is a product of discourses or sets of knowledge, for Shilling (1993) and Giddens (1991) it is a resource to be exploited and managed in social interaction. For Foucault, the body is constructed through the structures of power relations; for Shilling and Giddens, the role of agency is significant, albeit subject to social, cultural and biological constraints. Let us consider each of these approaches.

Foucault (1977) argued that the body was a product of social practices and discourses – that it had no prior existence. As such it is subject to powerful structures in society and is itself understood only through sets of knowledge that regulate bodies (for example, medicine). Foucault used the discourses around punishment in Europe in the eighteenth and nineteenth centuries to illustrate his argument and to show how disciplinary regimes concerned with punishing and rehabilitating criminal offenders focused their attention and power on the body. Through mechanisms such as the treadmill and techniques such as isolation and constant surveillance, the body of the criminal was disciplined and regulated. Armstrong (1983) extended this analysis in the context of medicine to argue that nineteenth- and early twentieth-century public health discourses surveilled not only bodies but also the spaces between them. This means that the physical body became a focus of medical attention but also the relationship between bodies came under scrutiny. This was achieved by health education initiatives such as vaccination programmes, by the establishment of isolation hospitals and by monitoring relationships between people that might result in the spread of infection. In this way, ill-health and infectious diseases could be controlled.

Porter (1991) takes a similar approach and asserts that the self should be understood in relation to the body, and that the latter should be sited within the wider body politic. Transformations in the nature of the self are constitutive of broader social and cultural relations. Bodies also have personal histories that must themselves be located within longer-term historical processes (Hallam et al., 1999). Thus, as moral, religious and value systems change over time, so do the relationships between the body, the mind and the soul. However, once again, this analysis emphasizes the impact of structures that are external to individuals. It fails to accord any significance to individual agency and tends to neglect the embodied experiences of social life.

Turner (1992) and Featherstone (1995) have highlighted the way in which contemporary Western societies prioritize and prize youthful bodies whilst stigmatizing ageing ones. For Featherstone, the significance of the body reflects the emergence of the 'performing self', where 'appearance, gesture and bodily demeanour become taken as expressions of self, with bodily imperfections and lack of attention carrying penalties in everyday interactions' (Featherstone, 1995: 189). He also suggested that the 'performing self' is a twentieth-century response to the emphasis of public health in the nineteenth and early twentieth centuries, which highlighted the importance of exercise regimes and care of the body, and witnessed the growth of a consumer culture of the body that developed goods and services such as beauty aids. Chapter 3 has discussed the more recent developments in terms of the 'new public health' (Peterson and Lupton, 1996) that focus on individual responsibility for bodily well-being, and have placed even greater emphasis on the manner in which individuals construct and care for their bodies.

Rather than focusing on structural factors, Shilling (1993) considers agency and argues that in high modernity the body is increasingly central to the construction of self-identity. According to his thesis, the body is a project to be worked on, and in this context, death is the inevitable failure. The body is a project worked on by individuals in the construction of self and is always in the process of 'becoming'. In an analysis reminiscent of Mauss (1935), in which he argued that physical deportment was influenced by cultural factors, Shilling contends that the body undergoes changes throughout the life course and that, as a result, bodily postures (for example, facial expressions) become ingrained and imprinted on the flesh. These postures or bodily habits are themselves developed and affected by social structures which impact on individual lifestyle, for example, the effect of poverty on diet, housing patterns and so on. As such, they may be said to be a form of 'habitus' (Bourdieu, 1977), a set of durable 'dispositions' that are often developed as a consequence of inequality in resources and result in particular practices and bodily attitudes. In this respect, habitus provides the link between structure and agency in as much as it demonstrates the way in which social structures assist in shaping bodily experiences.

Giddens (1991) further develops this link between structure and agency in relation to the body by arguing that bodies are not simply the product of social and cultural processes, but are the outcome of reflexive processes in which individuals utilize their bodies as a resource in the conscious construction of self-identity. Examples of this which are particularly prevalent in contemporary consumer cultures might be the use of cosmetic surgery, exercise and diet regimes, all of which are relevant to self-perception and to the way in which individuals mould and shape their bodies and identities and project these to the outside world. It is worth remembering, however, that the values that individuals draw upon to make decisions about preferred body image are subject to social structures and cultural expectations.

For the purposes of this chapter, with its emphasis on the dying and the dead body, we will now consider theories that have attempted to understand the body in crisis.

The body in crisis

Bury (1982) has identified illness as a disruptive event in the construction of the individual biography. Illness and pain threaten a separation of mind and body and are perceived as enemies to the self, having 'let down' the individual and betrayed a biography of good health and well-being. As such, the body in crisis can be regarded 'as a problematic site for social identity' (Hallam et al., 1999: 13). In ageing, chronic illness and dying, individuals must physically adjust to the more limited capabilities of their bodies. For Charmaz (1983) this leads to a loss of self and a further need for individuals to reconstruct their biographies and self-identity to make new meaning in life. Whilst the healthy body is a marker for self-identity and its projection, disease and old age are signs, visible to outsiders, of the split between self and social identity. Thus others 'read off ' an identity from the body that might be inauthentic for the individual (Featherstone and Hepworth, 1991). As Shilling (1993) notes, theorists need to engage with the body's materiality and, in the case of sick, elderly or dying people, to recognize that the 'body project' requires much more work than it does for those with young, healthy bodies. In the case of the former, individuals may no longer be able to actively construct their biography and identity around the body. The self may become fragmented due to the lack of fit between 'my' identity and 'your' perception of my identity as read off the body, and this leads to a need for self-identity to be recast. In societies where the biographical continuity of individuals is given high priority (Giddens, 1991), this fragmentation or disruption, which, for dying and ageing individuals may be irrecoverable, is particularly disturbing. It highlights the processes of transformation and the inevitable failure of the body project.

Furthermore, in contemporary Western societies, technology, such as photography and video, has facilitated the ability for individuals to reflect on the transforming nature of the body as it ages or becomes diseased (Turner, 1995). This has resulted in 'a necessary disjuncture between the inner self and the image of the body' (Turner, 1995: 250) and can lead to a sense of being trapped in a body which is perceived as the enemy and separated from the individual's sense of self. This might also be true of individuals who are socially perceived as 'failing' in the body project, believing themselves, for example, to be thin people trapped in fat bodies. As the body deteriorates and fails to respond to attempts to regain health and youth, individuals may experience a sense of alienation from their bodies, particularly in times of crisis, pain and dysfunction. For Csordas (1994), the body in crisis becomes objectified and ungovernable. As Becker (1995) contends, when experiencing pain the body appears to take on agency against the self. Moreover, in terms of society, bodies that appear to be failing to aspire to the stereotypical images of a healthy body (be that slim and youthful, as in most Western societies, or large as in Fijian society, where size is a symbol of status and well-being) are considered immoral, unkempt or pitiful. For instance, in cases of obesity or heart disease triggered by smoking or alcohol consumption, the illness is frequently represented as self-imposed and caused by the individual's inability to exert control over his or her body. The individual may then be perceived as degenerate rather than a victim of illness.

The dislocation of body and self is also assumed to be prevalent in illnesses such as dementia, in which the focus of care is on the body rather than the self of the individual. People with dementia are commonly perceived to be 'socially dead' and as having experienced a separation between body and self. As Jonathan Miller, President of the Alzheimer's Disease Society in the United Kingdom, expressed it, such diseases exemplify a form of living death where an individual may be depicted as 'an uncollected corpse ... which the undertaker has cruelly forgotten to collect' (1990: 230). According to this depiction, people with dementia or Alzheimer's disease are essentially bodies without selves.

A further example of the problematic relationship between

body and self is that of the individual in a coma who is kept alive with the use of medical technology. A comatose individual, medically identified as having entered persistent vegetative state (PVS), may continue to appear to be very much alive. Relatives may be faced with the decision to switch off the machinery that keeps organs functioning despite brain death. In cases such as this there is a lack of clarity as to when death has occurred and, commonly, a sense that it is switching off the technology that actually leads to death. An additional complication here may be the request from medical personnel for the removal of organs.

Once the person is found to be clinically dead, relatives may be asked to donate the organs of the deceased. For some minority ethnic cultures and religious groups, organ donation is not encouraged and it is unlikely, for example, that Muslims and Jehovah's Witnesses would agree to organ donation. For people of all ethnic and religious backgrounds, the decision whether to accede to the hospital's request for organs may be difficult or may later lead to trauma as, although clinical death has been announced, relatives may continue to perceive the body as the site of the self. Despite campaigns that depict organ donation as an uncontested good and representations of donors as heroes who allow others to live on after their own death, studies have shown that families may feel ambivalent about donation and some later regret having agreed to the removal of organs from the body of the deceased (Robbins, 1996; Younger et al., 1996; Wilson, 2001). The request for organs assumes that the body and the self are entirely separate. Only by accepting this body/self separation can organ donation be made possible. Thus the body is constituted as an object that is owned by the individual rather than as an entity that comprises the self. Although the dead body cannot legally be owned by anyone, body parts can be gifted either before or after death. However, as Robbins (1996) contends, this simple mind/body dichotomy may inform medical practice but has little validity for relatives, who tend to view the body and its parts as more than the discarded shell or vehicle of the soul. As Wilson points out, whilst people often take a pragmatic approach to the continued use of their own organs after death, bereaved survivors 'are more deeply concerned with what happens to the body of a loved one' (2001: 339).

The boundaries of body

The theories we have so far considered all assume that the living body is bounded – each person lives within a physical body that is separate from the bodies of others. They also assume that individual agency requires an embodied self. The problem with this approach is that it assumes individuals to be autonomous entities who are able to utilize their bodies for the construction of self-identity. Hallam et al. (1999) argue to the contrary: that bodies and selves may not be bounded and autonomous, separate from other bodies and selves, and, furthermore, that after death they may continue to have a significant social presence that is separate from their material bodies. They cite the examples of dead or (yet) unlived bodies that nevertheless exert a social influence on the living.

The stillborn baby has not experienced life outside the boundaries of its mother's body, although others, such as the prospective parents, will have constructed an identity for it. A baby born dead or miscarried represents the loss of a future self whose life course may not only have been anticipated by its parents but whose anniversaries (birth/death date, eighteenth or twenty-first birthday) may be remembered and celebrated by the family. In this respect, the baby will have a social presence that may continue long after its death (Hockey, 1996; Lovell, 1997). In Japan, stillborn, miscarried or aborted babies are thought to disturb the natural life–death balance. A feature of many temples of religion is the statues dedicated to the god Jizo. Jizo is considered to be a god who cares for babies who have never lived. Mothers, particularly of aborted babies, commonly place gifts (such as red woollen hats and child bibs) on and around these statues in order that the god may take care of their infants in the other world.

The privileging of the idea of the body as the container of the self (and hence its bounded and temporary nature) is, argued Battersby (1993), a reflection of modern, Western patriarchal societies. In these societies it is assumed that the body and the self are fixed and solid rather than fluid and permeated by others; that there are strict boundaries between self and non-self, inside and outside, and also between life and death. This is clearly contrary to experience, and specifically to the experiences of women, who, for example, in pregnancy carry around the body of another within their own. For them, the body is not bounded but physically shared.

Csordas (1994) contends that this Western emphasis on the objectification of the body is a consequence of the impact of a combination of consumer culture, biological science and Christianity – all of which assume a bounded body, separate from the bodies of others. Once dead, the body and the self become permanently disconnected.

The dead body

Whether survivors believe in an afterlife and/or soul, at death the material body is usually perceived as having transformed from a sacred to a profane entity, from body to corpse. This is common across a range of ethnic and religious groups. Defining the moment at which this transformation occurs has been problematic both historically and culturally. For centuries in Western societies, death has been variously associated with the terminal function of the heart, the organs and, more recently, the brain. In non-Western cultures it may be determined according to ritual. For example, in Hindu societies death is considered to occur when the skull of the deceased splits, thus releasing the soul – an event that takes place during cremation (Bloch and Parry, 1982).

When death occurs, the material body is subject to a number of procedures. If the death was expected, a doctor or physician will sign the death certificate stating cause of death. If death took place in hospital, the body is transferred to the mortuary where it may undergo an autopsy or post-mortem (see the discussion in chapter 8). As Sudnow (1967) notes, the hospital mortuary is usually located in the bowels of the building, away from prying eyes and unlikely to be a place that unsuspecting members of the public may encounter. Whether an autopsy is to be held will be determined by the nature of the death – for example, whether it was expected and if it was unusual in any way. If, when death occurs, it was unexpected, or if a doctor has not recently examined the deceased, the body is taken to the public or hospital mortuary for autopsy. The autopsy is an external and internal examination of the body of the deceased, carried out in order to ascertain the cause, or causes, of death. This is the medical validation of death.

When death has been medically certified, and if there are no suspicious circumstances, the body is usually moved to the funeral home or mortuary, where it is likely to undergo a number of procedures instigated either by funeral operatives, embalmers, or by family members who may want to wash and prepare the corpse according to their customs.

The dead body is a signifier of mortality and as such is deemed dangerous at two levels: physically it is polluting, and symbolically it represents dysfunction and disorder. The corpse has long been associated with pollution and disease. In some cultures, such as Cantonese society, mere proximity to the dead body or inhalation of the 'killing airs' can cause illness (Watson, 1982) and, potentially, death. In Western societies, it was during the nineteenth century that the cadaver was identified as a source of infection and disease. Following the development of pathology, which located disease within the dead body, public health systems regarded the decaying corpse as a carrier of disease and subsequently argued for a clearer separation between the living and the dead. As a potential danger to public health the corpse has since become the domain of experts who deal with the latent contamination associated with its disposal.

The dead body, in contrast with social perceptions of the living body, is unbounded. It is no longer able to contain body fluids and other potentially contaminating elements. It is the 'abject body' (Kristeva, 1982). 'It is no longer a secure, bounded body. Its orifices threaten to contaminate the external world with internal body matter and fluids; its surfaces cannot be relied upon to remain intact. It has lost its integrity and its wholeness' (Hallam et al., 1999: 127). As such it becomes physically and symbolically dangerous and disordered. As experts in the disposal of human remains, funeral directors, morticians and embalmers are tasked with the job of sealing leaks and temporarily re-establishing the body's boundaries. In order to achieve this, the outer surface of the corpse is cleansed, and in many societies the body may be embalmed. This process entails draining the fluids from the cadaver and replacing them with formalin, a chemical designed to ensure temporary preservation. Wounds are closed, orifices plugged, and the body is made to appear intact. This process is promoted to clients as the 'hygienic treatment' of the deceased. It temporarily removes the dangerous, polluting elements of death and facilitates relatives' contact with the deceased during the period prior to burial. This allows them to view the body of their loved one and to say their final farewells – a ritual that may be encouraged by psychologists as a mechanism for coming to terms with the death.

On another level, the work of embalmers and morticians effectively 'humanizes' the corpse by making it appear more lifelike and transforming the body from a defiling object to a representation of its former self (Howarth, 1996). Whilst embalming temporarily arrests decay and re-establishes the body's boundaries, it also restores colour and elasticity to the skin. Together with techniques that calm and reorder bodily features (closing eyes, brushing and arranging the hair, shaving facial hair and, on occasion, sewing lips together to enhance an expression of peacefulness) the corpse is made to resemble its former self and to appear to be asleep rather than dead. According to one manual of funeral directing this is an extremely important aspect of the mortician's work: '[G]one is the deathly pallor. . . . Instead the family sees a life-like presentation of their loved one appearing as though peacefully sleeping' (NAFD, 1988: 59).

There are times when the mortician makes mistakes, for example, in applying the wrong colour of make-up or setting the hair in ways never worn during life. This can be extremely traumatic for the family, who are, as a consequence, unable to recognize the person they have lost. For the most part, however, the reconstruction is successful and through this process the body transcends its materiality and enables bereaved relatives and friends to read signs of the self on the body of the deceased. The clothed body, whose skin colour and texture have been re-established, and hairstyle restored, enables visitors who knew the deceased to recognize central features of their identity. Thus, the disruption and disorder caused by the death of the body is halted and the self restored, albeit temporarily. This can be perceived as a 'finishing' of the body – not possible to achieve during life, but completed by the mortician.

'The reconstruction of the body in death is a particularly stark process of finishing, as the body becomes an object to be rescued and returned to an imagined subjectivity' (Hallam et al., 1999: 132).

These procedures, adopted in contemporary Western societies, stand in marked contrast to attitudes towards the decomposing corpse prevalent in medieval Europe. During that period the corpse was perceived and promulgated as a reminder of mortality, adopted as a memento mori. Images of the decaying corpse were particularly associated with tombs, and effigies of decaying bodies can still be found on tomb architecture from that period. According to Huizinga (1954) these representations were used to remind the living that the body was temporary and would be subject to decay and corruption. Within Christian eschatology the body is simply a vehicle for the soul and it is the latter that should be kept in good order in anticipation of eternal life. In increasingly individualist societies, the body has become more significant to continuing narratives and biographies of the deceased as constructed by others (Walter, 1996). For example, since the end of the nineteenth century, wherever possible, when people die in war, it has been considered important to return the body to the homeland. During the First World War the emerging embalming industry argued that the bodies of dead soldiers should be embalmed and returned to the UK (although this could be viewed as a mechanism for marketing a new industry, and also a fundamental lack of understanding of the nature of that war). In the late twentieth century the United States government spent in the region of $100 million per annum to bring home the remains of US soldiers (Nakashima, 2004). There are undoubtedly issues of nationalism and morale at work here, but these strengthen, rather than weaken, the argument that the dead body has social significance for both individuals and society.

Dead but not gone

The dead often continue to be important to both bereaved individuals and also to societies in general. With the assistance of modern technology, the faces, voices and sentiments of key political figures, such as J. F. Kennedy and Martin Luther King, do not lose their significance in death – on the contrary they may become even more powerful. Celebrities such as Diana, Princess of Wales and the popular musician Kurt Cobain retain an important position in society and culture, living on in the social memory. Martyrs or victims (for example of political violence) continue to play an important role in religious and political movements.

It would appear that the dead might continue to have social presence among the living. At the level of personal loss, bereaved individuals commonly speak of having some form of continuing relationship with the deceased. This may be a sense of presence as the bereaved person feels that the deceased is watching over them, or simply continuing to exist and connect to their world. At times, the deceased may appear in dreams, and at other times and to other people may take the form of a ghost or spirit. In a study conducted with older people, I found that continued presence was not uncommon (Howarth, 1998; Hallam et al., 1999) and this has been noted in a number of other studies (Bennett and Bennett, 2000; Rees, 1971). This phenomenon is discussed in greater depth in the next chapter. Here, it is raised as an example of the continuing agency of the dead in the lives of the living. Bereaved individuals often refer to the death of a loved one as a loss of some part of their own self, a loss that may require a reconstruction of self-identity. Moreover, they may also continue to connect with the deceased, not only for companionship but also when seeking guidance for actions in everyday life. For example, following the loss of a partner or close friend, a person may make a decision or engage in an action according to how they believe their partner or friend might have acted. In other cases, bereaved individuals may consult spiritualists or mediums in order to make contact with the dead to attain assistance with decision-making or simply to ascertain the well-being of their loved ones (Hallam et al., 1999). In instances such as these, and after the death of socially significant people, although the material body is gone, the self continues to exert influence in the world.

Summary

This chapter has considered the relationship between the body and the self in relation to dying, death and bereavement. A range of theories has been examined that challenge early sociological thinking that assumed a mind–body separation. The theories of Foucault (1977) and Turner (1985) have been particularly important in this context, and that of Shilling (1993) in exploring the significance of dying and death in terms of the contemporary Western emphasis on the 'body project'. The discussion has raised questions about the nature of embodiment and has argued that these need to be set alongside disembodiment (Hallam et al., 1999) if we are to understand the complexities of the body/self dichotomy and to contest the hitherto accepted boundaries between life and death.

Conditions such as dementia and PVS, and the continuing presence of the dead within societies have been examined and it is argued that these phenomena highlight the complexities of the relationship between body and self and undermine notions of a clear distinction between the two. This is particularly disturbing for societies that maintain a sharp boundary between the living and dead and results in the generation of categories that attempt to retain social order, to explain and to locate the dying and the dead within rational, scientific frameworks. The derivation of finer lines of demarcation between life and death (for example, the adoption of brain-stem rather than organ failure to identify the moment of death) and the development of psychological categories to explain contact with the dead as pathological or illusory assist in retaining this distinction. Yet, bodies and selves continue to exist at the margins or in the borderlands of social experience and these have the potential to destabilize the social order. However, this potential instability is smoothed away by the continuity of existence in collective and individual memories as the dead maintain elements of agency in both social and individual experiences.

The boundaries that are created and maintained between life and death, body and mind, self and other, are reflected in the dominant modernist approaches of science and medicine. At a more micro, individual level these boundaries are less rigid and the activities that take place at the margins, such as retaining contact with the deceased through sensory perceptions such as smell or sounds (accessed via the material body) or pursuit of spiritual connections (accessed via the bodies of mediums and clairvoyants), challenge these dominant frameworks and threaten to destabilize the life–death dualism.

Part III

Post-Death Rituals of Remembrance and Survival Beliefs

10

Grief and Loss

Introduction

It is important at the very start of this discussion to distinguish between grief and mourning. As Seale points out, the first 'may be said to describe the feelings (or feeling actions) of the bereaved; the second concerns the behaviour socially prescribed in a culture as appropriate for those who have been bereaved' (Seale, 1998: 198). The focus in this chapter is on grief and the theoretical models that have been used to understand grief in modern, Western societies. Mourning as culturally prescribed behaviour will be considered in the next chapter in the context of memorialization and also in chapter 12 in the context of funeral rituals.

Until relatively recently, the study of loss and grief had been regarded as the domain of psychiatrists and psychologists. As a consequence, professional and lay understandings of grief have been dominated by talk of 'normal' and 'pathological' states that rely for their validity on the biomedical model and assume that the grief experience is universal. Measuring its impact in relation to other events that bring change in personal life, 'The Social Readjustment Rating Scale' (a psychological tool) has found 'death of spouse' to be the most stressful life event. It is allocated a mean value of 100 as compared, for example, with 'marital separation' at 73, 'jail term' at 63, 'retirement' at 45, and 'wife begins or stops work' at 26 (Holmes and Rahne, 1967). From the last of these examples, we can assume that the scale was devised from a study of bereavement in males. In somewhat contradictory fashion, however, most of the foundation work on grief, which is still regarded by psychiatrists and psychologists as having established the basic principles for the field, was based on studies of women. For example, Colin Murray Parkes's (1972) work, *Bereavement: Studies of Grief in Later Life*, was based on research with widows, and John Bowlby's (1973–82) *Attachment and Loss*, took mothers as its focus. The findings from studies such as these have since been used as the basis for interpreting and distinguishing 'normal' and 'pathological' grief in the wider population.

This chapter will begin by looking more closely at the psychological study of loss and grief and identifying some of the established wisdoms about the 'transitions' through the loss experience. In so doing it will trace the psychological approach to grief to an individual systems model, a model that takes little or no account of social explanations that emphasize the significance of social structures and agency on the nature and experience of grief. In focusing on the mental health of the individual, it particularly neglects the analysis of agency – that is, the manner in which people construct grief in order to make sense of it. This typically results in the creation of reductionist theories that tend to view diversity in terms of medical models of pathology. To flesh out this argument, the discussion will consider the basic tenets and utilization of stage theories of grief together with a critique of these approaches. We will then turn to examine, in some depth, an attempt by Parkes (1988) to bring together psychological and social aspects of grief. Finally, the chapter will explore more recent theorizing that has rejected the idea that grief resolution necessarily requires the bereaved to 'let go' of the deceased. According to this approach, bereaved people do not ordinarily relinquish their attachments to the deceased in order to reattach to others. Rather, as Klass et al. (1996) assert, they may retain their ties with the dead. This is epitomized as a 'continuing bond'.

Early conceptualizations of psychological pathways through grief

In 1944 Eric Lindemann formulated the concept of 'grief-work', arguing that bereaved individuals had to 'work through' their loss in order to reassimilate into their established social roles. He asserted that grief was a syndrome, the outcome of which could be either 'normal' or 'morbid', implying reintegration or pathology. Based on studies of survivors of a nightclub fire and of ulcerative colitis, Lindemann argued that the nature of death was significant in determining the outcome of grief-work. The more traumatic the death, the more likely grief would be pathological.

Lindemann's theories were extremely influential in establishing a structure for the study of grief. Much of the later research adopted his framework and viewed grief as *work*, and as a *process of transition*, which could be regarded as either normal or pathological depending on the outcome. This way of thinking resulted in the development of stage theories of grief that regarded bereaved individuals as having to pass through a number of stages, phases or tasks before they were able to reach a successful outcome. In keeping with Lindemann's principles, a 'normal' or 'successful' outcome entailed the survivor giving up their relationship with the deceased and reintegrating or reinvesting their emotional energy in others around them. The box below outlines some examples of stage theories.

The basic assumption of each of these theories is that of the re-assimilation of the individual into social life. Western models of grief have tended to frame grief within a biomedical model of illness. As Stroebe remarks, it 'emerges as something like an ailment that needs to be recovered from as quickly and easily as possible' (1997: 257). Grief is resolved when survivors are able to emotionally detach from the deceased (Bowlby, 1969, 1973, 1980; Parkes, 1996; Raphael, 1984; Worden, 1991). This detachment does not require the bereaved to forget the dead person but, rather, to find a place for them within their own biography, as a memory. 'By definition, this place must be located in a past existence; a past from which the bereaved person will move on to a present, and

Some examples of stage theories of grief

John Bowlby (1969, 1973, 1980) *Attachment and Loss.*

    (1)   numbness

    (2)   urge to recover the lost object followed by disorganization

    (3)   adaptive reorganisation

William Worden (1991 [1982]) *Grief Counselling and Grief Therapy.*

    (1)   accept the reality of the loss

    (2)   experience and process the pain

    (3)   adjust to an environment where the deceased is missing

    (4)   withdraw emotional energy from the deceased and reinvest

Beverley Raphael (1984) *The Anatomy of Bereavement.*

    (1)   shock, numbness, disbelief

    (2)   separation pain

    (3)   psychological mourning process

    (4)   reintegration

Therese Rando (1993) *The Treatment of Complicated Mourning.*

    (1)   recognize loss

    (2)   react to separation

    (3)   recollect and re-experience deceased and the relationship

    (4)   relinquish old attachments of the old assumptive world

    (5)   readjust to move adaptively to new world without forgetting

    (6)   reinvest

forward to a future which does not include the deceased as an *active* participant' (Howarth, 2000b: 127).

If the successful outcome of grief is reassimilation, a 'pathological' outcome is one in which the bereaved person is unable or unwilling to give up their ties with the deceased. In other words, it is a situation where they do not 'work through' their grief and may find themselves 'stuck' in one or other of the stages. In these cases, grief may be referred to as delayed, inhibited or chronic. For example, a person may be unable to 'move on' from an early 'refusal to accept the reality' of their loss; they may experience prolonged and intense reactions that continue to cause them ongoing pain and despair; or, individuals who appear to be coping well in the early stages may become depressed and anxious later on. From a more sociological perspective Blauner's notion of 'unfinished business' (1966) presumes that grief will be resolved and the dead 'released' once 'business' has been completed.

Recognition of the importance of social factors in grief and loss

The importance of social factors has not gone unrecognized. An attempt to draw on both psychological and social aspects of grief is illustrated by Parkes (1988). His discussion of grief, however, takes illness as the starting point. He remarks that major life events are now seen as being implicated in the development of mental illness and that such illness is likely to result if:

- the event forces the individual to undertake a major review and revision of their assumptive world;

- individuals become lost in the implications of the event rather than transiting through it;

- the event occurs over a relatively short period of time entailing little or no preparation.

In establishing these potential routes to illness, however, he does acknowledge that major life events may impact differently on different people and that, 'each person's experience of grief is individual and unique' (1988: 242). For Parkes, the three features he outlines are the defining characteristics of 'psychosocial transitions' (PSTs). He considers the impact of bereavement as a PST and that people must undertake grief-work if a 'successful outcome' is to be achieved. His discussion considers four areas: assumptive world changes, the pain of change, coping and defence, and taking stock. Let us consider each in turn.

Assumptive world changes

For psychologists, the assumptive world refers to the habits of daily living. Sociologists might refer to this as the taken–for–granted world. Parkes argues that, following bereavement, people must reappraise the assumptive world in which they live. For example, he asserts that a woman will need to cease to turn to her husband for advice if she is to successfully revise her status from wife to widow. (This is an assertion that we will critique later in this chapter.)

Pain of change

Parkes acknowledges that there is tremendous pain in loss. Part of this pain is the loss of confidence that results when our perceptions of the world have been shattered. Sociologists may refer to this as the loss of 'ontological security' or the loss of meaning. Furthermore, Parkes notes that people also experience the pain of change as they embark on the work that must be carried out if they are to adapt to what he refers to as the requirements of the 'real' world.

Coping and defence

People in transition may withdraw from the challenges of the outside world, preferring to remain in the familiar private world in order to distract themselves from the 'reality' of loss. Although Parkes suggests that this may alleviate anxiety, he also believes that it is likely to delay the 'relearning' process.

Taking stock

Finally, Parkes argues that bereavement, as one of the major traumatic life events, affects the fundamental functions of everyday life and forces the individual to 'take stock'. For example, the loss of a spouse might also mean loss of a sexual partner, a companion, an income, status and so on.

These are all aspects of social life that alert the bereaved person to the tension between their familiar world and their new status within it. For Parkes, this tension is only resolved when the individual has completed their grief-work and made psychological adjustments that bring change in their social expectations.

A further attempt to acknowledge the role of social factors in grief was the 'dual-process' model developed by Stroebe and Schut (1999). They argued the need to move away from a focus on psychodynamic theories of attachment (which generated stage and phase theories) and to consider instead psychological theories of stress and coping (Field and Payne, 2003). Like Parkes, they emphasized the importance of understanding how people adapt to psychosocial changes, and they also suggested that research had shown that dwelling on loss (as associated with cognitive processing) might actually be harmful. Stroebe and Schut proposed a model of grief that encouraged a balance between 'loss orientation' and 'restoration orientation'. This model moves away from many of the earlier approaches in that it does not view grief as a linear process (the individual progressing through time from one stage or phase of grief to the next), but points instead to a process whereby individuals experience a range of emotional states and engage in a range of 'coping tasks' as they adjust to bereavement. Thus in this 'dual-process' model, social factors are acknowledged but the emphasis on the psychological adaptation of the individual remains.

Criticisms of psychological theories of grief

As psychological theorizing of death has developed, social factors have come to be viewed as significant to the nature and outcome of grief. Although the frameworks utilized are essentially unchanged, they have begun to recognize that the way in which society responds to the bereaved person and the manner in which the individual reorganizes their social roles will affect the loss experience and its 'resolution'. For example, Doka (1989) has formulated the concept of 'disenfranchised grief'. This is grief that is not publicly acknowledged or socially supported. Disenfranchised grief may occur in many situations of loss, including miscarriage and abortion (Lovell, 1997; Hey et al., 1989), loss of a homosexual partner (Shernoff, 1998), the death of a pet (Kellehear and Fook, 1997; Straube, 2004). Although there is a social element to disenfranchised grief, there is also an 'intrapsychic' dimension which assumes that the bereaved person is psychologically disenfranchising themselves either by not recognizing their grief or by framing it with shame or guilt. Thus, it is clearly important to take account of social structures that impact on bereavement and to be aware that structures such as gender, age, ethnicity, sexuality, disability and others will inevitably influence the individual's experience of grief and the way in which they frame it. Doka's concept of disenfranchised grief, for example, highlights the diversity in social recognition and support for bereaved people; social responses to different types of death will affect the support available to bereaved people. So, for example, the nature and extent of social support offered to people will vary according to a number of factors such as the socially perceived 'timeliness' of death, the cultural context in which it occurs and the nature of social prohibitions on relationship types. Thus the social context of grief and the support mechanisms available will differ for parents bereaved of young children, a woman bereaved of her female partner, a middle-aged man bereaved of his brother with dementia, an elderly working-class woman bereaved of her male spouse, a young woman bereaved of her Sikh grandfather, or a middle-aged couple bereaved by the suicide of their teenage son.

Although psychologists are now attempting to integrate social perspectives into their understandings of grief, most continue to emphasize the need to progress through grief, and for bereaved people to reintegrate into the 'real' world where the deceased is missing. These theoretical approaches have been heavily criticized for the assumptions they make about the nature of relationships between the living and the dead (this will be a focus for discussion later). On a more practical level, and in a similar fashion to the criticisms levelled at Kübler-Ross's stage theory of dying (1970) (see chapter 7), they have been condemned for their inflexibility and for the fact that these models have become prescriptive in professional practice. Stage theories often imply that each phase or task must be completed in sequence before the bereaved person can move on to the next. Whilst the recognition of different phases of grief might be helpful to our understanding, professionals have commonly interpreted these processes too rigidly. The consequences of this are that whilst some bereaved people may have been encouraged to 'move on', others have been identified as experiencing complicated or pathological grief because of their inability to do so.

In response to criticisms such as these, some theorists have begun to modify their approach (see for example, Worden, 1991) by stating that the stages may not be experienced sequentially and that individuals may express a range of emotions at different times. Furthermore, the assumption that bereaved people need to readjust their psyche by leaving the deceased behind them has more recently been questioned (see for example, Klass et al., 1996; Walter, 1996; Stroebe, 1997).

Sociological perspectives on grief

With the renewed interest in issues of death and dying, sociologists are beginning to recognize that loss and grief are not simply matters of psychological adjustment but, rather, that grief experiences are profoundly social. In order to understand bereavement better we need to reject the idea that grief is universally experienced and focus instead on the social construction of loss in all its cultural diversity.

Small (2001c) traces the history of thinking on grief and bereavement during the twentieth century. He explores the way in which theories of grief can be linked to social changes and to the dominant discourses of distinct periods. He argues against the notion that grief is experienced universally and suggests that a greater appreciation of the different manifestations of grief is required. The physical, spiritual and intellectual experiences of grief and bereavement need to be understood in the context of social norms, personal styles and cultural prescriptions (Kellehear, 2002). The significance of cultural scripts for grief is now increasingly acknowledged, with literature being produced that focuses on multicultural approaches, particularly within a Western social context (Kalish, 1980; Kalish and Reynolds, 1981; Irish, 1997; Parkes et al., 1997). The emphasis on the Western context is important as cultural norms and rituals are dynamic and inevitably adapt to changing social environments. The potential problem with such texts is that discussed in chapter 7 on the good death, that these insights into cultural diversity can become 'factfiles' that are then used by professionals to determine the appropriateness of grieving behaviour. For this reason it is important that cultural norms are understood in the context of personal styles and social experiences and expectations.

For Small, it is also important to recognize that we cannot really know what goes on in people's heads any more than we can know how people experience grief in the privacy of their family. He refers to this lack of knowledge as the strangeness or 'mystery' of the familiar. He encourages us to refrain from focusing on what we perceive as the 'exotic' or unusual experiences of grief in order to gain a better understanding of the diversity of loss. 'If we do this then we can approach bereavement not as a prompt for "tasks" or as a "problem" but as part of the sociality of our existence' (Small, 2001c: 21). So, for example, if we focus on gender, studies suggest that men and women express their grief in different ways and that grieving styles are culturally determined and influenced by the social expectations associated with sex-role behaviour (Cline, 1996; Parkes, 1996; Thomas and Striegel, 1995). Others argue that grief responses are not determined by gender per se but by culturally prescribed 'masculine' and 'feminine' styles of grief (Thompson, 1997). In order to flesh out this example, let us now briefly consider an empirical study of the social context of grief that highlights bereavement experiences according to gender.

Gendered grief and the death of children

Riches and Dawson (1997, 2000) conducted a sociological study of the impact on parents of the death of an unborn infant or that of a child. Working from a theoretical perspective that focuses on the social world of the individual, the authors examined the experiences of bereaved parents. Their study was based on research with parents whose children were either unborn or stillborn, who had died accidentally, or as a result of illness or murder. Their intention was to explore the different coping strategies adopted by these parents and to question the extent to which traditional understandings of gender (and the roles of mother and father associated with these) affect experiences of loss and grief. They were also interested in the way in which grief is culturally produced, arguing that, '[a]lthough social relationships may facilitate the process of grieving, culture provides the content of grieving' (1997: 55). From their study they suggested that there are four broad 'identity orientations' or typical ways in which bereaved parents make sense of the death of a child: (1) isolation or fragmentation, (2) nomic repair, (3) sub-cultural alternation and (4) personal reconstruction. These orientations were produced from a combination of the sentiments expressed among individuals in personal relationships, and the dominant or mainstream social discourses or constructions of concepts such as family, gender and bereavement. Let us outline each in turn.

Isolation or fragmentation This orientation was found to occur when parents were overwhelmed by grief and unable to return to their normal role identities. They became preoccupied with loss, and grief became a permanent feature of their lives.

Nomic repair Here parents separated their loss from their usual role identity. For example, returning to work offered a distraction, confirming their role as worker and downplaying their role as parent. People adopting this orientation tended to the view that 'life must go on'.

Sub-cultural alternation This was essentially a rejection by parents of the sentiments expressed by friends and family and the discourses of mainstream society, and a refusal to be diverted or distracted from their grief. Rather than subscribing to the notion that 'life must go on', these parents believed that life had changed forever and everything within it was irrevocably altered. Many such bereaved individuals become involved with other, like-minded people in self-help groups (Klass et al., 1996; Riches, 2001). This enables them to focus on their loss and to share in the losses of others. Some well-known examples of self-help groups are Mothers Against Drunk Driving (MADD), The Compassionate Friends, and Stillbirth and Neo-natal Death Support (SANDS).

Personal reconstruction   Here parents reappraised their roles and relationships but did so independently of their social networks and of the sentiments of mainstream society. Their search for new meaning in life sometimes resulted in a dramatically changed lifestyle and social networks.

From the analysis of their data, Riches and Dawson suggest that gender differences in patterns of grief are fluid and that it is unreliable to equate an active style of grief with men and emotional coping strategies with women. Rather, they argue, both men and women draw from a range of sentiments. Whilst some of these may utilize 'patriarchal assumptions about "natural" differences between the sexes... many of them are derived from the post-feminist, post-industrial discourses of late modernity' (Riches and Dawson, 1997: 74).

New models of grief

Presenting a chronology of the development of thought on grief, Small (2001c) discusses the work of Klass et al. (1996), who challenge traditional models of grief, replacing them with a model of 'continuing bonds'. We will now consider this critique and address the concern that Small expresses: that this model may become the new orthodoxy.

   Approaches that reject the idea of grief as a universal experience necessarily encompass awareness of the need to address the impact of cultural diversity. The rejection of universalism is founded on the premise that although grief as a reaction to loss may exist in all societies, the social and cultural contexts in which it is found and the prevailing social norms will influence the nature of individual experiences. For example, if we think about crying as an expression of grief, it is easy to see how the behaviour of individuals may differ according to social expectations, for example, of gender. In some cultural contexts, women may be encouraged and men discouraged from crying. Crying as a public display of grief may also be regarded as either more or less appropriate for members of elite groups (Edwards, 2001).

Furthermore, studies have tended to emphasize the negative aspects of grief, focusing on loss and poor psychological health, rather than considering potentially positive experiences. As Kellehear outlines, the dead may continue to be 'significant others' for bereaved people, acting as role models, advisers in times of crisis and success:

> grief can create a positive social legacy – in advocacy (influencing policy and education), in political activism (giving rise to groups such as Mothers Against Drunk Driving), in foundations (supporting research or service development) and in careers (heightening the personal achievements and ambitions of survivors). (2002: 176)

In order to examine some of the new frameworks entailing positive aspects of grief and to elucidate the nature of the bond between the living and the dead, the discussion will now turn to consider the work of Silverman and Klass (1996) and Walter (1996). Research conducted by Bennett and Bennett (2000) will then further our understanding of these frameworks and relationships by exploring the continuing presence of the dead in the lives of the living.

Continuing relationships between the living and the dead

In the introduction to their edited collection of articles concerned with 'continuing bonds', Silverman and Klass (1996) present a synopsis and critique of traditional stage theories of grief. They see the problem with these theories as deriving from a belief in the primacy of independence in humans. Stage theories, they assert, have reified independence. As a consequence they require bereaved people to detach from relationships with the dead and thus reassert their autonomy. This perspective is typical of modernist thinking that is based on the premise of detachment and insists on viewing individuals as separate from one another. This separation is both physical, with each of us living in our own distinct and bounded bodies (Hallam et al., 1999), and it is mental, each of us with a discrete and autonomous self. Thus, the model of good mental health entails autonomy and independence. By contrast, poor mental health or pathological grieving has been identified with dependent personalities (Raphael, 1984) and a refusal to give up the deceased person. This leads Silverman and Klass to assert that the 'pathology of grief has essentially been associated with the stereotype of feminine behaviour' (1996: 16). So, paradoxically, although much psychological research has been based on studies of women and grief, the model of good mental health that has been utilized is a male model that privileges independence and autonomy.

Silverman and Klass offer an alternative paradigm in which interdependence is prioritized over independence. They refer to the studies of the other contributors to their book to show that people consider themselves to be intimately involved in the lives of others. This means that when a person dies, survivors have not only lost that person but also the part of themselves that was intricately bound up with the deceased (Howarth, 2000b: 130). As Marris argued, 'the fundamental crisis of bereavement arises, not from loss of others, but the loss of self' (1974: 33). Indeed, Giddens (1991) contends that in order to retain ontological security, individuals must avoid experiences that threaten the sense of self. Following the work of Marwit and Klass (1994–5) and Klass (1992–3) (both working from a psychological perspective), Silverman and Klass (1996) suggest that survivors develop psychological mechanisms to overcome or distract them from threats to their self-identity. They achieve this by creating 'inner representations' of the deceased as part of the normal grieving process. It is these inner representations that allow people to continue to interact with the dead and, in this way, to retain a sense of continuity of self. Moreover, these representations are not static memories, frozen in the past but are the basis of dynamic social relationships.

While the intensity of the relationship with the deceased may diminish with time, the relationship does not disappear. We are not talking about living in the past, but rather recognizing how bonds formed in the past can inform our present and our future. (Silverman and Klass, 1996: 17)

Silverman and Klass argue against the need for people to seek to 'resolve' their grief experiences and instead recommend that bereavement might better be perceived as an ongoing process of negotiation and meaning making. The significance of loss and the place of the deceased in the life of survivors will be continually renegotiated as feelings lessen or intensify.

I have argued elsewhere (Howarth, 2000b) that continuing bonds may reflect a proclivity in contemporary Western societies to blur the boundaries between the living and the dead. This may in part have been stimulated by greater cultural diversity, an increased interest in ancestors, and a disillusionment with traditional forms of Christianity. This challenge to the hitherto strict separation between life and death is illustrated in the range and variety of ways in which bereaved people sometimes work to keep the dead alive. These may include displaying photographs, talking about the dead, visiting mediums or spiritualists, and celebrating or acknowledging anniversaries such as birthdays. Bennett and Bennett (2000), in their studies with elderly women, alert us to experiences of the continued presence of the dead. They observe that there are many well-documented accounts of the continued presence of the deceased found in a range of literatures, including medical, counselling and psychology texts. Their research in the UK revealed that the experience of sensing the presence of the dead could range in intensity: 'At its weakest this is a feeling that one is somehow being watched; at its strongest it is a full-blown sensory experience' (2000: 139). Whatever the force of the experience, they found that the sense of presence could occur at any time after the death of their loved one: that is, shortly after the death, or days, weeks, months or, in some cases, years later. For some, this was felt on only one occasion, for others it might entail ongoing communication and interaction with the deceased. Their findings contradict the orthodox literature that suggests that these 'illusory' perceptions occur only during a specific time period or stage of grief when the bereaved person is 'in transition', for example, whilst psychologically transferring their status from that of wife to that of widow.

Bennett and Bennett were especially interested in how respondents interpreted their experiences. There are two accepted perspectives on any form of extra-sensory perception. The first suggests that these experiences are illusory and/or stem from chemical changes in the brain (for example, Blackmore, 1993); the second that they are evidence of survival after death (see for example, Eadie, 1992). Bennett and Bennett refer to these respectively as the 'material' discourse and the 'supernatural' discourse. Both, they assert, are cultural artefacts and both are used by bereaved people to explain their experiences. In analysing the explanations their respondents gave, they found that people did not select and consistently use either one or other of these discourses. Rather, the accounts they gave were ambiguous as they moved back and forth between the two, at times asserting that their encounter was 'real' and at other times suggesting that it might have been a 'dream'. The authors argue that this apparent uncertainty results from an assessment of their audience. In other words, whether or not the narrator is personally certain of the nature of their experience, the account they give will be heavily influenced by what they perceive to be the characteristics of their audience.[1] For example, in the company of other widows they may claim the experience to be real; when responding to researchers' questions their interpretation of events is more likely to appear ambiguous or to lean towards a materialist analysis. Thus:

> [E]xpressions like 'dream' and 'as if he was there' on the one hand, and 'I really saw him' and 'he was there' on the other, should not be taken too literally. They may not reflect differences in the quality of the experience (or even necessarily of speakers' private interpretations, if they have any). It may be that they are choosing their language according to their assessment of the audience. (Bennett and Bennett, 2000: 155)

As a footnote to this research, it is interesting to note that much of the empirical evidence for the continuing presence of the dead among the living is based on research conducted with elderly women. An important question in this context, and one worthy of further research, is whether this is simply a reflection of the people that researchers choose to study, or whether this points to a pattern in society – with older women more likely to be experiencing continued presence, possibly as a consequence of the effects of social death (Howarth, 1998) as well as an outcome of different patterns of longevity between men and women (see chapter 2).

Conceptual understandings of continuing bonds: imagination or reality?

One significant feature of continuing bonds, highlighted by the Bennett and Bennett study is a sense of the continued presence of the deceased in the lives of survivors. This presence may be expressed in dreams, in communication, or in face-to-face interaction. The phenomenon has been variously interpreted as hallucination, make-belief (Bowlby, 1969, 1973, 1980; Marris, 1974; Rees, 1971), or, more recently, as interaction and negotiation between the survivor and an inner representation (Marwit and Klass, 1994–5; Silverman and Klass, 1996). This raises the question as to whether this continued presence is 'real' or imaginary. The concept of 'inner representation' has been helpful in avoiding the pejorative identification of continued presence as hallucination and its association with connotations of poor mental health. However, by creating a psychological concept to explain the mental mechanics of continuing bonds, the emphasis is still placed on the idea that 'it's all in the mind'. Thus, once again, and irrespective of how sympathetic we are towards the experience, the assumption of psychologists is that these experiences are imaginary.

Whilst Silverman and Klass (1996) rely for their understanding of continuing relationships on the psychological concept of an inner representation, others have been able to identify and explain these bonds without recourse to psychology (Howarth, 1998; Walter, 1996; Bennett and Bennett, 2000). A sociological analysis in which theorizing privileges individual experience or agency does not assume that continuing presence is a deception of the mind. A perspective that focuses on the way in which individuals construct and make sense of the world around them has no need to ask if such phenomena are real or imaginary. This is because this approach assumes that what people perceive as real *is real* in its consequences (Thomas, 1966). Therefore, the question of reality is not at issue, because those who experience the continued presence of the dead will themselves decide whether or not it is real and act accordingly. Furthermore, if by exploring the nature of continuing relationships our purpose is to understand experiences of grief, rather than to identify grieving behaviour as 'normal' or 'pathological', then the issue of objectivity (whether something is 'real' or not) is redundant.

Biographical reconstruction: the new orthodoxy?

Klass et al. (1996) are not alone in encouraging a rethink of models of grief. Using a sociological perspective, Walter (1996), arguing along similar lines, suggests that grief resolution should not be regarded as requiring the bereaved to leave the deceased behind. He believes that grief should be extracted from a medical framework and bereavement recognized as a normal life experience. His position is that in the late twentieth century the social context of grief changed. The impact of this change, as Stroebe summarizes, is that, 'instead of working through feelings, moving on and living without the deceased, the bereaved of the 1990s go about integrating the memory of the deceased into their ongoing lives' (1997: 257). This entails the construction of a durable biography of the deceased, which, Walter argues, is achieved through conversations with others who knew them. These biographical constructions, particularly in the context of sudden or violent death, might then be utilized by the bereaved to transform the death into a positive event through narratives of hope, change and so on (Seale, 1998; Bradbury, 1999). In viewing grief as an ongoing process that necessitates a 'rewriting' of the biography of both the bereaved and the deceased, Silverman and Klass (1996) and Walter (1996) argue for a 'new', more social model of grief that incorporates the capacity for continuing bonds between the living and the dead.

Whilst this approach has been important in acknowledging and theorizing relationships between the living and the dead, the idea that a new model should be developed is, for some (Howarth, 2000b; Small, 2001c), cause for concern. Models, whatever the original purpose of their construction, may become prescriptive as health professionals search for new and better ways to manage grief. As Small (2001c) remarks, however progressive the model, if it becomes the orthodoxy, it will necessarily privilege some people's experiences over others. As we noted earlier in this chapter, theoretical frameworks and professional practice must recognize cultural diversity. One-dimensional models of dying or of grief may be unhelpful in meeting the needs and expectations of the heterogenous individuals who make up modern multicultural societies. The nature of any ongoing relationship with the dead will be tempered by relationships in life, by the nature of the death itself, by social class, ethnicity, age, gender, sexuality and so on. Furthermore, relationships with the deceased may not always be welcomed. As I have suggested elsewhere, the dead also resist control.

> They may continue to surprise us with their presence – suddenly brought to life on hearing a special piece of music, encountering the waft of perfume, the fleeting sight of a familiar face or expression. For the dead are mobile, resisting practices that 'pin them down' in cemeteries or consign them to past relationships, fading photographs or lost memories. The dead may also impose themselves where they are not wanted, their presence being neither welcome nor comforting. (Howarth, 2000b: 135)

Rather than a new model of grief, there is a requirement for more flexible approaches to understanding grief that take account of cultural diversity, social norms, personal experiences and styles. Notwithstanding the criticism of producing models, it is important to acknowledge that professionals have a need for frameworks for practice. These must be more sensitive, flexible and responsive to individual, social and cultural contexts.

Summary

This chapter began by outlining some of the traditional theories of grief that have been developed by psychologists and psychiatrists working in the field of bereavement care. Many of these theories have posited the idea that in order to grieve, 'healthily' bereaved people must pass through a number of psychological or emotional stages with the aim of resolving their grief and letting go of the deceased. These theories, which derive from medical models of health and pathology, are now being challenged and more social models of grieving are being developed. The discussion has explored the model of continuing bonds and has illustrated the nature of the continuing presence of the dead by examining research into the experiences of elderly women. Whilst recognizing the important change of direction in understanding the nature of grief and bereavement, the chapter concluded with a concern with the prescriptive nature of such frameworks and the fear that models, almost inevitably, form the basis of practice for professionals who are themselves struggling to make sense of, and support people through the crisis of bereavement.

11

Relationships Between the Living and the Dead

Introduction

Relationships between the living and the dead, where the dead are placed and how they are remembered in each society, depend upon cultural representations of mortality. There are three main components to this in relation to the location and memorialization of the deceased: religious perspectives and beliefs about the destiny of the soul and the nature of ancestry; how the corpse is perceived; and prevailing practices around grief.

In some societies, such as the Soro of east India (Vitebsky, 1990) and in Japan (Yamamoto et al., 1969), the dead are venerated as ancestors and this enables a continuing dialogue between them and the living. Other cultures may perceive of the relationship between the living and the newly dead as one in which the living perform rituals to assist the soul of the deceased on its journey to the afterlife and this can be related to the practice of secondary burial such as that of rural Greece (Danforth, 1982). Yet others fear the dead and their return as ghosts. Of these, some work to pin them down in cemeteries (as found by Okely (1983) in her study of gypsies) whilst others such as the Apache (Opler, 1996 [1936]) banish them from the world of the living by obliterating any material trace of their existence.

The key to understanding these different practices lies in beliefs about the relationship between the living and the dead. Some ethnic and religious groups perceive of life and death as a form of continuum, with life merging into death and the omnipresence of death highlighting the scarcity of life. As Bloch argues of the Merina culture of Madagascar, such a continuum relies upon the notion that death and birth, or fertility, are interrelated, 'that it is the dead who have been and will be the suppliers of life' (1971: 222). In other societies, and dominant within modern Western societies, is a belief in a binary opposition between life and death, the living and the dead, which assumes that the dead are permanently removed – both physically and spiritually – from the society of the living and have little or no impact on the lifeworld. According to this system, which has been particularly significant in Western Protestant societies since the rejection of the doctrine of purgatory (LeGoff, 1984), whatever the belief in an afterlife, the living cannot intercede on behalf of the dead nor vice versa.

This chapter will explore the way these two belief systems affect the manner in which societies dispose of and remember their dead. It begins with a brief examination of traditional rituals that tend to focus on the needs of the dead and their journey to the afterlife. The emphasis here is on the importance of the dead as ancestors and the roles they may be expected to play in the destinies of the living. Attitudes to the corpse will also be considered, as these are significant in determining both the location and nature of disposal. In this context, the development of the cemetery in Western societies during the late eighteenth and nineteenth centuries, coupled with the changing nature of grief, will form the basis for a discussion of disposal ritual and memorialization in the modern world. The chapter will conclude with some tentative remarks about the way in which more innovative contemporary rituals might suggest that some elements in Western societies are moving, whether consciously or not, towards a view of life and death as a continuum.

Traditional disposal rituals and the veneration of the dead

The disposal of the dead in traditional societies is commonly ritualized in ways designed to meet the needs of the deceased on their journey to the afterlife, or to protect the living from the unwanted return of the dead. For example, exhumations of Bronze Age burials frequently uncover remains carefully placed in the grave together with tools, weapons or other implements assumed to assist the dead in the next world. This may take the form of practical help (sustenance or weapons) or symbolic help (depositing items such as valuable jewellery or similar artefacts) that reflect the high status of the deceased. In ancient Egypt the body of the deceased was believed to be significant in assisting the spirit and soul to live on after death. Following the deaths of powerful and wealthy people, the body would be carefully preserved and entombed together with provisions for the journey and riches needed in the next life.

In Chinese and Japanese societies, which have traditionally engaged in ancestor worship and considered the dead to be important in determining the fate of the living, funeral rituals are enacted to facilitate an easy transition for the soul into the spirit world (Loewe, 1982). In so doing, the dead undergo a rite of passage from living elders to ancestors and thereby continue to have a relationship with the living – one which enables them to assist their families in times of difficulty. Such practices can, of course, be viewed not only as endeavours to assist the dead but also as devices for meeting the needs of the bereaved. When ancestors are assumed to be helpful to the fate of the living, it is important to take good care of them and to perform whatever rites may be necessary to ensure that they reciprocate in kind.

For the Merina of Madagascar the relationship between the living and the dead is a continuum, rather than a binary opposition; one where life and death necessarily imply each other (Bloch, 1971). According to Bloch, the Merina live in two worlds: the society in which they are alive and the society of the ancestors. Participating in funeral rites and exhumation ceremonies (*famadihana*) assists in creating an 'ancestral fold' and in returning the dead to the society of the ancestors. Furthermore, touching things that have been in contact with the dead (rather than touching the body itself) are thought to promote fertility. He also notes that when referring to people, the Merina make the distinction between those who are living and thus 'imply the other type of existence of people as being dead' (1971: 221).

Whilst many societies and communities desire a continuing relationship with the dead, there are others who fear the dead and perform rituals to encourage them to quit this world and move rapidly to the next. The gypsy tradition of 'pinning' the dead down in local burial grounds for fear of them continuing to travel alongside the living (Okely, 1983) has already been mentioned. A further example of fear of the return of the dead is noted by DeSpelder and Strickland (2005) who cite research by Mandel-baum (1959). He suggests that among the native American tribes of the Cocopa and Hopi, funeral rites are designed to help the soul to take leave of its earthly connections and to not return. The Hopi, as a tribe with a clear binary perspective on life and death, are especially keen to avoid the dead and to discourage further communication with them. DeSpelder and Strickland (2005: 107) reproduce a burial oration of the Wintu tribe that also reflects this insistence on separation between the living and dead.

> You are dead.
> You will go above there to the trail.
> That is the spirit trail.
> Go there to the beautiful trail.
> May it please you not to walk about where I am.
> You are dead.

In medieval Christian Europe, the dead were to be found in burial grounds in the community, usually alongside or actually within the local church. With a belief in an afterlife, the resurrection of the body, and constant reminders (memento mori) of the temporary and fleeting nature of life on earth, it was important for the destiny of the soul that people were buried in consecrated ground and as close as possible to the altar of the church. Wealth and status dictated positioning, with the bodies of the rich and powerful sited under the church floor or within the walls of the building, proximity to the altar or the door being determined according to high or low status respectively. The churchyard accommodated those unable to afford a burial space inside the church; again, status determined proximity to the church building, with the poor buried at the greatest distance. The bodies of murderers and suicides, deemed to have taken life that was the prerogative of God and, therefore, not entitled to eternal salvation, were not permitted burial in consecrated ground (Gittings, 1984). In some European countries, an ossuary or charnel house would be used as a repository for bones once the flesh had decayed, thus enabling reuse of burial space.

During this pre-modern period there was relatively little geographical mobility among the populace and this meant that the churchyard was a focal point for recognition of linear descent as graves and intramural burials stood as fixed and permanent memorials for generations of local people. A belief in purgatory (a place where the souls of the dead may reside whilst undergoing purification) meant that through prayer the living could intercede on behalf of the deceased to assist their soul to attain purity and entry into heaven. This resulted in practices (for the wealthy) such as employing a chantry priest and distributing doles (small amounts of money) to the poor to engage their services in prayer. In the sixteenth century Protestants rejected the doctrine of purgatory and the belief that the living could mediate for the dead.[1] This was undoubtedly an important factor in the development of a philosophy (prevalent in modern Western societies) that perceived of life and death as binary opposites rather than a continuum.

Burial grounds as 'sacred space'

Places where the dead are buried commonly become viewed as sacred spaces. This is true of many cultures and religions. Lefebvre alerts us to the concept of 'absolute space', a space that, through the actions of powerful people, 'henceforth appears as transcendent, as sacred (i.e. inhabited by divine forces), as magical and cosmic' (1974: 234). Although determined by political forces, this space is perceived as being part of nature and its sacredness is attributed to natural forces. The places where the dead are located frequently take on this mantle of absolute or sacred space where the dead are bound to the living, and, for Lefebvre, where the absolute power of death over life is realized. There are many examples in the archaeological record of human burials that appear to acknowledge such power. The skeletons of children, for example, have been unearthed below ancient buildings and bridges, presumably placed there either as a sacrifice to nature or in a bid to protect the structure from the anger and displeasure of gods who might otherwise seek to destroy it.

In exploring the notion of sacred space Lefebvre also points to early burial pits, and in particular to the '*mundus*' in the Italian township. Originally the public rubbish dump, these ditches were used to discard the bodies of criminals and newborn, but unwanted, babies. As a repository for both 'the greatest foulness and the greatest purity', he argues, these pits were simultaneously associated with birth and death, with the sacred and the accursed, and thereby connected the spaces above ground (the city and its territories) with the hidden, mystical or clandestine spaces below ground (the subterranean spaces). The later Christian cemetery, he asserts, performs a similar function.

Drawing from a Durkheimian, structuralist perspective, Warner (1965) argued that during the twentieth century cemeteries became expressions of a community's beliefs and values and illustrated the significance of the dead for the world of the living. As enduring symbols of mortality, he asserted that these spaces, physically bounded by walls and fences, nevertheless spiritually connected or joined the living to the dead through ceremonies and rituals. He recognized a binary division between life and death, the social time of life and the eternal time of death. Thus, the time-bound, social individual in death is transferred to the 'eternal stillness' of the timeless and uncontrollable space of the dead. By placing the dead in cemeteries, which themselves are located among the living, humans attempt to retain control over death by keeping the dead 'alive' in the memories of the living through rituals and systems of meaning and so decrease their own anxieties about future extinction. Cemeteries, he maintained, are meeting places for the living and the dead in which inhere a complex mix of the secular and sacred; for example, they are repositories for the polluting corpse which, at the same time, is being transformed into a sacred entity. As we will see later in this discussion, it is acts of remembrance that allow the living to keep the dead 'alive': 'physical lifetime is ended but social existence continues. It exists so long as memory of it is felt by the living members of the group' (Warner, 1965: 369).

The development of the modern, Western cemetery

The post-Enlightenment period of early modern Europe was a time of great social and economic change. The emphasis on science and technology led to industrialization and new ways of thinking about the relationship between life and death. In the late eighteenth and during the nineteenth century, the sacred quality of the urban burial ground or churchyard became tarnished as rapid population growth led to an increasing concern with public health and the dangers of decaying corpses.

It was during this period that attitudes to the corpse changed, viewing it as potentially dangerous to the living. At the same time concern was expressed about its proper treatment. This resulted in the development of extramural cemeteries throughout Europe (Ariès, 1981; Kselman, 1993), first established in the early decades of the nineteenth century. Rapid urbanization, with its associated problems of poverty, disease and infection, meant that urban burial grounds became overcrowded, as the authorities were unable to find sufficient space comfortably to locate the dead. Bodies were buried close to the surface, and decaying flesh and bones were commonly unearthed by grazing animals and other natural forces that pushed them to ground level. Outbreaks of infections close to burial grounds led to the establishment of scientific theories that cited the corpse as a source of disease. According to Rugg, the idea that graveyard overcrowding caused fever was imported to the UK from France, 'where an orthodoxy on graveyard "emanations" had been developing since the 1730s' (1998: 114). The developing public and environmental health movements (see chapter 3) led the way to calls for better sanitation and an increased awareness of urban miasmas that cited the corpse as dangerous to health, 'alongside other "undesirables" for a civilized urban environment – effluvia, dead animals, and the sick and dying' (Rugg, 1998: 115). Rugg also cites the work of Leaney (1989) and draws on Richardson's (1987) study to suggest that it was not only public health concerns that encouraged cemetery development, but also anxieties about disturbing the dead, and in commercial quarters, the entrepreneurial commodification of the corpse.

The embryonic medical profession developed a requirement for corpses for dissection and examination in order to enhance their knowledge of the nature of illness and to further understand the functioning of the human body. In England, the only legal source of cadavers were those of executed murderers. Insufficient in number, the shortfall led to the practice of body-snatching, whereby corpses of the recently dead were robbed or 'snatched', usually from the grave, and sold to the surgeons and anatomists. Although not a criminal offence (as in law no one can own a dead body), the 'theft' of corpses deeply offended the relatives of the deceased, whilst the potential fate of dissection filled people with horror. According to Richardson (1987), a popular belief in the resurrection of the body continued to exist. Dissection would, therefore, extinguish hopes of an afterlife.

She further asserts that this trade in dead bodies is evidence of the commodification of corpses that was also reflected in the undertaking industry (see chapter 12). To deter the activities of the body-snatchers, relatives and friends would have acted as watchers at the grave and wealthier people would have purchased equipment from undertakers, such as strong coffins and spiked railings that were set deep into the ground around the grave.

Overcrowded burial grounds and the activities of the body-snatchers meant that the dead were frequently disturbed in their graves and this was contrary to beliefs about the sanctity of the dead and the right to 'rest in peace'. The undertaking industry had made a substantial profit from the fear of body-snatching, and the new commercial cemeteries were particularly attractive to people desiring protection for their dead.

These cemeteries effectively removed control of burial provision from the Church and transferred it to the municipal authorities or to the jurisdiction of private companies. Like the older local burial grounds, the cemeteries continued to perpetuate distinctions of wealth, social class and status (Jupp, 1997). Although it was no longer possible to arrange burials so that they radiated from the centre to the outer precincts of the church according to status, the wealthy were able to purchase larger and more striking memorials for their dead, whilst the poor, often unable to even secure grave markers, were frequently interred in common graves or pits. As Cannadine (1981) remarked, the large cemeteries of nineteenth-century England allowed the middle classes to establish burial estates with grand mausoleums, located in accessible and prominent positions. Lefebvre (1974) goes on to suggest that these highly visible, vertical monuments symbolized the power of their owners, whereas horizontal burials, without markers, symbolize submission. Working-class people who were able to afford a cheap grave and so escape the ignominy of communal burial, were allocated limited space. Indeed, Porter noted that such graves in Leeds were 'so tightly crammed together that they became for all the world like a mocking reproduction of the back-to-backs in which their tenants once had dwelt' (1990: x).

During the second half of the twentieth century cemeteries became less flexible and allowed families reduced choice with regard to forms of memorialization. According to Rugg, the move to bland, indistinguishable memorials (reminiscent of the war graves from the First World War) might be regarded as attempts to suggest that the cemetery was beginning to reflect the 'classless' nature of society wherein all citizens were entitled, under the new welfare state, to expect care from the 'cradle to the grave' (1998: 124).

Nevertheless, cemeteries have retained ethnic and religious distinctions within their walls. There has always existed religious segregation both between cemeteries (for example, with cemeteries providing burial plots for either Catholics or Protestants) and within cemeteries (with space allocated according to ethnicity and religious preference). Thus, although some cemeteries may boast that they are multicultural, providing separate burial space, for example, for Muslim, Protestant and Greek Orthodox burials, this usually entails the spaces being laid out separately according to religious or ethnic divisions. In one of the largest cemeteries in the southern hemisphere, Rookwood Necropolis in Sydney, Australia, the land is divided according to religion and a walk around the grounds quickly alerts the visitor to the diverse styles of monuments and burial customs contained therein. In this respect, this city of the dead might be perceived as a mirror of the city of the living, whereby different ethnic groups tend to locate in particular geographical regions. For Nicol (2000) the status of migrants is significant in influencing the type of mortuary monument selected. In Australia, post-Second World War migration led to an evolution in monumental design and was extremely welcome to the failing monuments industry. A new style and scale of monument symbolized not only a connection with the migrant's homeland but also stood as a measure of success in the new world. As Walter, drawing on the work of Childe (1945), contends, 'it is those whose status is insecure who are likely to take most care over mortuary ritual and over memorialising their dead' (Walter, 1999: 49).

The changing nature of grief

From the late nineteenth century the nature of grief and Western practices around mourning began to change. Walter argues that, 'since Freud, bereavement theory has effectively abolished the dead' (1999: 24). This, he asserts, has occurred because society has become ever more individualized and the growth of anonymous urban centres has resulted in an emphasis on individual or private, rather than communal, loss. This privatization is reflected in the internalization of grief and the accompanying psychological rather than social focus on loss. Relocating the dead from the communities of the living to spaces on the edges of the cities has compounded this new way of thinking about, and dealing with, grief. For Walter, bereavement was an invention of the nineteenth-century Romantic Movement that, in quasi-secular form, focused on the death of others rather than concentrating (as encouraged by the Christian Church in the medieval period) on death as memento mori, a reminder that we all must die. In a period when middle-class women were afforded more leisure time, grief became feminized as they indulged their sorrow in public expressions such as the wearing of mourning clothing and making highly visible excursions to visit tombs in the new cemeteries. Conversely, men were expected to display emotional control and to distract themselves with work (Jalland, 1996). The gendered separation of spheres – with men associated with reason, work and the public sphere and women with emotion, family and the private sphere – identified women as grievers (Hockey, 2001a) and according to Morley (1971) women complained that this placed a heavy burden of mourning on their shoulders.

McManners (1981) supports Walter's assertion that the Victorian period witnessed a growing sentimentalization of death – for the middle classes at least. This period has been identified as a time characterized by a social and economic celebration of death (Curl, 1972; Morley, 1971) and something that the funeral industry and the cemetery movement exploited. For example, the necessary journey of the funeral procession from the home to the distant cemetery was (as is noted in chapter 12) an opportunity to utilize extravagant displays to project wealth and status. However, the new cemeteries may also have provided an opportunity for middle-class Victorians to satisfy their needs to visit and grieve at the graveside in a way that had not been possible at the former overcrowded and distasteful burial grounds (Rugg, 1998; Jalland, 1996). Memorialization was central to this expression of grief, as it gave mourners both a symbolic and a material focus.

The importance of memorialization in the social expression of grief can perhaps be best illustrated by the creation of public monuments of remembrance following the First World War. Almost every town or village in England and in many other countries in Europe, Australia and the USA erected public memorials to the dead of the First (and subsequently the Second) World War. Winter (1998) argues that war memorials are symbols of nationalism that provide a focus for the recognition of heroism in the service of the country. On specific occasions each year (such as Armistice Day in the UK, or Anzac Day in Australia), these memorials become the forum for ritual acts of public remembrance when nations engage in ceremonies designed to remember the dead and the sacrifice that they made. For Davies (1994), in Western societies these acts of remembrance are reminiscent of Christian rituals that emphasize sacrifice (the dead are fallen rather than killed) and redemption (having died that others [we] might live). Moreover, he argues that the efficacy of these rituals is conditional upon remembrance (lest we forget) and that to fail to remember is an act of betrayal (1994: 155). This accent on remembrance can also be observed in private acts of grief that focus on the memorial (or gravestone) of the individual and require visits to the grave, and other acts of remembrance. For example, in Victorian times these might include the wearing of mourning clothes, mourning jewellery and display of other physical reminders of the deceased. During the twentieth century, widow's 'weeds' became less commonplace, but visits to the graveside continued and the insertion of entries in the 'in memoriam' pages of local newspapers on the anniversary of deaths may be perceived as ongoing acts of remembrance.

Cremation

A further significant development in many Western societies during the nineteenth and twentieth centuries was the turn to cremation as a method of human disposal. Charting its establishment in the UK, Jupp (1990, 1997, 2001) tentatively suggests that an increase in secularization and the Protestant rejection of purgatory, which outlawed communion between the living and the dead, may have encouraged cremation in ostensibly Protestant, yet secular, countries such as Britain and Sweden. The late nineteenth-century cremation movement can be linked to public health concerns about the proper sanitary disposal of the corpse. Proponents of cremation tended to be utilitarian and secular in their beliefs and argued that cremation had advantages for public health as well as social and economic benefits. Thus, whilst disposing of the corpse in a clean and sanitary fashion, the practice would also be less costly and would, furthermore, save on valuable land space. In the UK a cremation society was established in 1874 and this was followed in Australia by the creation of similar societies in New South Wales and South Australia in 1890 and in the State of Victoria in 1892 (Nicol, 2000: 98). In Britain, the Cremation Act of 1902 provided the legal basis for the practice, although the cremation rate remained low until after the Second World War. Much of the opposition to cremation came from the funeral and cemetery industries and religious organizations, particularly the Catholic Church. Indeed, in countries such as Russia and China, cremation was used as an anti-religious tool (Jupp, 2001).

Although there were a number of cremations prior to the Second World War (some of which were not within the guidelines of the Cremation Act of 1902; see White, 1990), in the United Kingdom its increasing popularity has been explained by a number of factors. These are its utilization as a public health measure, as a response to secularization, by the pressure on land in urban and suburban areas, and the post-Second World War support from doctors, clergy and funeral directors (Jupp, 2001). Larger-scale immigration in the second half of the twentieth century from countries where cremation is preferred was undoubtedly a further factor that accounted for cremation rates soaring from 0.2 per cent in 1914 to 71 per cent in 1998/9.

There are many ethnic and religious groups for whom cremation is the preferred form of disposal of human remains. For example, cremation is the usual practice for Hindus, Sikhs and Buddhists. In the UK, cremation provision and uptake has undoubtedly been influenced by the presence of these groups. For example, many crematoria have built viewing platforms where Hindus are able to see the body of their loved one placed in the cremator, thereby adhering to their religious requirement to witness the body consigned to the flames. Although these platforms were originally provided for this religious purpose, non-Hindus now frequently use them. This Hindu disposal ritual has, therefore, not only altered the architecture of crematoria, but has also impacted on the funeral rituals of other ethnic groups in the UK and reflects the dynamic nature of death rituals.

As a relatively new practice in Western societies, the implications for the memorialization of the cremated dead are unclear. A study by Davies (1997) revealed that 86 per cent of those surveyed felt that there was no difference in terms of their memories of the dead between those who were buried and those cremated. If it remains the case that a tomb is important as a place for the bereaved to visit and commune with the dead, then, unless cremated ashes are subsequently buried in a churchyard (as happens in Wales) or in a cemetery, it could be that the bereaved will have no sacred space to visit. Nicol (2000) suggests that the scattering of ashes means that the dead may go unmemorialized. However, ethnic groups that have traditionally cremated appear to be no less able to remember the dead even if they remove the ashes, sometimes long distances, or return them to the 'homeland'. Similarly, families may retain ashes in the home or may scatter them in a place that was significant to the deceased. All of these practices allow the bereaved to memorialize the dead, usually in a physical location, whether or not this is within a place designed for the purpose. The dead may also be memorialized in books of remembrance held at the cemetery or crematorium, in plaques erected in public places (such as park benches) or, increasingly, on internet websites dedicated to the life and memory of the deceased.

This leads us to the important issue of the social implications of the nature of disposal and remembrance practices in contemporary Western societies.

Present and future directions in locating and remembering the dead

In our discussion so far we have noted that dedicated burial grounds of whatever nature are conducive to societies that are relatively fixed geographically and stable socially. These may be characterized by unilinear lines of descent whereby the dead are placed in the local graveyard or cemetery, visited by the living and form part of the nexus between the society of the living and the world of the dead. As Warner suggests, these social forms facilitate a belief in continuity and a reassurance that in death the individual will not be forgotten: 'The living's assurance of life everlasting is dependent on their keeping the dead alive.' The cemetery represents a 'visible symbol of this agreement among men [*sic*] that they will not let each other die' (1965: 365).

In contemporary Western societies the place of the dead is not so clearly defined. This can be illustrated by the rise in cremation, a practice that separates the funeral ceremony from the disposal ritual and requires the bereaved to make a decision about where the dead should be located. In societies characterized as secular, burial in consecrated ground is only one option among many. Moreover, the dead are ever more visible and ever more mobile. The latter is particularly apt following cremation where the heavy body is no longer pinned down in the ground but rather, as lightweight ashes, can travel easily from one location to another. Indeed, it may even be divided up amongst relatives and thus allow the dead to be in more than one place at any time. Hindus living in the UK, for example, may send a portion of the ashes to friends or relatives in India so that they may be deposited in the Holy River Ganges.

This mobility and visibility of the dead is not confined to the disposal practice of cremation, but is also recognizable in new forms of memorialization. The cemetery is no longer the only place for positioning flowers in commemoration of a death. For example, it is now common to find bouquets of flowers located at the scene of a tragic death, often by the roadside where a fatal accident has occurred. These symbols of grief, sorrow and loss are not only offered by the family and friends of the deceased but are also frequently brought to the scene by others who may not have known the person but nevertheless recognize the tragedy of the loss. This form of commemoration has been particularly noticeable at the scenes of major disasters where whole streets or whole football fields may be filled with flowers. A further example of the enhanced visibility of the dead is illustrated by a popular trend in cemeteries that now allow for a ceramic plaque with a photograph of the deceased to be displayed on the gravestone. In the USA some families have moved a step further by attaching a video monitor to the grave that contains a visual and textual record of the life of the deceased. Such video technology has also enabled dying people to leave memory images and messages for their loved ones to view after death. T-shirts exhibiting photographs of the dead (whether personally connected or those of celebrities such as Kurt Cobain and Che Guevara); lockets or pendants containing photographs, locks of hair, or small pieces of cremated remains (reminiscent of the mourning jewellery worn during the Victorian celebration of death); and memorial wall painting on buildings (DeSpelder and Strickland, 2005) are all testimony to the mobility of the dead and their increasing refusal to be restricted to the confines of burial plots.

Bloch (1971), in his discussion of the burial practices of Merina culture, argues that the fixed burial practices of unilinear descent groups enable people to achieve a sense of belonging to a community that has always existed and that has value and meaning beyond the immediate events of the present. These descent patterns require fixed and stable communities such as those prevalent in pre-twentieth-century Western societies. During the twentieth century, however, and some would argue with the beginnings of postmodernity, Western societies have become increasingly socially fragmented. Populations are more mobile, both geographically and socially, and the traditions of fixed communities in which individuals are known to each other largely dissipated after the 1950s and '60s. Moreover, traditional kinship networks have changed radically with family networks demonstrating significant trends towards patterns of single-parent and second-family households. Minority ethnic communities may retain strong kinship networks but although these have developed from traditional forms they have adapted to Western social environments, and many relationships may be conducted across thousands of miles. This has implications for our relationships with the dead. The unilinear lines of descent that assume traditional nuclear or extended family kinship networks, firmly located within a specific geographical area, are no longer the norm in contemporary Western societies. Bloch cites Sahlins (1961), who points to the existence of segmentary lineages as an alternative to unilinear models that allow society members to retain their links with one another, and with the dead, whilst enabling them to 'foray far and wide' (Bloch, 1971: 217). It could be argued that this concept is pertinent to the analysis of descent lines in contemporary Western societies. It may be that rather than adopting the notion of segmentary lines, fragmentary lines of descent might be more appropriate as societies and communities within them are ever more socially and geographically disjointed. Such fragmented patterns enable mobility and visibility to both the living and the dead who may now accompany them. Moreover, it may be that rituals that are bringing the dead out of the cemeteries, together with fragmented descent groups, are forcing us to question the hitherto accepted boundaries between life and death.

Summary

This chapter has explored a range of practices and explanations for the manner in which humans dispose of their dead. It began by asking questions about the purpose of disposal rituals and the reasons for choosing to place the dead in particular locations. The discussion suggested that in pre-modern societies, disposal and remembrance rituals were usually designed to assist the dead on their journey to the afterlife. In so doing, for societies that engaged in ancestor worship the appropriate ritual treatment of the dead ensured their place in the ancestral fold and would result in the dead reciprocating by interceding on behalf of the living in times of crisis. We noted, however, that some communities feared the dead and that ritualizing disposal was important in order to guarantee that the dead would not return to the world of the living.

In turning to consider the role that attitudes to the corpse played in disposal and memorial practice, the chapter examined the late eighteenth-century and nineteenth-century development of the extramural cemetery in Western societies. A public health movement that was concerned about the risk to health emanating from the overcrowded burial grounds in part prompted this. It was also suggested that social disquiet about the disturbance of bodies in their graves was a further element in abandoning local urban churchyards. The commodification of the corpse, cited by Richardson in her study of body-snatchers, and the commercialization of funerals and memorialization also contributed to this dramatic change in the location of the dead which further encouraged a binary division between life and death.

Changing patterns of grief during the nineteenth century were also examined, as was the gendered and class-ridden nature of grief-work and memorialization. Agitation for cremation, which began in the latter part of the nineteenth century, reflected concerns with public health but was also testimony to secularization trends and to increasing multicultural influences, which grew during the second half of the twentieth century. The turn to cremation that was witnessed in both secular and historically Protestant societies has prompted questions about the appropriate disposal of cremated remains or ashes.

The final section of the chapter explored the implications of the increased mobility and visibility of the dead. It argued that rather than being characterized by unilinear descent groups (that are fixed and stable over generations) contemporary Western societies may be more appropriately perceived as having segmentary or fragmented descent groups that reflect the social mobility of the living and of the dead. The chapter concluded by asking whether the development of fragmented descent groups and rituals for placing and memorializing the dead that enable the dead to be more mobile are effectively beginning to break down the boundaries between life and death. This is a question to which we will return in the final chapter.

12

Mortuary Rituals

Introduction

In the last chapter we considered the nature of relationships between the living and the dead and how these impact on practices of remembrance. Here we will build on that discussion and that of chapter 10, which looked at the nature of grief, to examine after-death rituals. The concept of mortuary rituals covers a range of behaviours and ceremonies. There are rituals that are primarily designed to deal with the social impact of death, and others that are of a more personal nature that help the individual to deal with loss. Rituals may also be public or private; some may combine public and private acts; some rituals may be personal. An obvious example of a public ritual is the funeral. Funerals are public ceremonies that allow bereaved people to make the death public, to make sense of their loss according to whatever cultural, religious or personal framework they use for the ceremony, to place the dead person in their social context, and to mark their own changing status. On occasions the funeral may publicly re-establish social hierarchies. In some communities there may be two funerals – one which takes place soon after death and a second which occurs after a set period time when the body has largely decomposed and the soul completed its journey to the afterlife (Danforth, 1982). All these rituals can be perceived as strategies for the symbolic transformation of death from an event that creates disorder to one that reinforces social structures and personal meaning systems.

A further element in an exploration of death rituals must bring an awareness of their dynamic nature. Society is dynamic and continually changing, and this is also true of the rituals it adopts to generate meaning as it relates to death. As societies become more culturally diverse, death rituals become more differentiated and numerous. Cultural groups may discard, retain or revise traditional rituals as well as develop new ones. This is particularly the case in modern, increasingly multicultural societies where rituals may be adapted to take account of the practices of dominant or minority ethnic groups.

The discussion that follows will examine the nature of funeral rituals in traditional and contemporary societies. In so doing it will utilize some of the theoretical insights offered from anthropology and history, and will draw attention to the political nature of state funerals and the way in which mortuary rituals can be employed as a resistance to political systems. Mortuary rites will then be considered in the context of the Western funeral industry. Critiques of contemporary funeral expertise have, like those that critique medicalization, tended to focus on the disempowerment of their clients. A further feature of the condemnation has been the commercialization of funeral practice in Western societies. Both of these concerns will be examined in depth. The chapter ends by addressing the natural death movement and related attempts to undermine both the professionalization and the commercialization of after-death rituals.

Some theoretical frameworks for understanding mortuary rites

Much sociological theorizing of mortuary rituals derives from the anthropological record. The groundbreaking work of Robert Hertz (1960 [1907]) (a student of Durkheim who identified himself as a sociologist) outlined three primary explanations for the nature and purpose of funerals: the disposal of the corpse, to intercede in the fate of the soul and to reintegrate mourners into the social fabric. Let us briefly consider each.

Disposal of the corpse

Hertz suggested that in traditional societies such as the Dayak of Borneo, the dead body is considered to be a source of pollution and requires double burial. After death the body would be isolated from the community and left for a number of years, exposed on a platform in the branches of trees. This, Hertz referred to as the 'wet' stage, when the flesh was in the process of decay. During this time the corpse would slowly lose its contaminating elements as the flesh decomposed leaving only the bones. Once the bones were dry (the 'dry' stage) the corpse would undergo a second burial. Secondary burials are not an uncommon feature of traditional societies, especially in a rural context. According to this practice, the body is left either exposed, in a container, or sometimes buried in the earth, and subsequently removed from this place in order for any remaining flesh to be removed from the skeleton. Once the bones are clean, they undergo a secondary burial, usually with an appropriate burial ritual. Danforth (1982) has found that secondary burials continue to take place in some areas of the Mediterranean. According to Greek Orthodox practice, relatives may exhume the bodies of their dead in order to clean the bones and reinter the deceased in the village ossuary. Of particular note here is that the ritual cleaning of bones is undertaken by the women of the family. It has been argued elsewhere (Harding, 1986) that women are perceived as being closer to nature than men. As a consequence of this they are viewed as being less at risk of pollution than men, and, as the natural arbiters between the sacred and the profane, they are able to perform otherwise polluting tasks.

The fate of the soul

In his discussion of the fate of the soul, Hertz shows how the corpse, mourners and soul are interconnected. Each undergoes transition from the everyday world of the profane to the separate realm of the sacred. In the context of the soul, following secondary burial the deceased has been fully released from the material world and is relocated among the ancestors. As such, the dead take on a new identity as a benevolent forebear with the duties and responsibilities that this may entail. In this way, Hertz demonstrated that the dead continue to 'live on as social beings in the memory of survivors, despite the demise of their bodies' (Hockey, 2001b: 237).

The reintegration of mourners

The journey of transition undertaken by the deceased is reflected in the changing status of the mourners, whose proximity to the profane (in the guise of the corpse) is perceived as a source of danger for the community. Once the deceased has been transformed to the afterlife and charged with ancestral responsibilities, the mourners may become fully reintegrated into the social life of the group.

Implicit within Hertz's analysis is the concept of transition. Van Gennep (1960 [1909]), an anthropologist, demonstrated that rituals of transition share a similar structure and could be utilized to understand the key rites of passage in societies. These might include birth, initiation rites, marriage and death, and were identified as containing a tripartite structure. This structure encompassed rituals of separation, threshold rites and rites of aggregation or incorporation. In other words, people lost a particular status then entered a period of liminality or ambiguous time before, finally, entering the third stage of re-entry into a new social status. Whilst in traditional societies, such as the Dayak, the liminal status of the bereaved may last from the death of a loved one until the second burial (possibly some years later), among secular groups in Western societies it may be regarded as the period between death and the completion of the funeral ceremony. In the transition from the social status of wife to widow, for example, there are now few rituals to acknowledge the ambiguities and struggles that may take place in such a liminal and time-limited period (Littlewood, 1993). This can be compared to periods of mourning established in the nineteenth century when the liminal period may have spanned a number of years.

A further theoretical strand to the understanding of mortuary rituals is that they serve to repair the social order. Douglas (1966) pointed to the problem of pollution that was associated with disorder. Thus, rather than viewing 'dirt' as something inherently flawed or polluted, she argued that it was simply 'matter out of place', defined negatively as a consequence of the social disorder it generated. Death has a similar effect in that it disrupts the social order. Funeral rites can, from this perspective, be regarded as attempts to achieve symbolic resolution of ambiguous social and political relations. This is particularly resonant with the death of kings (Metcalf and Huntington, 1991) and other elite or notable public figures. During the medieval period in Western Europe and in some indigenous societies, effigies were constructed to substitute the decaying bodies of royalty and aristocracy (Giesey, 1960; Gittings, 1984; Evans-Pritchard, 1948). As Metcalf and Huntington comment:

> In many respects, the meaning of the royal effigy in France ... [was that] it came to stand for the perpetuity of kingship, and the French nation ... [t]he triumph of death versus the triumph over death, church ritual versus state ritual, grief versus joy, all revolving around the body of the mortal king and the effigy of the immortal royal dignity. (1991: 174)

This analysis might be summed up in the English cry following the death of the king: 'The king is dead, long live the king!'

Although effigies may no longer be commonplace in elite funerals, mortuary rites do continue to perform a role in nation building and the construction of political discourses. Death in war frequently gives rise to public funeral rites (especially when the bodies of those killed are returned to their homeland) or rituals of commemoration of war dead. These may occur annually or on specific anniversaries. For example, in Australia and New Zealand Anzac Day is celebrated on 25 April each year as this was the day in 1915 when soldiers from Australia and New Zealand landed at a geographical location in Gallipoli, later renamed 'Anzac Cove'. The personal and social losses that resulted from the Gallipoli Campaign are ritualized by dawn ceremonies and street parades. These rituals service a political/nation (public) building purpose, but can also be meaningful on an individual (personal or private) level. A further example of the political uses of mortuary rituals was the state funeral of the USA President John F. Kennedy, when the US nation was unified in its grief. A similar political interpretation of death is that inherent in the North American response to the deaths that occurred as a result of the destruction of the World Trade Center on 11 September 2001. Whilst the nation grieved, it also committed to the continuance of social order and resolutely condemned any action that might be perceived as dragging it into the type of chaos identified by the government as the goal of the terrorists. Funeral rites may also serve political purposes that are contrary to the maintenance of social order. For example, in South Africa during the apartheid regime and throughout 'the troubles' in Northern Ireland, public funeral rites were utilized as symbols of struggle and resistance to the establishment.

Let us now turn to consider the development of mortuary rites in contemporary Western societies and, in particular, to the changing role and position of funeral workers.

The development of the funeral industry

There are very few societies that dispose of their dead without ceremony. In Western societies, when it is not possible to hold a funeral due to the loss of the body of the deceased, family and friends may feel emotionally and ritually disabled. Funeral rituals help society and bereaved individuals to acknowledge publicly the loss of the deceased. In Western societies the dominant trend in funerals is for these to be organised by an expert funeral director, some of whom may specialize in funerals for specific ethnic groups, such as Muslims or Jews. Funeral directors are usually delegated responsibility for taking custody of the corpse, preparing the body for the funeral, organizing the funeral ceremony and ensuring that everything runs smoothly and according to 'acceptable' ritual practice. For some minority ethnic groups, however, the bereaved family may take control of certain elements of the ritual. For example, it is usual for Muslims to prepare the body of the deceased. Ritual washing and purification may be carried out by a professional washer or by family members (of the same sex as the deceased). I have argued elsewhere (Howarth, 1996) that funeral directors are the key to understanding the structure of funeral rituals. They advise and guide the bereaved family and friends in their choice of disposal ritual and then direct the drama of the funeral ceremony. Although rituals vary according to ethnic, religious and social class expectations, bereaved people commonly rely on the expertise of the funeral directors to deal with bureaucratic tasks and to give them cues to appropriate behaviour. In geographical areas that lack a funeral director with expertise in minority ethnic rituals, relatives may use the premises of a less specialized funeral director and instruct him or her in important elements of funeral ritual and organization. Indeed, practice manuals for funeral directors commonly adopt a 'factfile' (see chapter 7) approach to the rituals of minority ethnic groups.

The roots of the modern Western funeral director can be found in the heraldic traditions of early Europe with its emphasis, in the funerals of the elite, on pomp and ceremony. Whilst artisans were responsible for making coffins, the first distinct undertaking business in England was not established until the latter decades of the seventeenth century. This development needs to be understood as a consequence of a combination of factors. These include a lessening of the emphasis on funerals as providing assistance to the dead (that is, a concern for the fate of the soul), and consequent reduction in the role of the priest; increased individualism and the effects of urbanization; and the commercialization of death (Howarth, 1997a). We will consider each.

From care of the dead to care of the living

In Protestant Europe, the rejection of purgatory led people to question the value of death rites for the salvation of the deceased. Thus, the efficacy of practices such as praying for the souls of the dead came to be viewed with scepticism. In time, funerals came to be viewed less from the perspective of the future of the deceased and more as rituals for providing assistance to the bereaved. Efforts previously employed in praying for the dead were transferred to the care and protection of the corpse (Houlbrooke, 1989). Furthermore, the deathbed rituals of the Middle Ages, where the priest had performed such a central role, began to lose their authority as the sickroom and dying came to be viewed as the domain of the doctor. In keeping with this development towards the secularization of death, the undertaker came to take responsibility for the care, protection and control of the corpse.

Increasing individualism and urbanization

Gittings (1984) argues that a growth in individualism heightened awareness of the significance of the distinction between life and death. An expanding consciousness of the self led to a desire to mark and mourn loss in a new, more privatized fashion, resulting in an expression of grief that was affirmed through an intensified nuclear family (McManners, 1981). With rapid urbanization and industrialization, there was less time and fewer individuals available to organize funeral rituals. In this social environment, handing over the role to an expert would recoup time and unburden the family (Howarth, 1997a).

The commercialization of death

With the spiralling demand for a specialist agency to release individuals from the tasks of funeral organization, the funeral industry came, initially, to be viewed as a trade of convenience. As such, the embryonic industry developed four commercial strands to its

practice: the promotion of funereal goods and services; the purchase of corpses for dissection; the provision of cemeteries; and the
burial club movement (Howarth, 1997a). Each of those enabled the
industry to play a controlling role in after-death rituals and led to
the increased commercialization of funeral practices. Notably, each
of these elements neglected the care of the soul of the deceased
and, in modern societies, the industry has come to focus on the
disposal of the corpse and the needs of mourners.

It was the increasing commercial extravagance of funerals during
the Victorian period that resulted in calls for reform. By the early
decades of the nineteenth century funerals were becoming more
elaborate. After death the family would consult the undertaker and
associated trades (such as the carpenter and draper) to determine
the design of the funeral and the extent of expenditure according
to social status. Funeral rituals involved adherence to strict social
codes that dictated the nature of the ritual and the extent of display
and exhibition associated with it. The undertakers of the emerging
funeral industry would advise mourners of the funeral requirements appropriate to their social status. At the poorer end of the
social scale, and at great cost relative to their income, families might
purchase or hire hats, hatbands, gloves and scarves for the mourners
in attendance. Cannon (1969) reproduces the report of John
Stanley James, of the funeral of a young boy in Australia:

> It was attended only by a 'meek and careworn-looking
> woman ... [and] a little child' who were clad in old rustic black
> garments, apparently bought from a pawn or second-hand shop.
> The single mourning coach did double duty as a hearse. There
> was nothing and no-one else. (Cannon, 1969: 70)

At the other end of the social hierarchy, funerals could be
extremely elaborate affairs, and mutes, pages and feathermen would
accompany black-clad mourners in the funeral procession. The
coffin resided in an ornate hearse, pulled by horses with black
plumes of feathers on their heads (Morley, 1971; Griffin and Tobin,
1997).[1] Thus, the cost and nature of funerals demonstrated the
social class status of the deceased and their family. As such, these
nineteenth-century funerals were utilized as a means of displaying

status and power in society. The pauper funeral, entailing anony-mous burial in a mass grave, underscored the class basis of society.

By the middle of the nineteenth century there was growing concern, in the UK in particular, about expenditure on funerals. According to Chadwick's 1843 Report, the sum of £4–5 million was 'annually thrown into the grave' – a sizeable sum for the period. Perhaps surprisingly, a substantial element of this expenditure was devoted to the funerals of the poor who, through the provision of burial insurance, had finally managed to secure 'decent' funerals akin to those long enjoyed by the middle classes. Their expenditure, however, was readily condemned by the wealthier sectors of society who adopted the stereotype of a working class that would rather see their children starve than undergo a pauper burial. In all likeli-hood, one element of this condemnation was a fear of the risk of contamination by a diseased poor (who provided labour and serv-ices to the wealthier classes) who were said to be storing dead bodies until they were able to pay for the funeral.

Most campaigners for reform laid the primary responsibility for extravagance at the door of the undertaker. These deathworkers were depicted as greedy, heartless men feeding from the anxieties of people subsumed within an entrenched system of social class with its accompanying expectations of status-linked behaviour.[2]

Reform and expertise

Declining infant mortality rates

Towards the end of the nineteenth century the work of the reform-ers started to take effect as death began to go out of fashion (Jacobs, 1899). Greater understanding of nutrition, public health and sanita-tion contributed to a radical shift in mortality, with infant mortality rates declining from the end of the century. Thus, for the first time in history, adults (from the wealthier classes) could expect their children to outlive them (Mitchison, 1977). As mortality came to loosen its grip on life, romantic representations of death, prevalent in the nineteenth century, held less attraction. The flamboyance and ceremony of funeral rites dissipated and they became much quieter and simpler affairs. However, whilst extravagant funerals became less familiar among the middle class, many of the practices with which they were associated survived in the funerals of the poor until well into the twentieth century. The discrepancy in changing patterns of mortality may partly explain this, as the improvements to health that accompanied the decline in mortality rates was negligible among the working classes until the interwar period of the twentieth century (Mitchison, 1977). Death continued to be a familiar event for working–class people and, therefore, was given a significant place symbolically, in both the appropriate disposal of the corpse and the reintegration of mourners into the social order (Howarth, 1997a).

The modern funeral expert

The twentieth century witnessed a great deal of innovation in funeral practice. The criticisms of the reform movement of the nineteenth century meant that if the industry was to survive it had to reinvent itself. It achieved this by adopting the language of the reformers and by focusing on a potential role in protecting public health. In so doing, it relinquished much of the flamboyance associated with Victorian funerals and chose instead to emphasize scientific expertise in the sanitary disposal of remains, and the psychological care of mourners. As I have elsewhere contended, '[i]n responding to the nineteenth-century reform movement undertakers adopted the rhetoric of public health and protection, and (like the medical profession) they have exposed death to science. Rather than tame it, they have sanitised it' (Howarth, 1997a: 132).

In harnessing the discourse of twentieth-century medical science, undertakers (or funeral directors as they became known in the 1930s and 1940s[3]) aspired to achieve professional respectability. Millerson (1964) lists a number of characteristics that distinguish an occupation as professional. These are: skill based on theoretical knowledge; training and education; demonstration of competence by passing an exam; maintenance of integrity by adhering to a code of conduct; developing a professional organization; and the provision of a service for the public good. Funeral directors in Western societies have, throughout the twentieth century, cultivated each of these characteristics, with most notable success in the USA, where funeral directors have developed professional education and training courses and successfully lobbied governments to legislate the requirements for practitioners. The combination of these elements of professionalism reflects the acquisition of knowledge and power by groups of experts. Foucault (1980) draws our attention to the development of dominant discourses built on the creation and acquisition of expert knowledge. This knowledge is restricted to members of the expert group and its exclusivity invests it with power. Thus, those who are familiar with the discourses of expert knowledge have access to the power that is its corollary. In the case of funeral directors, knowledge was created in two ways. First, responsibility was removed from lay people and thereby common knowledge of practices associated with the care of the dead was undermined. Second, the funeral industry developed new forms of knowledge that utilized technology and science in the care of the dead and, in so doing, drew from medico-psychological knowledge of the care of the bereaved.

A primary example of the use of medical science frameworks in the furtherance of professionalization is clear in the case of deathworkers in the USA. A central plank in their drive to professionalization was the technique of embalming, with its requirement for specialist knowledge and training. In the early part of the twentieth century in the USA, embalming was considered to provide a key to professional respectability. As a technique for the temporary preservation of dead bodies, it was regarded as a visible demonstration of the expertise of the funeral director. Indeed, so powerful was this tool that Professor George B. Dodge, President of the Massachusetts College of Embalming, found it difficult to understand why the British industry had not wholeheartedly embraced the technique.

> Why every undertaker in this country does not prepare himself to use these methods . . . is something that is very hard to understand. The reputation he would gain for keeping bodies in good condition would rapidly spread and give him a vast advantage

over his competitors who do absolutely nothing to prevent those most disagreeable conditions. (*Undertakers Journal*, January 1910; cited in Howarth, 1997a: 129)

A related feature of funeral practice is the provision of housing for the corpse – a service assumed both to be welcomed by the bereaved and to reduce the danger to public health posed by the dead body. In Britain, during the interwar years in the first half of the twentieth century, the corpse was gradually relocated from the home to the funeral parlour. In tandem with this was legislation that barred midwives from laying out dead bodies (the traditional neighbourhood layer-out) and the exclusion by male funeral directors of women from body-handling work. The effect of this was to establish tasks associated with the care of the body as the work of male experts. Their preference to acquire and utilize scientific techniques not only redefined their knowledge base, it also functioned to exclude 'non-professionals' from their trade.

The modern funeral industry

Organizing a funeral is something most people in Western societies are rarely required to do. It is considered normal, and indeed expected, that bereaved people will turn to the funeral director to organize the ritual and to provide information about the appropriate nature of the ceremony. This includes advice on the type and extent of funeral goods and services, whether or not embalming and viewing should be recommended and guidance in making 'appropriate' funeral decisions that reflect their concern to do, and be seen to have done, the 'right thing' for the deceased (Howarth, 1996). For some, this might be regarded as an important time-saving service that provides essential clues to ritual conduct. For others, the funeral industry is viewed as a centre of expertise that not only creates but also polices social expectations around funeral ritual. From this latter perspective, these deathworkers are perceived as utilizing scientific techniques to establish norms, and in so doing are disempowering their clients (Smale, 1997; Young, 1996).

In similar vein to the criticisms levelled at the medical profession during the 1960s, '70s and '80s, the funeral director has been lambasted as a source of unreasonable expenditure and disempowerment of the bereaved (Mitford, 1963). At the end of the twentieth century funeral reformers were once again at work in exposing the unprofessional practices within the industry. They condemned what they regarded as exorbitant expenditure on funerals (see, for example, the Office of Fair Trading Report, 1989) but, perhaps more significantly, they pointed to the lack of meaning in current ritual practice (Albery et al., 1993; Walter, 1994; Young, 1996). This loss of meaning has been associated with the attempts to professionalize deathwork (Clark, 1982; Smale, 1997) and with the loss of individual control over the ritual preparation of the body and the organization of the funeral ceremony (Spottiswood, 1991). Others have remarked on the perfunctory manner in which the ceremony is conducted and the limited time allocated for use of the cemetery or crematorium chapel (Walter, 1990; Young, 1996).

By the 1960s a movement to reduce the cost of funerals was under way, expounding the virtues of cheap, low-profile and predominantly functional funerals. These funeral packages appear to be attractive to all economic classes, some preferring them for their simplicity and others for the accessibility of the prices. There are those, however, who would argue that taken to its logical conclusion, simplicity becomes the opposite extreme to extravagance. For them, the purely functional disposal of human remains, seen in some parts of the USA, is considered even more abhorrent than the wasteful expenditure and opulence of the nineteenth century. Funeral rituals affirm social and individual relationships and values; to bury or cremate with little or no preceding ceremony may be regarded as a degradation of human life and a devaluation of ethnic, religious and national identities.

These rushed ceremonies that appear to lack ritual substance are not usually found in funerals of minority ethnic groups where funeral directors and cemetery and crematorium staff expect that traditional religious preferences should be honoured. As a result, funerals are often lengthy and may be considered by people from other ethnic groups to be flamboyant. Indeed, it may be that 'outsider' observations of the apparent depth of meaning in minority ethnic funerals have fuelled the sense of dissatisfaction with Protestant and secular rituals noted above.

A further movement that emerged in the 1980s as a critique and alternative to the high-cost, professionally controlled funeral was the 'natural death movement' (Albery et al., 1993). This gained a foothold in countries such as the UK, Australia and in some parts of the USA and Canada. Its remit was to undermine the control of the experts in after-death rituals and to allow individuals to exert greater control. As the title suggests, the objective was to move away from scientific techniques and return to a more 'natural' way of death. Whilst the question of what is 'natural' is debatable, it is clear these attempts to challenge the monopoly of the funeral profession have had some successes. For example, there is now provision in many Western countries for woodland burials and other forms of disposal that are more environmentally friendly than the traditional grave-plot or cremation in an urban crematorium.

A further key development in funeral practice is the growth of multinational funeral companies. For example, by the end of the twentieth century Service Corporation International, a company established in the USA, owned 14 per cent of the British funeral industry, 25 per cent of the Australian funeral industry and 28 per cent of the French industry. Whilst companies like this can offer clients the benefits of economies of scale, there is, nevertheless, a risk that funerals will become less personalized and less culturally distinct. In a world increasingly depicted as a global society, these multinational companies may work to undermine cultural traditions and possibly stimulate a 'McDonaldization' (Ritzer, 1996) of mortuary rituals.

Diversity in funeral rituals

Whilst many of these criticisms of the modern funeral profession are valid, it is worth considering the extent to which the critics of current practice are aware of the diverse nature of funeral rites in Western societies. I have argued (Howarth, 1997b) that it may be that many of those who criticize modern funeral rites do so from a perspective that assumes (1) that all funerals take the same form, and (2) that a return to former, more religious obsequies may offer a more satisfactory solution to the problems of corpse disposal and social reintegration.

The assumption that, due to the input of the funeral industry, most funerals adhere to the same pattern is fallacious. If, for example, we examine the migrant societies of the USA and Australia, it is clear that it is not possible to speak in any meaningful way of a singular contemporary disposal ritual. At the most basic level, funerals will differ according to a preference for cremation or burial, and in line with religious affiliation. Further distinctions emerge that reflect migration patterns and religious and ethnic preferences established during the nineteenth and twentieth centuries, and other social characteristics such as class, age and gender.

Western societies are increasingly multicultural, peopled by a diversity of ethnic and religious communities each of which is likely to uphold more or less distinct rites of passage that have been adapted to meet the social and environmental demands of the society in which they live. Funeral ceremonies, like other transition rituals, provide opportunities for preserving cultural traditions and also for providing a sense of continuity with the old world. Funerals are important in preserving cultural traditions, but traditional rituals are rarely as static as they may sometimes appear. When groups migrate from one location or country to another, they bring with them distinct rituals. Furthermore, these rituals are adapted to take account of the physical, social and cultural climate of the land and communities in which they are practised. For example, when Anglo-Saxon funeral rituals were transported from England to Australia and the USA in the late eighteenth and nineteenth centuries, they evolved to suit the climate and social requirements of the emerging nation (Howarth, 2000a). In Australia, the religious dominance of the Anglican Church eventually succumbed to recognition of other denominations. The scarcity of priests in the early days of the colony meant that certain public officials and other lay people were empowered to conduct the rituals and read the burial service. Indeed, this may have been significant in the trend towards secularization and a general resistance to religious dominance over death rituals.[4] The official monopoly of the Church to conduct funeral rituals was finally broken in 1973, and by 1988 funeral celebrants were conducting 25 per cent of funerals in Melbourne (Spender, 1988: 46). The lack of formal places of worship meant that funerals were normally conducted in the home, again undermining the dominance of the Church, which had been such an emblem of English funeral rituals. This example illustrates that it is possible for distinct ethnic groups to retain their cultural traditions whilst adapting, and contributing to, the developing social climate of the nation.

Migrants to other Western nations have brought with them the funeral traditions of their national, ethnic and religious communities. The Anglican dominance within ostensibly Protestant countries such as Britain and the USA has been undermined by the Orthodox traditions of Greek, Russian and Macedonian migrants, with Irish Catholicism augmented by the Roman Catholicism of Italian communities. Later migrants brought Muslim funeral rituals from countries such as Turkey and Albania; immigrants have introduced Hindu ceremonies from India and Sri Lanka, and Buddhist practices from Vietnam and Malaysia. In the USA, people from Mexican communities tend to view life as transient and their seemingly flamboyant mortuary rituals represent a mix of Catholic and indigenous traditions (Irish, 1997).

Social class, age and gender

The funeral ceremonies of all ethnic groups inevitably vary according to a range of social factors such as social class or status, age and gender. The importance of social class in the provision of nineteenth-century funerals and the move towards low-cost, simple funerals has already been noted. Although social class may not be such a clearly differentiating factor in contemporary funerals, it is certain that the cost of funeral goods and services will privilege the purchasing power of wealthier sections of society.

A further factor in differential mortality practice is the change in mortality rates, with death now more likely to come in old age rather than infancy. This phenomenon has resulted in the existence of large and increasingly aged, often relatively poor, sectors of populations. In terms of funerals, this has led to the success of the pre-paid package. As people approach late middle age, they are not only prompted to consider later life and their pension needs, but also to contemplate death and the purchase of a personal funeral plan. The most frequently stated advantages of the pre-paid packages are that tomorrow's funeral may be purchased at today's prices; and that they allow elderly people to design their own ceremonies and make their funeral wishes known rather than leaving the decisions and burden to grief-stricken relatives.

Gender differences may also account for variations in the contemporary funeral rituals of modern societies. For example, some ethnic and religious practices may stipulate the appropriate gender of those who wash the body, attend the religious service and accompany the corpse to the grave, women commonly being excluded from many of these rituals. Griffin and Tobin (1997) also remark on gendered assumptions about the relationship that men and women have with death. They note, with reference to a nineteenth-century Australian engraving of a funeral ceremony, that, 'the women are shown to be grieving while the men celebrate the continuity of life. This sex-role stereotyping was an accurate reflection of social practice. It still tends to be true, particularly in that part of the Australian community which is heavily Anglo-Saxon in its style' (1997: 165). With respect to the funeral industry itself, we have already observed that, since its creation, the industry has been a largely male preserve. This, however, is beginning to change, as the image projected by the industry is now more concerned with care and counselling than with retaining a more objective, male detached persona.

Summary

This chapter has explored some of the key characteristics of mortuary rituals in both traditional and modern societies. It has examined the classic work of Hertz, an anthropologist who drew attention to the interconnections between the fate of the soul of the deceased and the social reintegration of mourners. The potentially polluting nature of the corpse was also discussed in the context of Douglas's (1966) theories of social order and disorder. The political potential of funeral rituals was also noted. Examples were given of the significant use of effigies and the transference of power in the funerals of medieval kings. The importance of funeral rituals in nation building, during wars and following events that stimulate national crises such as the destruction of the World Trade Center in New York in September 2001, were also discussed.

The creation and development of Western funeral industries were considered, with particular emphasis placed on their emergence in seventeenth-century England. This development was explored in the context of a reduction in the prominence of the role of the priest, increased individualism, urbanization and the commodification of death. Campaigns to reform the funeral industry – to curb extravagance in the nineteenth and early twentieth centuries, and to undermine their control over after-death rituals in the late twentieth century – were also explored. The chapter concluded by suggesting that some of the recent calls for reform have been voiced by commentators with little understanding of the diverse nature of funeral rituals. The effect of ethnic, religious and social class identity was discussed together with recognition of the significance of age and gender in the composition and direction of funeral rituals.

Conclusion:
Resurrecting Death?

Introduction

This book began by asking the question of how societies make meaning in the face of mortality. Our examination of this question has been set in the context of changing societies and has focused on contemporary Western societies. In a book entitled *The Revival of Death*, Walter (1994) argued that there has been a revival of interest in death, especially in relation to the care of dying and bereaved people. This growing recognition of the importance of death in contemporary Western societies has been explored in this text through attitudes to mortality; religious, spiritual and media approaches; the care of dying and bereaved people; understandings of the dying and dead body; and the nature of memorialization and funeral rituals. This concluding chapter will look more closely at the apparent resurgence of interest in mortality and consider what this suggests about the nature of Western societies and the modern expectation of a strict boundary between life and death. The discussion will also address three key theoretical positions that have arisen in the detailed discussions of aspects of mortality. First, that contemporary societies have been conceptualized as 'risk' societies and, more precisely, Prior's (1989) assertion that in Western societies death has come to be seen as a risk rather than a certainty. Second, that contemporary Western societies have been identified as individualist (as opposed to collectivist) in that mortality is made sense of at the level of the individual with each person constructing their own meaning rather than as members of communities. Third, in conjunction with the issue of individualism, the discussion will also address the question as to whether a 'psychologized self' (which incorporates a 'denial of death') is the defining characteristic of the Western relationship with death.

Risk and certainty

Modernity: a separation of spheres

The transitional nature of death in pre-modern societies, where rites of passage influenced the fate of the soul and its journey into the next life, has been replaced in modernity with rites of passage that account for the exit from this life without fully engaging with, or arguably, denying, the transit to the next. In modern societies rites of passage for the dead (found, for example, in the hospital, the coroner's court and the crematorium) have tended to focus on a change in status from 'dying' to 'dead' or 'alive' to 'dead' (depending on whether the death was protracted or sudden). An afterlife is no longer a certainty, only a possibility.

Throughout modernity death has progressively been seen as final, as an end to life, and has been located within a framework of control and separation. With the supreme dominance of science there has been a separation between the known and the unknown (or even the unknowable). Scientific models of understanding have been based on concepts of 'knowledge' and 'truth' and, as Popper (1945) has suggested, although we may not know when we have found truth we nevertheless acknowledge it as an objective reality. This does not mean that religion has been rejected per se but that it has been constructed as a belief system rather than a scientific truth. The implication is that the status of religion has lessened and been pitted against the high status of scientific, knowable truths in society. Religious experiences (including those, such as near-death experiences, which connect this world with the next) have been broadly categorized as separate from the material concerns of our earthly existence.

As a consequence of this separation between spiritual and material matters and the striving to control the mortal world, life and death have been constructed as a dualism, a central element of which has been the creation of boundaries between the two. These boundaries have been built and policed within structures of professional expertise, for example, in the form of the priest, the coroner and the psychiatrist.

One feature of this separation of spheres is the refusal by the established Christian Church to embrace, acknowledge or countenance communication between the living and the dead. On occasions when the two worlds appear to meet, such as the occurrence of ghostly apparitions or other occult phenomena, these are usually dealt with in one of two ways. First, in extreme cases of haunting, the Church may consider some form of exorcism, requiring the professional skills of a priest. As Hockey observed in her study of Anglican responses to the occult, the 'minister's starting point is the authority of the Church of England. He invokes a privileged access to the sacred' (Hallam et al., 1999: 175). The second mechanism for dealing with such phenomena is medical science in the guise of psychiatry. Again, Hockey reports that the minister acknowledged the similarity between him and the psychiatrist.

> 'Somebody comes for laying on of hands and starts shaking and screaming and speaking in a foreign language ... you think is this possession or is this person schizophrenic ... let's get somebody else ... and see if we can get some medical reports on him.' (Hallam et al., 1999: 177)

This coordinated response from the minister and the psychiatrist demonstrates the strength of the barrier between life and death in that only an expert can intervene in the risky business of communicating between the two worlds. It also reflects perceptions of the nature of order in this world and the potential problems of disorder that might ensue if the spheres of life and death do not remain separate. The appearance of other worldly phenomena in this world is, in modernity, viewed as disorderly and potentially dangerous and, therefore, as requiring remedial action. Attempts to classify the phenomenon with labels such as fantasy, '"madness", "trickery", "bad plumbing" or a "ghost" ... can be seen as an important dimension of returning the matter to its right place, of wielding expert power' (Hallam et al., 1999: 178).

A further example of the modern emphasis on scientific knowledge in relation to other worlds was the emergence of parapsychology in the late nineteenth century. This was an attempt to 'uncover rigorous scientific evidence for the survival of biological death' (Irwin, 2001: 345) and led to the establishment of the Society for Psychical Research (SPR) in England in 1882, a period of increased popular interest in spiritualism and communication with the dead. It was during the interwar years of the twentieth century, which Cannadine (1981) identified as a period of obsession with death, that the popular spiritualist church movement[1] was tolerated on the fringes or margins of orthodox Christianity. This movement became particularly important after the First World War as people struggled to make sense and to bring order to the devastation brought about by the deaths of so many young men in battle; confirmation that their loved ones continued to exist brought solace to many.

Spiritualism and continuing communication with the dead

It could be argued that the need to link life and death, or to be more precise, the living and the dead, forms the basis of spiritualism. Parallels between Western spiritualism and African traditions of spirit guidance and shamanism clearly exist. Spiritualists believe that it is possible for the living to communicate with the spirits of the dead; the living may learn about the afterlife and the status of their loved ones and the deceased sometimes assist in the lives of the living by providing advice or support (Walliss, 2001). Spiritualism reached its peak in the mid-nineteenth century in Britain and North America and, after a decline, grew again in numbers following the First World War as bereaved people reached out to the spirit world in an effort to contact those who had perished in the hostilities (Cannadine, 1981). Winter (1998) located its popularity at that time among people for whom the traditional churches could not provide appropriate responses to such an apocalyptic occurrence. He also argued that during the nineteenth century it was particularly attractive to people who had rejected mainstream religion and looked to spiritualism as a way of 'reconciling science, deism and socialism' (Winter, 1998). Hallam (2001) further contends that in contemporary Western societies spiritualism has grown in a climate of rejection of the materialism of modern industrial, scientific societies. In denouncing the omnipotence of science, however, spiritualists have harnessed technology to enhance their relationships with the other world. So, for example, telegraphy and photography have been particularly significant in recording contacts with the dead.

This belief system does not have the tenets of an established religion but sits at the margins of orthodox Christian beliefs (Walliss, 2001). Further, in contrast to many established world religions women have played an important role as mediums and this has allowed them a position of authority in an otherwise male-dominated system. In addition to allowing communication between the two worlds, Skultans (1974) asserts that spiritualism has also provided a mechanism for deceased spirits to assist with the physical and emotional well-being of the living.

Contemporary Western societies: life and death intertwined

In pre-modern societies religion is the dominant discourse for making sense of death. As Berger (1969) suggests, religion forms a 'sacred canopy' under which humans shelter and make meaning in relation to mortality. In these societies death exists alongside life – the two worlds are closely intertwined. As such, death is a certainty, but then so is the afterlife, and it could be argued that this is what makes death meaningful. Put another way, the termination of mortal existence is not perceived as an end of life itself. Rather, it is a transition from one state of being to another and the latter is commonly constructed as a better existence (spiritually) with a promise of eternal life. Thus although death is a certainty rather than a risk, it is not necessarily perceived as the end and may, indeed, be viewed as a beginning.

In contemporary Western societies, identified by some as postmodern, death is both a risk and a certainty. Patterns of mortality were transformed during the twentieth century with old age replacing infancy as the most likely time to die. Life expectancy in the West now stands at around 70–80 years, depending on gender, class, ethnicity and in which country or region of the country one lives. 'Premature death', that is, death in infancy, youth or middle-age, is now less prominent in Western societies than in the developing societies of the world, and the way in which it is constructed by individuals and structured by society has changed and continues to change. For example, during the Victorian period, characterized by high mortality rates, people celebrated death (Curl, 1972; Morley, 1971) and subsequently lost their interest in elaborate funeral and mourning rituals when death rates reduced. In contemporary Western societies these altered patterns of mortality have brought with them a reconstruction of the meaning of death and the afterlife. This, combined with a questioning of the power of science and medicine, and the declining power of the established Christian Church, has meant that the search for spiritual meaning and the interest in an afterlife has been resurrected.

Medical science continues to work to improve health and to increase longevity and, on the fringes occasionally provides a mirage of immortality. Nevertheless, death is all around us and we are aware of this through media coverage. Media presentations of death, however, tend to report untimely death of a nature that we expect to happen to others rather than to us or to those we love. The promise of control over mortality is extended in the shape of medical advances and risk-aversion strategies that focus on individual mental and physical health. These commonly involve diet and exercise programmes for healthy living and warnings about not travelling to places around the globe where we might put ourselves in danger. They also rely on the promise of medical intervention, such as heart surgery or dialysis, if we are not able to control the personal health risks.

Alongside a declining faith in the power of science has been a decline in adherence to orthodox religion. This decline in established religion has been identified as a move to secularization and yet, at the same time these so-called secular societies of the West have witnessed the introduction of Eastern religions such as Hinduism, Sikhism and Buddhism; the rise of Christian fundamentalism (especially in the USA); and other new forms of spirituality (see the discussion in chapter 4) – many of which do not require intercession from religious ministers. Thus, although Western societies have been characterized as secular, it would be more accurate to say that this is largely a rejection of the established Christian Church rather than a rejection of spiritual concerns.

Whilst the afterlife continues to be largely perceived as uncertain, because it is unknowable and therefore a risk, what is now emerging is recognition of a range of beliefs that challenge the modern separation between the living and the dying, and the living and the dead. Furthermore, identifying a social trend (that the existence of an afterlife is uncertain) does not detract from the beliefs and experiences of people who believe in life after death.

Afterlife beliefs and near-death experiences

In Kellehear's (1996) model of spiritual needs (which was explored in chapter 4), religious needs may entail questions about an afterlife. Although afterlife beliefs do not necessitate a religious framework they are often set in the context of religious traditions. For example, a belief in purgatory, a place where the dead await judgement, was common in medieval Europe. Reincarnation is an accepted philosophy in Buddhism; heaven may be the final destination of good souls in Christian, Islamic and Buddhist eschatology. Some of those who believe in life after death may do so as a result of a chance visit to other worlds during near-death experiences (NDEs). Whether or not they stem from religious thinking, these different perspectives may be collectively referred to as 'survival beliefs'.

In a study conducted among urban and rural groups in the UK, Davies (1996) found that around 47 per cent of people believed in some form of life after death. Unsurprisingly, active churchgoers were more likely to believe in an afterlife (69 per cent). Although this latter figure is understandably high, it does suggest that there is a large minority of people who may lack a religious framework and yet continue to believe in life after death.

Irwin (2000) explored the nature of afterlife beliefs in Australia. He considered a range of experiences or practices, including communication with spirits, out-of-body and near-death experiences, apparitional experiences and reincarnation. Each of these may be perceived as signs of afterlife survival. He noted, however, that like all other modern Western societies the dominant discourse surrounding survival beliefs is that of science. This can be illustrated most clearly by focusing on NDEs. As Kellehear (1996) has pointed out in a sociological discussion of NDEs, academic explanations for these experiences have tended to utilize either the framework of medical science, and assume that these are hallucinations, or, alternatively, beliefs in the supernatural which argue that they are evidence of survival.

A Gallup Poll in the USA in the early 1980s found that around 10 million people had experienced some form of near-death or out-of-body experience (Irwin 2000). A NDE most commonly occurred when the individual was seriously ill or injured, although Howarth and Kellehear (2001) have shown that people intimately connected with a dying or a seriously ill individual may also undergo a NDE. The encounter can take a number of different forms, but usually incorporates a journey from the location of the physical body to a 'transcendent realm' such as heaven that forms the setting for an experience of the afterlife. In a modern Western social context, the NDE may incorporate one or a combination of the following features: a sense of peace, absence of physical pain, an out-of-body sensation, drifting through darkness or a tunnel, awareness of a golden light, meeting with spirit beings or religious figures, a life review, encountering a beautiful world (Irwin, 2000).[2]

The NDE often has a profound effect on the near-death traveller. Following a survey of Australian NDErs, Sutherland (1990) showed that these experiences have a significant impact on people's attitudes to life and death. For example, fear of death was lower after a NDE. This does not mean that NDErs become more religious in a traditional sense, but that their normal systems of making sense of things have been disrupted and reconstructed as a consequence of their 'otherworld journey' (Zaleski, 1987). This reconstruction commonly takes the form of a belief in an afterlife.

Experiences of other-wordly phenomena such as spiritualism and near-death experiences suggest that in the early twenty-first century, the rational model of reason, science and expertise that is associated with modernity is being challenged in respect of the separation of the living and the dead and dying. As this book has argued, the voices of dying people are now more likely to be heard as societies reject the medicalization of dying, so prevalent in the 1950s, '60s and '70s, and attempt to re-empower individuals via the introduction of hospice, dying at home, the natural death movement and euthanasia. Lay experiences of bereavement and grief are also coming to the foreground in the bereavement literature because of unease with the structures for identifying, classifying and categorizing sudden death. In this respect the voices of the bereaved are not now so easily subsumed by professional discourse. With the assistance of technology, the voices of the dead are also resurfacing through messages left for the living, for example, in video and audio recordings, and through ongoing relationships with the living (recently identified as continuing bonds: Klass et al., 1996). The preserve of the dead is also becoming more familiar to the living through innovative memorial practices (such as roadside tributes) and disposal techniques (such as cremation) that allow them to be more visible in the world of the living.[3] Significantly, many of these contemporary rituals or practices are developing without the assistance of established experts.

In an attempt to understand these developments, let us turn to examine the assertion that contemporary societies have become more individualistic. The discussion will question whether it is a focus on the psychological needs of the individual and a rejection of collectivism that has led to these new approaches to making sense of mortality.

Individualism versus collectivism and the psychologized self

In keeping with the dominant framework of modernity, contemporary Western societies have been labelled as individualistic rather than collectivist. Walter (1996) claims that in postmodern Western societies the authority for mortality is 'personal choice' and choice is commonly associated with individualism. The significance of choice may have been enhanced by the growth of social and cultural diversity in Western societies. As societies become more diverse, with a concomitant awareness of the wide variety of possible meanings and rituals associated with mortality, so the range of choices available is increased. Yet it is difficult to see how choices can be made without reference to social and cultural norms and experience. In modernity, choices such as those involved in end-of-life decision-making are frequently made with the assistance of experts, as individuals cannot so easily make choices in a world of infinite choice and in situations where they have no previous experience. In contemporary societies, in addition to relying on expertise and lay experience, individuals look for cues to meaning and beliefs, ritual practices and behaviour by referring to books, films, the internet and other media to assess how others have made meaning and choices around life and death. Surrogate experiences are now available more widely, for example, through mass media, electronic communications and greater access to the 'global community'. In other words, whilst individuals may be empowered to choose, this does not necessarily imply that they do so independently of others. Rather than being societies of disparate individuals, people continue to live in communities and to have collectivist outlooks.

These communities may be difficult to recognize because they do not resemble traditional communities, often defined according to geographical and social space. In this respect, Anderson (1983) identifies the growth of 'imagined' or virtual communities that engender new forms of collective practices. These new forms of collectivism may challenge modernist frameworks or they may not. Moreover, at one and the same time, they build on the structures of modernity whilst utilizing traditional or pre-modern forms of community and thereby produce a rich tapestry of beliefs and practices around mortality. This is a reflection of the dynamic nature of societies – which have always contained a range of beliefs and practices (some of which are currently being heralded as new) but have merely been silenced by the dominant discourses of modernity.

The assumption that collectivism is lost once traditional forms of community fragment reflects a framework privileging modern discourses that take for granted the concept of the bounded self. As was noted in chapter 9, the efficient functioning of the body and the correlated development of self-identify presumed a bounded entity with a self contained therein. The construction of self-identity (which relies on and influences bodily form) has emphasized the bounded nature of individuals, seen as separate from others. This representation of the body and self as distinct from other bodies and selves relies upon a modernist notion of separation and individuality. This is at odds with perceptions of traditional or pre-modern communities where selves are not bounded but intertwine with the selves both of significant and anonymous others. As individuals interact with and reach out to others to construct self-identity as well as to search for meaning, they become part of a community, not as an isolated self but constructed in relation to the selves of others – both alive and dead. This conjoining of selves may entail engaging with others who have similar experiences. For example, parents whose children have died may create self-help groups with the aim of sharing and supporting each other in grief. People may also continue to connect with the selves of the dead, perhaps through memory, by seeking communication or through other forms of continuing bonds.

These communities may meet in traditional spaces (such as the church) and also in virtual space, through the media or via information technology and communication systems such as the internet. The media assists virtual communities to become aware of death and to learn appropriate responses to it. Communities may also congregate in real space to protest against violent death (as in demonstrations against the Iraq War). They may meet to commemorate the dead (in public ceremonies of remembrance for those killed in war or disaster). They may also engage in communal acts of mourning such as ceremonies held to celebrate the lives of innocent people killed violently. These are occasions when the virtual communities of television viewers and newspaper readers can physically come together as a community of caring individuals. This congregation may utilize the symbolic structures already available and in regular use within modernity. For example, religious buildings such as churches, may bring together mourners for celebrities, such as Diana, Princess of Wales, or people not known personally but killed in tragic, 'unholy' or 'evil' circumstances. The mourning community may not be religious, but may nevertheless assemble in religious buildings where generations before them have met to shelter against the meaninglessness of a cruel world. They come together in a manifestation of shared experience. Recognized as sacred structures, these physical spaces continue to be used in communal acts of mourning because of the power of their sacred symbols. Equally, traditional rituals of remembrance, for example, in the UK the ritual of the two-minute silence – to mark remembrance for those dead in war – is now widely acknowledged as a ritual that marks respect for the dead. This ritual may be held at the start of a football match to mark the loss of a member of either the football community or a local or national personality; in towns and cities when people are asked via the media to stand in silence at 11 am[4] in public places to share their concern after an incident of particularly untimely or tragic death (such as the Asian tsunami in 2004). In other words, these new forms of community are employing earlier structures and rituals, adapting them for purpose and, in this way, deriving meaning in death. This practice effectively superimposes new frameworks for meaning onto pre-existing structures and rituals.

These new and adapted forms of spirituality and public mourning pose a challenge to theories of grief that suggest that death is now a private event, sequestered from public space. The phenomenon of communal mourning in both real and virtual space demonstrates the resurgence of mourning as a collective activity and a public event.

Chapter 5 discussed Walter's (2004) assertion that the media are replacing religion by informing their audiences of the existence of

evil and offering salvation. In this respect the media are implicated
in the virtual communities of mourners who attend rituals for the
dead they did not know, who engage with virtual rituals, and leave
flowers at the scene of a tragic death or disaster. The media are cat-
alysts in the development of these communities. They are also
important in providing information and explanations of dominant
theories and practices in relation to dying and loss. By focusing on
individual experiences, they frequently invoke the knowledge and
expertise of psychology as a mechanism for understanding and
meaning-making. As modernity continues to inform contemporary interpretations of death, medical dominance of dying persists
and this is combined with psychological discourses. Much psychological theorizing continues to emphasize the need for individuals
to speak of their emotions and to work through the various stages
of dying and grief in order to achieve separation, either from this
life or from those who have died. These models of dying and grief
further underline the power of the professionals and their ability to
define and mould the experiences of dying and bereaved people.

Yet, whilst appearing to support the dominant frameworks of
modernity, the media are also crucial to the development of alternative approaches. They examine human mortality and individual
spirituality from standpoints, such as new age perspectives, that promote alternative paradigms in which the individual is the expert,
though often in community with others. Although psychology
(with its claim to scientific status) has become a prominent discourse in social understandings of dying and grief, this is now being
subverted by alternative approaches that acknowledge spirituality
and the connected nature of selves, one with another, with common bonds and experiences. These new forms of spirituality are
commonly collectivist forms, existing within virtual communities
where relationships with the dead (who might also be members of
the community) are also negotiable at an individual level and
where previously hidden practices are increasingly visible.

Dismantling boundaries – death resurrected?

In modern Western societies the frameworks of religion and medical science have, rather curiously perhaps, worked side by side to marginalize experiences of dying and death and to outlaw communication between the living and the dead. This has been achieved through a combination of religious and scientific discourses that have established systems of expertise that effectively police the boundary that separates life and death. These two frameworks have defined and shaped human relationship with death. Yet, in contemporary Western societies new perspectives are emerging, and previously hidden attitudes to mortality are being uncovered that challenge this separation. As Kuhn (1962) might argue, we are now seeing the development of a new paradigm that is changing the manner in which societies make sense of mortality. This new paradigm welcomes a closer relationship between life and death. It exists alongside, and in some respects is intertwined and in tension with, the old paradigm of separation so central to the production of meaning in modernity.

Returning once again to Walter's (1996a) typology of mortality in pre-modern, modern and postmodern societies (discussed in chapter 1) it is now possible to argue that the individualization he identifies as a phenomenon of postmodernity, expressed in the authority of the self, is little more than an attempt to reassert the authority of science via psychology. As I have argued, modernity has established a separation between life and death and medical science has held out the promise of pushing back the boundaries between the two by extending longevity and by assuming that all illness and disease will eventually be curable. In contemporary or postmodern Western societies psychology is now the foremost discipline for understanding mortality in virtue of its focus on emotions and the self. Furthermore, it is psychology that has proposed the thesis of death denial as a framework for understanding a society's relationship with mortality. However, what is perceived as denial may be a failure to recognize and acknowledge new (or previously marginalized) ways of making sense of mortality.

In other words, attitudes to mortality in contemporary Western societies are neither singularly modern nor postmodern. This is not, as Walter (1996) would argue, because contemporary societies are postmodern and fragmented, opting for a pick-and-mix of rituals and behaviours. Rather, it is because Western societies are increasingly socially and culturally diverse. There is a range of religious and cultural beliefs and practices surrounding mortality, some of which have been introduced into Western societies as a consequence of growing multiculturalism. Furthermore, traditional Western beliefs are dynamic, developing according to the changing nature of societies (for example, changing perceptions of risk) and relationships with mortality. New beliefs and practices develop from dissatisfactions with old ones. Beliefs, rituals and practices are also rediscovered or resurrected from much earlier activities that have been prohibited or marginalized within modern societies. Some apparently 'new' practices have pre-existed at the margins or fringes of modernity and have been covered and hidden by the dominant frameworks of modernity. For example, the concept of 'continuing bonds' is unlikely to be a depiction of new forms of continuing relationships with the dead. Such relationships were identified by psychologists in the 1970s but were considered to be hallucination, transitional or abnormal forms of grief (Rees, 1971). What is currently emerging in contemporary Western societies is a rich fusion of beliefs, practices and rituals that is resurrecting death and beginning to embrace mortality as central to life. A crucial feature of these approaches is a rejection of the notion of death as necessarily the end of existence and, as a consequence, a challenge to the dualistic separation of life and death, so dominant in modernity. By pursuing alternative forms of spirituality and continued relationships with the dead, individuals and societies are making sense of death anew and with that are creating new meanings in their relationship with mortality.

Notes

Chapter 1:   Death, Denial and Diversity

1   Doles took the form of food, clothing or money that were given to the poor in return for their prayers for the soul of the deceased.
2   Chantry chapels were usually located in churches and normally sponsored by wealthy people with the express purpose of holding masses, chants and prayers to aid the founder's soul through purgatory.

Chapter 3   Life and Death in 'Risk Society'

1   <http://www.chernobyl.com/info.htm>
2   Source: website 'Saving Lives: Our Healthier Nation', prepared 5 July 1999, accessed 26 April 2002.

Chapter 4   Death, Religion and Spirituality

1   A vast amount of sociological literature is concerned with the media. It is not, however, the purpose of this chapter to explore this in depth. For further reading on the role of the media in modern societies see, for example, Golding, 1974; Glasgow University Media Group, 1982, 1985, 1996; Bausinger, 1984; Postman, 1987; Walter et al., 1995; Briggs and Cobley, 1998.
2   The death of the Pope in 2005, however, was mourned by large numbers of people across the globe and his funeral broadcast live in many

countries. This suggests that secularization is perhaps not so wide-spread or prevalent as acknowledged wisdom may have us believe.

3 There are, of course, many Western societies which have actually witnessed a resurgence of strong Christian beliefs, for example, Christian Fundamentalism in the USA. These beliefs may, however, be perceived as attempts to reassert tradition.

4 Hindus believe that a person's actions in life determine his/her status in the next life.

Chapter 6   Dying: Institutionalization and Medicalization

1 It could be argued that the early hospice movement might also constitute a NSM in the Habermasian sense. We will consider this in the next chapter.

Chapter 7   The Good Death

1 See for example, *Ars moriendi*, originally published in the Netherlands around 1430; William Caxton's *Arte and Crafte to Know Well to Dye* (1490); Thomas Lupset's *The Waye of Dyinge Well* (1534); and Jeremy Taylor's *The Rule and Exercises of Holy Dying* (1651).

2 This legislation was passed by the Parliament of the Northern Territory of Australia in 1995 but was subsequently overturned by the Australian Federal Parliament in 1997.

Chapter 8   The Social Organization of Sudden Death

1. A review of the procedures for investigation into sudden death has recently been undertaken in the UK. The draft report of this review has now been published and cites the reasons for the review as the recognition that, in the light of the age of the system, it 'must undergo radical change if [it is] to become fit for the purposes of a modern society'. Furthermore, two areas of change are regarded as essential: 'One is to restore public confidence in the protection afforded by the death certification process. The other is to improve the response of the coroner service to families' (Death Certification and Investigation in England, Wales and Northern Ireland. The Report of a Fundamental Review 2003, Cm.5831, London: HMSO: 3).

Chapter 9   The Dying and the Dead Body

1   See also Mulkay and Ernst (1991).

Chapter 10   Grief and Loss

1   This was also found to be the case in a study by Howarth and Kellehear (2001) of shared near-death and illness experiences.

Chapter 11   Relationships Between the Living and the Dead

1   For an illustrated discussion of purgatory and other historical aspects of death in England, see Jupp and Gittings (1999).

Chapter 12   Mortuary Rituals

1   See Morley (1971) for details of codes of status employed by English funeral firms. Also, Griffin and Tobin (1997) for details of Australian adaptations of English nineteenth-century rituals.
2   See, for example, the novels of Charles Dickens, who was a leading funeral reformer.
3   See Howarth (1997a) for a full account of the rise of the funeral profession in the UK during the early twentieth century.
4   13 per cent of Australians now identify themselves as having no religion.

Conclusion: Resurrecting Death?

1   Which, incidentally is dominated by women (Skultans, 1974).
2   NDEs can be distinguished from near-death visions as the latter are usually experienced by dying people who, being very close to death, may not subsequently be able to relate their experiences.
3   In chapter 11 we noted the increased use of media images, especially of celebrities, and private practices such as keeping and displaying photos, t-shirts with photos and names on them (for example, Che Guevara and Kurt Cobain). In some respects this could be viewed as a resurgence of Victorian practices where bereaved people would retain portraits, locks of hair and wear memorial brooches and other jewellery as public rites of remembrance.
4   Eleven o'clock in the morning is commonly chosen as the time for remembrance, and this stems from the first such rituals of

remembrance in the UK that aimed to commemorate the armistice of the First World War that occurred at eleven o'clock on the eleventh day of the eleventh month of 1918.

References

Abel, E. K. (1986) 'The hospice movement: institutionalizing innovation', *International Journal of Health Services*, 16, 1, 71–85.

Addy, T. and Silný, J. (2001) 'Globalization in Central and Eastern Europe. Responses to the ecological, economic and social consequences', *The Ecumenical Review*, 53, 4.

Alberry, N., Elliot, G. and Elliot, J. (eds) (1993) *The Natural Death Handbook*, London: Virgin.

Allik, J. and Realo, A. (2004) 'Individualism – collectivism and social capital', *Journal of Cross-Cultural Psychology*, 35, 1, 29–49.

Almond, B. (1990) 'Introduction: war of the world', in *AIDS: A Moral Issue. The ethical, legal and social aspects*, Basingstoke: Macmillan.

Anderson, B. (1983) *Imagined Communities: reflections on the origins and spread of nationalism*, London: Verso.

Arber, S. and Ginn, J. (1991) *Gender and Later Life*, London: Sage.

Arber, S. and Ginn, J. (1995) *Connecting Gender and Ageing*, Buckingham: Open University Press.

Ardener, S. (ed.) (1993) *Defining Female: the nature of women in society*, Oxford: Berg.

Ariès, P. (1974) *Western Attitudes toward Death from the Middle Ages to the Present*, London: Marion Boyars Publishers.

Ariès, P. (1981) *The Hour of Our Death*, London: Allen Lane.

Ariès, P. (1985) *Images of Man and Death*, Cambridge, MA: Harvard University Press.

Armstrong, D. (1983) *The Political Anatomy of the Body: medical knowledge in Britain in the twentieth century*, Cambridge: Cambridge University Press.

Armstrong, D. (1987) 'Silence and truth in death and dying', *Social Science and Medicine*, 24, 651–7.

Arney, W. and Bergen, B. (1984) *Medicine and the Management of Living: taming the last great beast*, Chicago: University of Chicago Press.

Ashby, M. (2001) 'Palliative care', in G. Howarth and O. Leaman (eds), *The Encyclopedia of Death and Dying*, London: Routledge.

Atkinson, J. Maxwell (1978) *Discovering Suicide: studies in the social organisation of sudden death*, London: Macmillan.

Awoonor-Renner, S. (1991) 'I desperately needed to see my son', in D. Dickenson and M. Johnson (eds), *Death, Dying and Bereavement*, London: Sage.

Baines, M. (1990) 'Tackling total pain', in C. Saunders (ed.), *Hospice and Palliative Care: an interdisciplinary approach*, London: Edward Arnold.

Barnard, D. (1988) 'Love and death: existential dimensions of physicians' difficulties with moral problems', *Journal of Medical Philosophy*, 13, 393–409.

Bartley, C. (2001) 'Ars moriendi', in G. Howarth and O. Leaman (eds), *The Encyclopedia of Death and Dying*, London: Routledge.

Battersby, C. (1993) 'Her body/her boundaries. Gender and the metaphysics of containment', *Journal of Philosophy and the Visual Arts*, 31–9.

Baudrillard, J. (1993) *Symbolic Exchange and Death*, London: Sage.

Bauman, Z. (1992) *Mortality, Immortality and other Life Strategies*, Cambridge: Polity.

Bausinger, H. (1984) 'Media, technology and daily life', *Media, Culture and Society*, 6, 4, 343–52.

Beck, U. (1992) *Risk Society: towards a new modernity*, London: Sage.

Beck, U. (1996) 'World risk society as a cosmopolitan society', *Theory, Culture and Society*, 13, 4, 1–32.

Beck, U., Giddens, A. and Lash, S. (1994) *Reflexive Modernization: politics, traditions and aesthetics in the modern order*, Cambridge: Polity.

Becker, A. (1995) *Body, Self and Society. A view from Fiji*, Philadelphia: University of Pennsylvania Press.

Becker, E. (1973) *The Denial of Death*, New York: Collier-Macmillan.

Bendiksen, R. (2001a) 'Assisted suicide', in G. Howarth and O. Leaman (eds), *The Encyclopedia of Death and Dying*, London: Routledge.

Bendiksen, R. (2001b) 'Living wills', in G. Howarth and O. Leaman (eds), *The Encyclopedia of Death and Dying*, London: Routledge.

Bennett, G. and Bennett, K. M. (2000) 'The presence of the dead: an empirical study', *Mortality*, 5, 2, 139–58.

Beres, L. (1999) 'Beauty and the Beast: the romanticization of abuse in popular culture', *European Journal of Cultural Studies*, 2, 2, 191–207.

Berger, P. (1969) *The Social Reality of Religion*, London: Faber.

Berger. P. L. and Luckmann, T. (1967) *The Social Construction of Reality*, London: Allen Lane, The Penguin Press.

Blackmore, S. J. (1993) *Dying to Live: science and the near-death experience*, London: Grafton.

Blauner, R. (1966) 'Death and social structure', *Psychiatry*, 29, 378–94.

Bloch, M. (1971) *Placing the Dead. Tombs, ancestral villages, and kinship organization in Madagascar*, Illinois: Waveland Press.

Bloch, M. and Parry, J. (1982) *Death and the Regeneration of Life*, Cambridge: Cambridge University Press.

Blumer, J. G. and Katz, E. (eds) (1974) *The Use of Mass Communications*, London: Sage.

Bourdieu, P. (1977) *Outline of a Theory of Practice*, Cambridge: Cambridge University Press.

Bowlby, J. (1969; 1973; 1980) *Attachment and Loss*, vols I, II, III, New York: Basic Books.

Bowlby, J. (1981) *Loss, Sadness and Depression*, Harmondsworth: Penguin.

Boyne, R. (2003) *Risk*, Buckingham: Open University Press.

Bradbury, M. (1999) *Representations of Death: a social and psychological perspective*, London: Routledge.

Briggs, A. and Cobley, P. (eds)(1998) *The Media: an introduction*, Harlow: Longman.

Bruce, S. (ed.) (1992) *Religion and Modernization: sociologists and historians debate the secularization thesis*, Oxford: Clarendon Press.

Burr, V. (2003) 'Ambiguity and sexuality in *Buffy the Vampire Slayer*: a Sartrean analysis', *Sexualities*, 6, 3–4, 343–60.

Bury, M. (1982) 'Chronic illness as biographical disruption', *Sociology of Health and Illness*, 4, 2, 167–82.

Bytheway, B. (1995) *Ageism*, Buckingham: Open University Press.

Campbell, D., Moore, G. and Small, D. (2000) 'Death and Australian cultural diversity', in A. Kellehear (ed.) *Death and Dying in Australia*, Melbourne: Oxford University Press.

Cannadine, D. (1981) 'War and death, grief and mourning in modern Britain', in J. Whaley (ed.), *Mirrors of Mortality*, London: Europa.

Cannon, M. (ed.) (1969) *The Vagabond Papers*, Melbourne: Melbourne University Press.

Cannon, M. (1978) *Who's Master? Who's Man? Australia in the Victorian Age*, Melbourne: Thomas Nelson.

Carroll, B. (1977) *Disasters, Horror and Fear in Australia*, Sydney: Bacchus Books

Cartwright, A. (1991) 'Changes in life and care in the year before death', *Journal of Public Health Medicine*, 13, 81–7.

Centeno-Cortes, C. and Nunez-Olarte, J. M. (1994) 'Questioning diagnosis in terminal cancer patients: a prospective study evaluating patients' responses', *Palliative Medicine*, 8, 39–44.

Chadwick, E. (1843) *Supplementary Report on the Results of the Special Inquiry into the Practice of Interment in Towns*, London.

Charmaz, K. (1980) *The Social Reality of Death: death in contemporary America*, Reading, MA: Addison-Wesley.

Charmaz, K. (1983) 'Loss of self: a fundamental form of suffering in the chronically ill', *Sociology of Health and Illness*, 5, 2, 168–91.

Childe, V. G. (1945) 'Directional changes in funerary practice during 50,000 years', *Man*, 45, 13–19.

Clark, D. (1982) *Between Pulpit and Pew*, Cambridge: Cambridge University Press.

Clark, D. (1993) 'Whither the hospices?', in D. Clark (ed.) *The Future for Palliative Care*, Buckingham: Open University Press.

Clark, D. (1998) 'Originating a movement: Cicely Saunders and the development of St Christopher's Hospice, 1957–1967', *Mortality*, 3, 1, 43–63.

Clark, D. (1999) '"Total Pain": disciplinary power and the body in the work of Cicely Saunders, 1958–1967', *Social Science and Medicine*, 49, 727–36.

Clark, V. (2001) 'Cinema', in G. Howarth and O. Leaman (eds), *The Encyclopedia of Death and Dying*, London: Routledge.

Cline, S. (1996) *Lifting the Taboo: women, death and dying*, London: Abacus.

Cohen, P. F. (2002) 'The New York Inferno: taking solace from the stories', *Journal of Religion and Health,* 41, 2, Summer, 113–20.

Connell, R. (1995) *Masculinities*, Berkeley: University of California Press.

Cooley, C. H. (1964 [1902]) *Human Nature and the Social Order*, New York: Scribner's.

Crawford, R. (1980) 'Healthism and the medicalisation of everyday life', *International Journal of Health Services*, 10, 3, 365–89.

Cross, S. E. and Madson, L. (1997) 'Models of the self: self-construal and gender', *Psychological Bulletin*, 122, 1, 5–37.

Csordas, T. (1994) *Embodiment and Experience*, Cambridge: Cambridge University Press.

Curl, J. (1972) *The Victorian Celebration of Death*, Detroit: Partridge.

Danforth, L. M. (1982) *The Death Rituals of Rural Greece*, Princeton, New Jersey: Princeton University Press.

Davies, D. (1996) 'The social facts of death', in G. Howarth and P. C. Jupp (eds), *Contemporary Issues in the Sociology of Death, Dying and Disposal*, Basingstoke: Macmillan.

Davies, D. (1997) *Death, Ritual and Belief: the rhetoric of funerary rites*, London: Cassell.

Davies, J. (1994) 'Introduction: Ancestors – living and dead', in J. Davies (ed.), *Ritual and Remembrance. Responses to death in human societies*, Sheffield: Sheffield Academic Press.

De Beauvoir, S. (1973) *A Very Easy Death*, trans. P. O'Brien, New York: Warner.

De Leo, D. (2002) 'Why are we not getting any closer to preventing suicide?', *British Journal of Psychiatry*, 181, 372–4.

DeSpelder, L. A. and Stickland, A. L. (2005) *The Last Dance. Encountering death and dying*, New York: McGraw-Hill.

Diamond, I. and McDonald, P. (1994) 'Mortality', in D. Lucas and P. Meyer (eds), *Beginning Population Studies*, 2nd edn, Canberra: The Australian National University.

Doka, K. J. (ed.) (1989) *Disenfranchised Grief: recognizing hidden sorrow*, Lexington, MA: Lexington Books.

Doka, K. J. and Morgan, J. D. (eds) (1993) *Death and Spirituality*, Amityville, NY: Baywood.

Douglas, J. D. (1967) *The Social Meaning of Suicide*, Princeton, NJ: Prince ton University Press.

Douglas, M. (1966) *Purity and Danger. An analysis of the concepts of pollution and taboo*, London: Routledge and Kegan Paul.

DuBois, P. (1980) *The Hospice Way of Death*, New York: Human Sciences Press.

Durkheim, E. (1951 [1897]) *Suicide: a study in sociology*, New York: Free Press.

Durkheim, E. (1954 [1915]) *The Elementary Forms of Religious Life*, trans. J. W. Swaine, London: Allen & Unwin.

Durkheim, E. (1964a [1893]) *The Division of Labour in Society*, New York: Free Press.

Durkheim, E. (1964b [1895]) *The Rules of Sociological Method*, trans. S. A. Solovay and J. H. Mueller, New York: Free Press.

Eadie, B. J. (1992) *Embraced by the Light*, London: The Aquarian Press.

Edwards, N. (2001) 'Crying', in G. Howarth and O. Leaman (eds), *The Encyclopedia of Death and Dying*, London: Routledge.

Elias, N. (1985) *The Loneliness of the Dying*, Oxford: Basil Blackwell.

Essex-Cater, A. J. (1967) *A Synopsis of Public Health and Social Medicine*, Bristol: John Wright and Sons.

Estes, C., Gerard, L. and Clarke, A. (1984) 'Women and the economics of aging', *International Journal of Health Service*, 14, 1, 55–68.

Evans-Pritchard, E. E. (1948) *The Divine Kingship of the Shilluk of the Nilotic Sudan*, Cambridge: Cambridge University Press.

Featherstone, M. (1995) 'The body in consumer culture', in M. Featherstone, M. Hepworth and B. S. Turner (eds), *The Body: social process and cultural theory*, London: Sage.

Featherstone, M. and Hepworth, M. (1991) 'The mask of ageing and the postmodern life course', in M. Featherstone, M. Hepworth and B. S. Turner (eds), *The Body. Social process and cultural theory*, London: Sage.

Feinberg, A. (1997) 'Editorials. The care of dying patients', *Annals of Internal Medicine*, 15 January, 126, 2, 164–5.

Field, D. (1995) 'Terminal illness: views of patients and their lay carers', *Palliative Medicine*, 9, 44–54.

Field, D. (1996) 'Awareness and modern dying', *Mortality*, 1, 3, 255–67.

Field, D. and Copp, G. (1999) 'Communication and awareness about dying in the 1990s', *Palliative Medicine*, 13, 459–68.

Field, D., Hockey, J. and Small, N. (1997) 'Making sense of difference: death, gender and ethnicity in modern Britain', in D. Field, J. Hockey and N. Small (eds), *Death, Gender and Ethnicity*, London: Routledge.

Field, D. and James, N. (1993) 'Where and How People Die', in D. Clark (ed.), *The Future for Palliative Care*, Buckingham: Open University Press.

Field, D. and Payne, S. (2003) 'Social aspects of bereavement', *Cancer Nursing Practice*, 2, 8, 21–5.

Finn Paradis, L. and Cummings, S. B. (1986) 'The evaluation of hospice in America towards organizational homogeneity', *Journal of Health and Social Behaviour*, 27, December, 370–86.

Foucault, M. (1973) *The Birth of the Clinic: an archaeology of medical perception*, New York: Vintage Books.

Foucault, M. (1977) *Discipline and Punish: birth of the prison*, London: Tavistock.

Foucault, M. (1980) *Power/Knowledge. Selected interviews and other writings 1972–1977*, ed. Colin Gordon, Sussex: The Harvester Press.

Foucault, M. (1982) 'Afterward: the subject and power', in H. Dreyfus and P. Rainbow (eds), *Michael Foucault: beyond structuralism and hermeneutics*, Chicago: University of Chicago Press.

Freud, S. (1940) *An Outline of Psychoanalysis*, trans. J. Strachey, New York: W. W. Norton.

Freud, S. (1957 [1915]) 'Thoughts for the times on war and death. Our attitudes towards death', in J. Strachey and A. Freud (eds), *The Standard Edition of the Complete Psychological Works of Sigmund Freud*, vol. XIV (1914–16), Hogarth Press.

Garner, D. and Mercer, S. (1989) *Women as they Age*, London: The Haworth Press.

Giddens, A. (1979) *Central Problems in Social Theory: action, structure, and contradiction in social analysis*, London: Macmillan.

Giddens, A. (1984) *The Constitution of Society: outline of a theory of structuration*, Cambridge: Polity.

Giddens, A. (1990) *The Consequences of Modernity*, Cambridge: Polity.

Giddens, A. (1991) *Modernity and Self-Identity. Self and society in the late modern age*, Cambridge: Polity.

Giddens, A. (1994) 'Living in a post traditional society', in U. Beck, A. Giddens and S. Lash, *Reflexive Modernization. Politics, tradition and aesthetics in the modern social order*, Cambridge: Polity.

Giddens, A. (1999) *The Runaway World. How globalisation is reshaping our lives*, London: Profile Books.

Giesey, R. E. (1960) *The Royal Funeral Ceremony in Renaissance France*, Librairie E. Droz.

Gilchrist, H., Howarth, G. and Sullivan, G. (forthcoming) 'The cultural context of youth suicide: the impact on youth of economic restructuring in Australia'.

Gittings, C. (1984) *Death, Burial and the Individual in Early Modern England*, London: Croom Helm.

Gittings, C. (1999) 'Sacred and secular: 1558–1660', in P. C. Jupp and C. Gittings (eds), *Death in England: an illustrated history*, Manchester: Manchester University Press.

Glaser, B. and Strauss, A. (1965) *Awareness of Dying*, Chicago: Aldine.

Glaser, B. and Strauss, A. (1967) *Time for Dying*, Chicago: Aldine.

Glasgow University Media Group (1982) *Really Bad News*, London: Writers and Readers.

Glasgow University Media Group (1985) *War and Peace News*, Milton Keynes: Open University Press.

Glasgow University Media Group (1996) *The Media and Mental Illness*, London: Longman.

Goffman, E. (1959) *The Presentation of Self in Everyday Life*, New York: Doubleday.

Goffman, E. (1974) *Frame Analysis. An essay on the organization of experience*, New York: Harper.

Goldberg, V. (1998) 'Death takes a holiday, sort of ', in J. Goldstein (ed.),

Why We Watch: the attractions of violent entertainment, New York: Oxford University Press.

Golding, P. (1974) *The Mass Media*, London: Longman.

Goodgame, R. W. (1990) 'AIDS in Uganda: clinical and social features', *New England Journal of Medicine*, 323, 383–9.

Gorer, G. (1955) 'The pornography of death', *Encounter*, October.

Gorer, G. (1965) *Death, Grief and Mourning in Contemporary Britain*, London: Cresset.

Grande, G. E. (1999) 'Does hospital at home for palliative care facilitate death at home?', *British Medical Journal*, 319, 1472–5.

Green, J. and Green, M. (1992) *Dealing with Death: practices and procedures*, London: Chapman & Hall.

Griffin, G. M. and Tobin, D. (1997) *In the Midst of Life . . . The Australian response to death*, revised edn, Melbourne: Melbourne University Press.

Gunaratnam, Y. (1997) 'Culture is not enough: a critique of multi-culturalism in palliative care', in D. Field, J. Hockey and N. Small (eds), *Death, Gender and Ethnicity*, London: Routledge.

Habermas, J. (1987) *Theory of Communicative Action*, Cambridge: Polity.

Hallam, E. (1996) 'Turning the hourglass: gender relations at the deathbed in early modern Canterbury', *Mortality*, 1, 1, 61–82.

Hallam, E. (2001) 'Spiritualism', *The Encyclopedia of Death and Dying*, London: Routledge, 427–9.

Hallam, E., Hockey, J. and Howarth, G. (1999) *Beyond the Body. Death and social identity*, London: Routledge.

Hammes, B. J. and Rooney, B. L. (1998) 'Death and end-of-life planning in one Midwestern community', *Archives of Internal Medicine*, 158, 383–90.

Harding, S. (1986) *The Science Question in Feminism*, Ithaca, NY: Cornell University Press.

Hardman, C. (2000) 'Introduction', in G. Harvey and C. Hardman (eds), *Pagan Pathways. A guide to the Ancient Earth Traditions*, London: Thorsons.

Hare, J., Pratt, C. and Nelson, C. (1992) 'Agreement between patients and their self-selected surrogates on difficult medical decisions', *Archives of Internal Medicine*, 152, 1049–54.

Harris, L. (1990) 'The disadvantaged dying', *Nursing Times*, 86, 22, 26–9.

Hart, B., Sainsbury, P. and Short, S. (1998) 'Whose dying? A sociological critique of the "good death"', *Mortality*, 3, 1, 65–77.

Hassan, R. (1995) 'Effects of newspaper stories on the incidence of suicide in Australia', *Australian and New Zealand Journal of Psychiatry*, 29, 3, 480–3.

Haynatzka,V. et al. (2002) 'Racial and ethnic disparities in infant mortality rates in 60 largest US cities', 1995–1998', *Morbidity and Mortality Weekly Report*, 19 April , 51, 329–332, 343.

Hazan, H. (1980) *The Limbo People. A study of constitution of the time universe among the aged*, London: Routledge, Kegan and Paul.

Henley, A. (1982) *Caring for Muslims and their Families*, London: DHSS/King's Fund.

Henley, A. (1987) *Caring in a Multiracial Society*, London: DHSS/King's Fund.

Herbert, C. (2002) 'Vampire religion', *Representations*, 79, 1, 100–21.

Hertz, R. (1960 [1907]) *Death and the Right Hand*, trans. R. and C. Needham, Cohen and West.

Hey,V. et al. (eds) (1989) *Hidden Loss: miscarriage and ectopic pregnancy*, London: The Women's Press.

Heyse-Moore, L. H. (1996) 'On spiritual pain in the dying', *Mortality*, 297–315.

Higginson, I. (1993) 'Palliative care: a review of past changes and future trends', *Journal of Public Health Medicine*, 15, 3–8.

Hittner, J. (2005) 'How robust is the Werther Effect? A re-examination of the suggestion–imitation model of suicide', *Mortality*, 10, 3, 193–201.

HMSO (2003) *Death Certification and Investigation in England, Wales and Northern Ireland. The Report of a Fundamental Review 2003*, Cm 5831, London: HMSO

Hochschild, A. R. (1983) *The Managed Heart: commercialization of human feeling*, California: University of California Press

Hockey, J. (1990) *Experiences of Death*, Edinburgh: Edinburgh University Press.

Hockey, J. (1996) 'The view from the West: reading the anthropology of non-western death ritual', in G. Howarth and P. C. Jupp (eds), *Contemporary Issues in the Sociology of Death, Dying and Disposal*, Basingstoke: Macmillan.

Hockey, J. (2001a) 'Changing death rituals', in J. Hockey, J. Katz and N. Small (eds) *Grief, Mourning and Death Ritual*, Milton Keynes: Open University Press.

Hockey, J. (2001b) 'Hertz, Robert', in G. Howarth and O. Leaman (eds), *Encyclopedia of Death and Dying*, London: Routledge.

Hockey, J. and James, A. (1993) *Growing Up and Growing Old. Ageing and dependency in the life course*, London: Sage.

Holmes, T. H. and Rahne, R. H. (1967) 'The social readjustment rating scale', *Journal of Psychosomatic Medicine*, 41, 503–14.

Hospice Information Service (1998) *Annual Survey*, London: Hospice Information Service.

Hossain, S. Z., Skinner, J. and Jensen, R. C. (1996) *Population Analysis*, Module CEA 8, Brisbane:The University of Queensland.

Hossain, Z. (2001) 'Mortality rates', in G. Howarth and O. Leaman (eds), *Encyclopedia of Death and Dying*, London: Routledge.

Houlbrooke, R. (ed.) (1989) *Death, Ritual and Bereavement*, London: Routledge.

Howarth, G. (1996) *Last Rites: the work of the modern funeral director*, Amityville, NY: Baywood.

Howarth, G. (1997a) 'Professionalising the funeral industry in England 1700–1960', in P. C. Jupp and G. Howarth (eds), *The Changing Face of Death: historical accounts of death and disposal*, Basingstoke: Macmillan.

Howarth, G. (1997b) 'Is there a British way of death?' in K. Charmaz, G. Howarth and A. Kellehear (eds), *The Unknown Country: death in Australia, Britain and the USA*, Basingstoke: Macmillan.

Howarth, G. (1997c) 'Death on the road.The role of the coroner's court in the social construction of an accident', in M. Mitchell (ed.), *The Aftermath of Road Accidents. Psychological, social and legal consequences of an everyday trauma*, London: Routledge.

Howarth, G. (1998) ' "Just live for today." Living, ageing, caring and dying', *Ageing and Society*, 18, 6, 673–89.

Howarth, G. (2000a) 'Australian funerals', in A. Kellehear (ed.), *Death and Dying in Australia*, Melbourne: Oxford University Press.

Howarth, G. (2000b) 'Dismantling the boundaries between life and death', *Mortality*, 5, 2, 127–38.

Howarth, G. (2001) 'Social class', in G. Howarth and O. Leaman (eds) *Encyclopedia of Death and Dying*, London: Routledge.

Howarth, G. and Jefferys, M. (1996) 'Euthanasia: sociological perspectives', *British Medical Bulletin*, 52, 2, 376–385.

Howarth, G. and Kellehear, A. (2001) 'Shared near-death and related illness experiences: steps on an unscheduled journey', *Journal of Near-Death Studies*, 20, 2, 71–87.

Huizinga, J. (1954) *The Waning of the Middle Ages*, New York: Doubleday.

Hurst, S. A. and Mauron, A. (2003) 'Assisted suicide and euthanasia in Switzerland: allowing a role for non-physicians', *British Medical Journal*, 326, 271–3.

Hutton, R. (2000) 'The roots of modern paganism', in G. Harvey and C. Hardman (eds), *Pagan Pathways. A guide to the Ancient Earth Traditions*, London:Thorsons.

Illich, I. (1976) *Limits to Medicine*, London: Marion Boyars.

Irish, D. P. (1997) 'Diversity in universality', in K. Charmaz, G. Howarth and A. Kellehear (eds), *The Unknown Country: death in Australia, Britain and the USA*, Basingstoke: Macmillan.

Irwin, H. (2000) 'The end: a view from parapsychology', in A. Kellehear (ed.), *Death and Dying in Australia*, Melbourne: Oxford University Press.

Irwin, H. J. (2001) 'Parapsychology', in G. Howarth and O. Leaman (eds), *The Encyclopedia of Death and Dying*, London: Routledge.

Jacobs, J. (1899) 'The dying of death', *Fortnightly Review*, LXXII.

Jalland, P. (1996) *Death in the Victorian Family*, Oxford: Oxford University Press.

James, N. and Field, D. (1992) 'The routinization of hospice: charisma and bureaucratization', *Social Science and Medicine*, 34, 12, 1363–75.

Jarvis, C. (2001) 'School is hell: gendered fears in teenage horror', *Educational Studies*, 27, 3, 257–67.

Jefferys, M. and Thane, P. (1989) 'Introduction: an ageing society and ageing people', in M. Jefferys (ed.), *Growing Old in the Twentieth Century*, London: Routledge.

Jupp, P. C. (1990) *From Dust to Ashes: the replacement of burial by cremation in England, 1840–1967*, London: The Congregational Memorial Hall Trust.

Jupp, P. C. (1997) 'The popularization of cremation in England', in K. Charmaz, G. Howarth and A. Kellehear (eds), *The Unknown Country: death in Australia, Britain and the USA*, Basingstoke: Macmillan.

Jupp, P. C. (2001) 'Cremation', in G. Howarth and O. Leaman (eds), *The Encyclopedia of Death and Dying*, London: Routledge.

Jupp, P. C. and Gittings, C., (eds) (1999) *Death in England: an illustrated history*, Manchester: Manchester University Press.

Kalish, R. A. (1980) *Death and Dying: views from many cultures*, Farmingdale, New York: Baywood.

Kalish, R. A. and Reynolds, D. K. (1981) *Death and Ethnicity: a psychocultural study*, Farmingdale, New York: Baywood.

Katz, J. (2001) 'Nursing homes', in G. Howarth and O. Leaman (eds) *The Encyclopedia of Death and Dying*, London: Routledge.

Katz, J. and Sidell, M. (1994) *Easeful Death. Caring for dying and bereaved people*, London: Hodder & Stoughton.

Kauffman, J. (2001) 'Denial', in G. Howarth and O. Leaman (eds) *The Encyclopedia of Death and Dying*, London: Routledge.

Kellehear, A. (1984) 'Are we a "death-denying" society? A sociological review', *Social Science and Medicine*, 18, 8, 713–23.

Kellehear, A. (1990) *Dying of Cancer. The final year of life*, London: Harwood Academic.

Kellehear, A. (1996) *Experience Near Death*, New York: Oxford University Press.

Kellehear, A. (1998) 'Health and the dying person', in A. Petersen and C. Waddell (eds), *Health Matters. A sociology of illness, prevention and care*, St Leonards: Allen & Unwin.

Kellehear, A. (1999a) 'Health-promoting palliative care: developing a social model for practice', *Mortality*, 4, 1, 75–83.

Kellehear, A. (1999b) *Health-Promoting Palliative Care*, Melbourne: Oxford University Press.

Kellehear, A. (2000) 'Spirituality and palliative care: a model of needs', *Palliative Medicine*, 14, 149–55.

Kellehear, A. (2001) 'Denial, criticisms of ', in G. Howarth and O. Leaman (eds), *The Encyclopedia of Death and Dying*, London: Routledge.

Kellehear, A. (2002) 'Grief and loss: past, present and future', *Medical Journal of Australia*, 177, 176.

Kellehear, A. and Anderson, I. (1997) 'Death in the country of Matilda', in K. Charmaz, G. Howarth and A. Kellehear (eds), *The Unknown Country: Death in Australia, Britain and the USA*, Basingstoke: Macmillan.

Kellehear, A. and Fook, J. (1997) 'Lassie come home: a study of "lost pet" notices', *Omega: Journal of Death and Dying*, 34, 3, 191–202.

Kennedy, L. (1994) 'Edwin Stevens Lecture', given at the Royal Society of Medicine (1993). Extract reprinted in *The Newsletter of the National Association of Bereavement Services*, 15, 4.

Klass, D. (1981) 'Elisabeth Kübler-Ross and the tradition of the private sphere: an analysis of symbols', *Omega*, 12, 3, 242–67.

Klass, D. (1992–3) 'The inner representation of the dead child and the worldviews of bereaved parents', *Omega*, 26, 255–72.

Klass, D., Silverman, P. R. and Nickman, S. L. (eds) (1996) *Continuing Bonds. New understandings of grief*, Washington, DC: Taylor & Francis.

Kristeva, J. (1982) *Powers of Horror. An essay on abjection*, New York: Columbia University Press.

Kselman, T. (1993) *Death and the Afterlife in Modern France*, Princeton: Princeton University Press.

Kübler-Ross, E. (1970) *On Death and Dying*, New York: Macmillan.

Kuhn, T. (1962) *The Structure of Scientific Revolutions*, Chicago: Chicago University Press.

Kuhse, H. and Singer, P. (1997) 'From the Editors. Bob Dent's decision', *Bioethics*, 11, 1, 3–5.

Kyokai, B. D. (1996) *The Teaching of Buddha*, Tokyo: Kosaido Printing Co.

Lawton, J. (2000) *The Dying Process: patients' experiences of palliative care*, London: Routledge.

Layder, D. (1994) *Understanding Social Theory*, London: Sage.

Leaney, J. (1989) 'Ashes to ashes: cremation and the celebration of death in nineteenth century Britain', in R. Houlbrooke (ed.), *Death, Ritual and Bereavement*, London: Routledge.

Lefebvre, H. (1974) *The Production of Space*, trans. D. Nicholson-Smith, Oxford: Basil Blackwell.

LeGoff, J. (1984) *The Birth of Purgatory*, London: Scolar.

Lester, D. (1994) 'Challenges in preventing suicide', *Death Studies*, 18, 6, 623–39.

Lindemann, E. (1944) 'Symptomatology and management of acute grief ', *American Journal of Psychiatry*, 101, 141–8.

Linsley, K. R., Schapira, K. and Kelly, T. P. (2001) 'Open verdict *v.* suicide', *British Journal of Psychiatry*, 178, 465–8.

Littlewood, J. (1993) 'The denial of rites of passage in contemporary societies', in D. Clark (ed.), *The Sociology of Death*, Oxford: Blackwell Publishers/Sociological Review.

Loewe, M. (1982) *Chinese Ideas of Life and Death*, London: George Allen and Unwin.

Lotland, L. (1978) *The Craft of Dying: the modern face of death*, Beverly Hills: Sage.

Lovell, A. (1997) 'Death at the beginning of life', in D. Field, J. Hockey and N. Small (eds), *Death, Gender and Ethnicity*, London: Routledge.

Loyn, D. (2005), 'Tsunami aid went to the richest', *BBC News, UK Edition*, <http://news.bbc.co.uk/1/hi/world/south_asia/4621365.stm>, accessed 25 June 2005.

Lundin, T. 'Long term outcomes of bereavement', *British Journal of Psychiatry*, 145, 424–8.

Lunt, B. and Neale, B. (1987) 'A comparison of hospice and hospital: care goals set by staff ', *Palliative Medicine*, 1, 136–48.

Lupton, D. (1999) *Risk*, London: Routledge.

Lynn, J., Teno, J. M., Phillips, R. S., Wu A. W., Desbiens, N., Harrold, J. et al. (1997) 'Perceptions by family members of the dying experience of older and seriously ill patients', *Annals of Internal Medicine*, 126, 97–106.

Lysaght, P. (1995) 'Visible death: attitudes to the dying in Ireland', *Marvels and Tales*, 9, 27–60.

MacConville, U. (2004) 'Mapping a social landscape: an exploration of lay and professional understandings of a "good death" and palliative care in an Irish setting', unpublished PhD thesis, University of Bath.

Malinowski, B. (1954) *Magic, Science and Religion and Other Essays*, Doubleday.

Mandelbaum, D. (1959) 'Social uses of funeral rites', in H. Feifel (ed.), *The Meaning of Death*, New York: McGraw-Hill.

Markides, K. S. and Miranda, M. R. (eds) (1997) *Minorities, Ageing and Health*, London: Sage.

Marris, P. (1974) *Loss and Change*, London: Routledge.

Mars (1982) *Cheats at Work: an anthology of workplace crime*, London: Allen and Unwin.

Martsolf, D. S. and Mickley, J. R. (1998) 'The concept of spirituality in nursing theories: differing world views and extent of focus', *Journal of Advanced Nursing*, 27, 294–303.

Marwit, S. J. and Klass, D. (1994–5) 'Grief and the role of the inner representation of the deceased', *Omega*, 30, 283–9.

Mason, B. (2004) 'World Health Report: Life expectancy falls in poor countries', *World Socialist Web Site*, <www.wsws.org/articles/2004/jan2004/whor-j12.shtml>, accessed 14 June 2004.

Matsumoto, D. (1999) 'Culture and self: an empirical assessment of Markus and Kitayama's theory of independent and inter-dependent self-construal', *Asian Journal of Psychology*, 2, 3, 289–310.

Matthews, P. and Foreman, J. (1993) *Jervis on the Office and Duties of Coroners*, 11th edn, London: Sweet and Maxwell.

Mauss, M. (1935) 'Body techniques', repr. in M. Mauss (1979) *Sociology and Psychology*, London: Routledge and Kegan Paul.

McCallum, J. (1997) 'Health and ageing: The last phase of the epidemiological transition', in A. Borowski, S. Encel and E. Ozanne (eds), *Ageing and Social Policy in Australia,* Cambridge: Cambridge University Press.

McGrath, P. (1999) 'Exploring spirituality through research: an important but challenging task', *Progess in Palliative Care*, 7, 310.

McInerney, F. (2000) 'Requested death: a new social movement', *Social Science and Medicine*, 50, 137–54.

McKeown, T. (1975) 'An interpretation of the decline of mortality in England and Wales during the twentieth century', *Population Studies*, 29, 3, 391–422.

McKinlay, J. B. and McKinlay, S. M. (1977) 'The questionable contribution of medical measures to the decline in mortality in the United States', *Millbank Memorial Fund Quarterly*, Summer, 405–28.

McManners, J. (1981) *Death and the Enlightenment: changing attitudes to death among Christians and unbelievers in eighteenth-century France*, Oxford: Clarendon.

McQuail, D. (1994) *Mass Communications Theory: an introduction*, London: Sage.

McSherry, W. and Draper, P. (1998) 'The debates emerging from the literature surrounding the concept of spirituality as applied to nursing', *Journal of Advanced Nursing*, 27, 683–91.

Mead, G. H. (1934) *Mind, Self and Society: from the standpoint of a social behaviorist*, Chicago: University of Chicago Press.

Mellor, P. (1993) 'Death in high modernity: the contemporary presence and absence of death', in D. Clark (ed.), *The Sociology of Death, Sociological Review Monograph*, Oxford: Blackwell, 11–31.

Mellor, P. and Shilling, C. (1993) 'Modernity, self identity and the sequestration of death', *Sociology*, 27, 411–32.

Merrin, W. (1999) 'Crash, bang, wallop! The death of Diana and the media', *Mortality*, 4, 1, 41–61.

Metcalf, P. and Huntington, R. (1991) *Celebrations of Death: the anthropology of mortuary ritual*, 2nd edn, Cambridge: Cambridge University Press.

Midgley, C. (2004) 'Spirited away: why the end is nigh for religion', *The Times, T2*, 4 November.

Miller, J. (1990) 'Interview', in R. Dinnage (ed.), *The Ruffian on the Stair*, Harmondsworth: Penguin.

Millerson, G. (1964) *The Qualifying Professions*, London: Routledge and Kegan Paul.

Mitchell, J. (1993) 'When disaster strikes ... the critical incident stress debriefing process', *Journal of Emergency Medical Services*, 8, 36–9.

Mitchell, M. (1996) 'Police coping with death: assumptions and rhetoric', in G. Howarth and P. C. Jupp (eds), *Contemporary Issues in the Sociology of Death, Dying and Disposal*, Basingstoke: Macmillan.

Mitchell, M. and Munro, A. (1996) 'The influence of the occupational culture on how police probationers learn to deal with sudden death', *Psychological Perspectives on Police and Custodial Culture and Organisation: issues in legal and criminological psychology* (special issue), 25, 47–53.

Mitchison, R. (1977) *British Population Change Since 1860*, London: Macmillan.

Mitford, J. (1963) *The American Way of Death*, New York: Simon and Schuster.

Montgomery, R. J. V. and McGlinn Datwyler, M. (1992) 'Women and men in the caregiving role', in L. Glasse and J. Hendricks (eds), *Gender and Ageing*, Amityville, NY: Baywood Publishing.

Moran, C. and Massam, M. (1997) 'An evaluation of humour in emergency work', *The Australasian Journal of Disaster and Trauma Studies*, 3 (online journal).

Morgan, R. (1989) *The Demon Lover: on the sexuality of terrorism*, London: Methuen.

Morley, J. (1971) *Death, Heaven and the Victorians*, London: Studio Vista.

Mulkay, M. (1993) 'Social death in Britain', in D. Clark (ed.), *The Sociology of Death, Sociological Review Monograph*, Oxford: Blackwell.

Mulkay, M. and Ernst, J. (1991) 'The changing profile of Social Death', *Arch. Europ. Sociol.*, XXII, 172–96.

Murphy, S. A. (1988) 'Mental distress and recovery in a high risk bereavement sample 3 years after untimely death', *Nursing Research*, 37, 1, 30–5.

Murray, C. (2000) 'WHO issues new healthy life expectancy rankings. Japan number one in new "healthy life" system', *Press Release WHO*, released in Washington DC and Geneva, Switzerland, 4 June.

NAFD (1988), *Manual of Funeral Directing*, London: National Association of Funeral Directors.

Najman, J. M. (2000) 'The demography of death: patterns of Australian mortality', in A. Kellehear (ed.), *Death and Dying in Australia*, Melbourne: Oxford University Press.

Nakashima, E. (2004) 'In Laos, sifting the earth for American Dead', *The Washington Post*, 1 May A01.

National Centre for Health Statistics (NCHS) (2000) 'Infant mortality rates vary by race and ethnicity', online: <www.cdc.gov/nchs/release/99facts/00sheets/infmort.html> accessed 13 october 2003.

Nettleton, S. (1995) *The Sociology of Health and Illness*, 2nd edn, Cambridge: Polity.

Neuberger, J. (1987) *Caring for Dying People of Different Faiths*, London: Austen Cornish and Lisa Sainsbury Foundations.

Nicol, R. (2000) 'Australian burial customs', in A. Kellehear (ed.) *Death and Dying in Australia*, Melbourne: Oxford University Press.

Noggle, B. (1995) 'Identifying and meeting needs of ethnic minority patients', *The Hospice Journal*, 10, 85–92.

Novack, D. H., Plumer, R., Smith, R. L., Ochitill, H., Morrow, G. R. and Bennett, J. M. (1979) 'Changes in physicians' attitudes towards telling the cancer patient', *Journal of the American Medical Association*, 241, 897–900.

OECD (2001) *Society at a Glance: OECD social indicators*, Paris: CI.

Office of Fair Trading Report (1989) *Funerals*, London: OFT.

Ohnuki-Tierney, E. (1984) *Illness and Culture in Contemporary Japan: an anthropological view*, Cambridge: Cambridge University Press.

Okely, J. (1983) *The Traveller Gypsies*, Cambridge: Cambridge University Press.

Opler, M. (1996 [1936]) *An Apache Life-Way: the economic, social and religious institutions of the Chiricahua Indians*, Nebraska, University of Nebraska Press.

Parker, J. and Aranda, S. (eds)(1998) *Palliative Care: explorations and challenges*, Sydney: MacLennon & Petty.

Parkes, C. M. (1972) *Bereavement: Studies of Grief in Later Life*, London: Tavistock.

Parkes, C. M. (1985) 'Terminal care: home, hospital or hospice?', *Lancet*, 1, 155–7.

Parkes, C. M. (1988) 'Bereavement as a psychosocial transition: processes of adaptation to change', Extract from *Journal of Social Issues*, 44, 3, published in D. Dickenson and M. Johnson, (eds), *Death, Dying and Bereavement*, London: Sage.

Parkes, C. M. (1996) *Bereavement: studies of grief in adult life*, 3rd edn, London: Routledge.

Parkes, C. M., Laungani, P. and Young, B. (1997). *Death and Bereavement Across Cultures*, New York: Routledge.

Parrott, W. G. and Harr, R. (2001) 'Princess Diana and the emotionology of contemporary Britain', *International Journal of Group Tensions*, 30, 1, 29–38.

Parsons, T. and Lidz, V. (1967) 'Death in American society', in E. Shneidman (ed.), *Essays in Self-Destruction*, New York: Science House.

Petersen, A. and Lupton, D. (1996) 'The New Public Health: a new morality', in A. Petersen and D. Lupton, *The New Public Health*, St Leonards: Allen & Unwin.

Phillips, D. (1974) 'The influence of suggestion on suicide; substantive and theoretical implications of the Werther effect', *American Sociological Review*, 39, 3, 340–54.

Phillips, D., and Carstensen, L. (1986) 'Clustering of teenage suicides after television news stories about suicide', *New England Journal of Medicine*, 315, 11, 685–9.

Phoenix, S. (1997) 'Death and dying', <http://www. geocities.com/ slvrphoenix/death. html>.

Pickerell, J. (2005), 'Facts and Figures: Asian Tsunami Disaster', <http:// www. christianaid. co. uk>, updated 20 January 2005.

Pirkis, J. and Blood, R. (2001). *Suicide and the Media: a critical review*, Canberra: Commonwealth Department of Health and Aged Care.

Pirkis, J., Blood, R., Francis, C., Putnis, P., Burgess, P., Morley, B., Stewart, A. and Payne, T. (2001) *The Media Monitoring Project; a baseline description of how the Australian media report and portray suicide and mental health and illness*, Canberra: Department of Health and Aged Care.

Pollard, A. H., Yusuf, F. and Pollard, G. N. (1990) *Demographic Techniques*, 3rd edn, Sydney: Pergamon Press.

Popper, K. (1945) *The Open Society and its Enemies*, London: Routledge & Kegan Paul.

Porter, R. (1989) 'Doctors and death in Georgian England', in R. Houlbrooke (ed.), *Death, Ritual and Bereavement*, London: Routledge.

Porter, R. (1990) 'Introduction', in S. Barnard, *To Prove I'm Not Forgot*, Manchester: Manchester University Press.

Porter, R. (1991) 'History of the body', in P. Burke (ed.), *New Perspectives on Historical Writings*, Cambridge: Polity.

Postman, N. (1987) *Amusing Ourselves to Death*, London: Methuen.

Powles, J. (1973) 'On the limitations of modern medicine', *Social Science and Medicine*, 1, 1–30.

Prior, L. (1989) *The Social Organization of Death. Medical discourses and social practices in Belfast*, Basingstoke: Macmillan.

Prior, L. (1997) 'Acturial visions of death: life, death and chance in the modern world', in P. C. Jupp and G. Howarth (eds), *The Changing Face of Death. Historical accounts of death and disposal*, Basingstoke: Macmillan.

Prior, L. and Bloor, M. (1993) 'Why people die: social representations of death and its causes', *Science as Culture*, 3, 3, 346–75.

Rando, T. (1993) *The Treatment of Complicated Mourning*, Champaign: Research Press.

Raphael, B. (1984) *The Anatomy of Bereavement: a handbook for the caring professions*, London: Hutchinson.

Raphael, B. (1997) 'Death and the great Australian disaster', in K. Charmaz, G. Howarth and A. Kellehear (eds), *The Unknown Country: death in Australia, Britain and the USA*, Basingstoke, UK: Macmillan.

Raphael, B., Meldrum, L. and MacFarlane, A. C. (1995) 'Does debriefing after psychological trauma work?', *British Medical Journal*, 310, 1479–80.

Rees, W. D. (1971) 'The hallucinations of widowhood', *British Medical Journal*, 4, 37–41.

Reykowski, J. (1994) 'Collectivism and individualism as dimensions of social change', in U. Kim, H. C. Triandis, C. Kagitçbasi, S. C. Choi and G. Yoon (eds), *Individualism and Collectivism: theory, method and applications*, Thousand Oaks, CA: Sage.

Richardson, R. (1987) *Death, Dissection and the Destitute*, London: Routledge and Kegan Paul.

Richardson, R. and Hurwitz, B. (1997) 'Death and the doctors', in K. Arnold, B. Hurwitz, F. McKee and R. Richardson (eds), *Doctor*

Death. Medicine at the end of life. An exhibition at the Wellcome Institute for the History of Medicine, London: The Wellcome Trust.

Riches, G. (2001) 'Self-help', in G. Howarth and O. Leaman (eds), *The Encyclopedia of Death and Dying*, London: Routledge.

Riches, G. and Dawson, P. (1997) '"Shoring up the walls of heartache": parental responses to the death of a child', in D. Field, J. Hockey and N. Small (eds) *Death, Gender and Ethnicity*, London: Routledge.

Riches, G. and Dawson, P. (2000) *An Intimate Loneliness. Supporting bereaved parents and siblings*, Buckingham: Open University Press.

Riley, J. C. (1989) *Sickness, Recovery and Death: a history and forecast of ill health*, Basingstoke: Macmillan.

Ritzer, G. (1996) *The McDonaldization of Society*, revised edn, Thousand Oaks, CA: Pineforge Press.

Robbins, M. (1996) 'The donation of organs for transplantation: the donor families', in G. Howarth and P. C. Jupp (eds), *Contemporary Issues in the Sociology of Death, Dying and Disposal*, Basingstoke: Macmillan.

Rose, H. and Bruce, E. (1995) 'Mutual care but differential esteem: caring between older couples', in S. Arber and J. Ginn (eds), *Connecting Gender and Ageing. A sociological approach*, Buckingham: Open University Press.

Roth, J. and Conrad, P. (1987) *Research in the Sociology of Health Care: the experience and management of chronic disease*, Greenwich, CT. and London: JAI Press.

Rowling, L. (2001) 'Critical incident debriefing', in G. Howarth and O. Leaman (eds), *The Encyclopedia of Death and Dying*, London: Routledge.

Rugg, J. (1998) '"A few remarks on modern sepulture": current trends and new directions in cemetery research', *Mortality*, 3, 2, 111–19.

Rumbold, B. (1998) 'Implications of mainstreaming hospice into palliative care services', in J. Parker and S. Aranda (eds), *Palliative Care: explorations and challenges*, Sydney: MacLennon & Petty.

Rumbold, B. (2002) 'From religion to spirituality', in B. Rumbold (ed.), *Spirituality and Palliative Care: social and pastoral perspectives*, Victoria, Australia: Oxford University Press.

Rutz, W. (2001) 'Mental health in Europe: problems, advances and challenges', *Acta Psychiatrica Scandinavica*, 104 (suppl. 410), 15, 20.

Sahlins, M. (1961) 'The segmentary lineage: an organisation of predatory expansion', *American Anthropologist*, 63, 322–45.

Saunders, C. (1988) 'Spiritual pain', *Hospital Chaplain*, March, 3–7.

Saunders, C. (1996) 'Guest contribution: hospice', *Mortality*, 1, 3, 317–22.

Scott, P. (2003) 'Sudden death processing: an ethnographic study of emergency care', unpublished PhD thesis, Durham University, UK.

Seale, C. (1998) *Constructing Death. The sociology of dying and bereavement*, Cambridge: Cambridge University Press.

Seale, C. and Addington-Hall, J. (1994) 'Euthanasia: why people want to die earlier', *Social Science and Medicine*, 39, 5, 647–54.

Seale, C. and Addington-Hall, J. (1995) 'Dying at the best time', *Social Science and Medicine*, 40, 5, 589–95.

Sen, K. and Bonita, R. (2000) 'Global health status: two steps forward, one step back', *The Lancet*, 356, 577–81.

Shernoff, M. (1998) 'Gay widowers: grieving in relation to trauma and social supports', *Journal of the Gay and Lesbian Medical Association*, 2, 1.

Shilling, C. (1993) *The Body and Social Theory*, London: Sage.

Silverman, P. R. and Klass, D. (1996) 'Introduction: what's the problem?', in D. Klass, P. R. Silverman and S. L. Nickman (eds), *Continuing Bonds. New understandings of grief*, Washington, DC: Taylor & Francis.

Simpson, M. A. (1972) *The Facts of Death: a complete guide for being prepared*, London: Prentice-Hall.

Sinclair, P. C. (2004) 'A Social Role Valorizing Model of Palliative Care: towards an alternative paradigm', unpublished PhD thesis, La Trobe University, Melbourne, Australia.

Singer, P. (1993) *Practical Ethics*, 2nd edn, Cambridge: Cambridge University Press.

Sinha, J. B. P., Sinha, T. N., Verma, J. and Sinha, R. B. N. (2001) 'Collectivism coexisting with individualism: an Indian scenario', *Asian Journal of Social Psychology*, 4, 2, 133–45.

Skultans, V. (1974) *Intimacy and Ritual: a study of spiritualism, mediums and groups*, London: Routledge and Kegan Paul.

Slapper, G. (1993) 'Corporate manslaughter: an examination of the determinants of prosecutorial policy', *Social and Legal Studies*, 2, 423–43.

Smale, B. (1997) 'The social construction of funerals in Britain', in K. Charmaz, G. Howarth and A. Kellehear (eds) *The Unknown Country: death in Australia, Britain and the USA*, Basingstoke: Macmillan.

Small, N. (1998) 'Spirituality and hospice care', in M. Cobb and V. Robshaw (eds), *The Spiritual Challenge of Health Care*, Edinburgh: Churchill Livingstone.

Small, N. (2001a) 'Acquired Immune Deficiency Syndrome', in G. Howarth and O. Leaman (eds), *Encyclopedia of Death and Dying*, London: Routledge.

Small, N. (2001b) 'Hospice', in G. Howarth and O. Leaman (eds), *Encyclopedia of Death and Dying*, London: Routledge.

Small, N. (2001c) 'Theories of grief: a critical review', in J. Hockey, J. Katz and N. Small (eds), *Grief, Mourning and Death Ritual*, Buckingham: Open University Press.

Smith, A. (1984) 'Problems of hospices', *British Medical Journal*, 304, 718.

Spender, L. (ed.) (1988) *Rest Assured: a guide to wills, estates and funerals*, Sydney: Redfern Legal Centre.

Spottiswood, J. (1991) *Undertaken with Love*, London: Robert Hale.

Stedeford, A. (1984) *Facing Death: Patients, Families and Professionals*, London: Heinemann.

Straube, S. H. (2004) *Pet Death*, New York: Baywood Publishing.

Strauss, A. L. (ed.) (1994) *Chronic Illness and the Quality of Life*, 2nd edn, St Louis: C. V. Mosby.

Stroebe, M. (1997) 'From mourning to melancholia to bereavement and biography: an assessment of Walter's new model of grief ', *Mortality*, 2, 3, 255–63.

Stroebe, M. and Schut, H. (1999) 'The dual process model of coping with bereavement: rationale and description', *Death Studies*, 23, 197–224.

Sudnow, D. (1967) *Passing On: the social organization of dying*, Englewood Cliffs: Prentice Hall.

Sullivan, G., Howarth, G. and Thomas, D. (forthcoming)

Surbone, A. (1992) 'Truth telling to the patient', *Journal of the American Medical Association*, 268, 1661–2.

Susser, M. (1973) *Causal Thinking in the Health Sciences*, New York: Oxford University Press.

Sutherland, C. (1990) 'Changes in religious beliefs, attitudes and practices following near-death experiences: an Australian study', *Journal of Near-Death Studies*, 9, 1, 21–31.

Tatz, C. (2001) *Aboriginal Suicide is Different: a portrait of life and self-destruction*, Canberra: Aboriginal Studies Press.

Taylor, C. (1989) *Sources of Self*, Cambridge: Cambridge University Press.

Taylor, D. A. (1979) 'Denial of death in close encounters', *Omega*, 10, 277–9.

Taylor, S. (1982) *Durkheim and the Study of Suicide*, London: Macmillan.

Thomas, W. I. (1966) *On Social Organization and Social Personality*, Chicago: University of Chicago Press.

Thomas, V. and Striegel, P. (1995) 'Stress and grief of a perinatal loss', *Omega*, 30, 4, 229–311.

Thompson, N. (1997) 'Masculinity and loss', in D. Field, J. Hockey and N. Small (eds), *Death, Gender and Ethnicity*, London: Routledge.

Townsend, P. and Davidson, N. (1982) *Inequalities in Health*, Harmondsworth: Penguin.

Triandis, H. (1990) 'Cross-cultural studies of individualism and collectivism', *Nebraska Symposium on Motivation, 1989*, 37, 41–133.

Tripathi, R. C. and Leviatan, U. (2003) 'Individualism and collectivism: in search of a product or process?', *Culture and Psychology*, 9, 1, 79–88.

Turner, B. S. (1984) *The Body and Society: explorations in social theory*, Oxford: Basil Blackwell.

Turner, B. S. (1992) *Regulating Bodies: essays in medical sociology*, London: Routledge.

Turner, B. S. (1995) 'Ageing and identity: some reflections on the somatization of self', in M. Featherstone and A. Wernick (eds), *Images of Aging: cultural representations of later life*, London: Routledge.

Turner, B. S. (1996) *The Body and Society*, London: Sage.

UNAIDS (2000) 'HIV/AIDS/STI surveillance', Regional information from <www. who. org/emc-hiv/fact_sheets/index. html>.

US Department of Health and Human Services (2002) Health Resources and Services Administration, Maternal and Child Health Bureau, *Women's Health USA, 2002*, Rockville, MD.

USAID (2005) *USAID's HIV/AIDS Program in Swaziland*, June 2005, <www.usaid.gov/our_work/global_health/aids/Countries/africa/swaziland.html>.

Van Gennep, A. (1960 [1909]) *Rites of Passage*, Chicago: University of Chicago Press.

Vitebsky, P. (1990) *Dialogues with the Dead: the discussion of mortality among the Sora of Central India*, Cambridge: Cambridge University Press.

Vogeler, I. (1996) 'Declining world mortality rates map', Online: <www.uwee/edu/Academic/Geography/Ivogeler/wIII/dempop.htm>.

Walliss, J. (2001) 'Continuing bonds: relationships between the living and the dead within contemporary spiritualism', *Mortality*, 6, 2, 127–46.

Walter, T. (1990) *Funerals: and how to improve them*, London: Hodder & Stoughton.

Walter, T. (1991) 'Modern death – taboo or not taboo?' *Sociology*, 25, 2, 293–310.

Walter, T. (1994) *The Revival of Death*, London: Routledge.

Walter, T. (1996a) 'Facing death without tradition', in G. Howarth and P. Jupp (eds), *Contemporary Issues in the Sociology of Death, Dying and Disposal*, Basingstoke: Macmillan.

Walter, T. (1996b) 'A new model of grief', *Mortality*, 1, 7–27.

Walter, T. (1997) 'The ideology and organization of spiritual care: three approaches', *Palliative Medicine*, 11, 21–30.

Walter, T. (1999) *On Bereavement. The culture of grief,* Buckingham: Open University Press.

Walter, T. (2004) 'Disaster, modernity, and the media', in K. Garces-Foley (ed.), *Death and Religion in a Changing World,* Armonk, NY: M. E. Sharpe.

Walter, T. (2006) 'Disaster, modernity, and the media', in K. Garces-Foley (ed.), *Death and Religion in a Changing World,* Armonk, NY: M. E. Sharpe.

Walter, T., Littlewood, J. and Pickering, M. (1995) 'Death in the news: the public invigilation of private emotion', *Sociology,* 29, 579–96.

Walvin, J. (1982) *A Child's World: a social history of English childhood 1800–1914,* Harmondsworth: Penguin.

Warner, W. L. (1965) 'The city of the dead', in R. Fulton (ed.), *Death and Identity,* New York: John Wiley and Sons.

Watson, J. L. (1982) 'Of flesh and bones: the management of death pollution in Cantonese society', in M. Bloch and J. Parry (eds), *Death and the Regeneration of Life,* Cambridge: Cambridge University Press.

Weber, M. (1968 [1914]) *Economy and Society,* vols I, II and III, Totowa, NJ: Bedminster Press.

White, S. (1990) 'A burning issue', *New Law Journal,* 10 August.

Wilkinson, R. G (1996) *Unhealthy Societies: from inequalities to well-being,* London: Routledge.

Wilson, J. (2001) 'Organ donation', in G. Howarth and O. Leaman (eds), *The Encyclopedia of Death and Dying,* London: Routledge.

Wines, M. and LaFraniere, S. (2004) 'Hut by hut, AIDS steals life in a southern Africa town', *New York Times,* 28 November.

Wing, N. (1996) 'Baudelaire's frisson: fraternal horror and enchantment in "Les Tableaux Parisiens"', *Neophilologus,* 81, 1, 21–33.

Winter, J. (1998) *Sites of Memory, Sites of Mourning: the Great War in European cultural history,* Cambridge: Cambridge University Press (Canto edn).

Woolacott, M. (1995) 'Three sides to every story', *Guardian,* 2 September.

Worden, W. (1982) *Grief Counselling and Grief Therapy,* New York: Springer.

Worden, W. (1991) *Grief Counselling and Grief Therapy,* 2nd edn, London: Routledge.

World Health Organization (1990) 'Pain relief and palliative care', *Technical Report Series 804,* Geneva: WHO.

World Health Organization (1992) *Psychosocial Consequences of Disasters: prevention and management,* Mental Health Division, Geneva: WHO.

Wright, B. (1991) *Sudden Death. A research base for practice,* 2nd edn, New York: Churchill Livingstone.

Yamamoto, J., Iyiwsaki, T. and Yoshimura, S. (1969) 'Mourning in Japan', *American Journal of Psychiatry*, 125, 1660–5.

Yates, D. W., Ellison, G. and McGuiness, S. (1993) 'Care of suddenly bereaved', in D. Dickenson and M. Johnson (eds), *Death, Dying and Bereavement*, London: Sage.

Young, M. (1996) 'What a rotten way to go', *Guardian*, 31 January, p. 2.

Young, M. and Cullen, L. (1996) *A Good Death. Conversations with East Londoners*, London: Routledge.

Younger, S. J., Fox, R. C. and O'Connell, L. J. (1996) *Organ Transplantation: meanings and realities*, Wisconsin: University of Wisconsin Press.

Zaleski, C. (1987) *Otherworld Journeys. Accounts of near-death experiences in medieval and modern times*, New York: Oxford University Press.

Zola, I. K. (1972) 'Medicine as an institution of social control', *Sociological Review*, 20, 487–504.

Index